BERNARD BARUCH

Park Bench Statesman

Press Association, Inc.

THE PARK BENCH STATESMAN

A Recent Photograph.

BERNARD BARUCH

Park Bench Statesman

BY
CARTER FIELD

WHITTLESEY HOUSE
MCGRAW-HILL BOOK COMPANY, INC.
New York - - - - - - - - - - *London*

This book is produced in full compliance with the government's regulations for conserving paper and other essential materials.

PUBLISHED BY WHITTLESEY HOUSE
A division of the McGraw-Hill Book Company, Inc.

Printed in the United States of America

ILLUSTRATIONS

CHAPTER . . . ONE

IT WAS election night in Camden, South Carolina. Down the dusty street came a mob—flourishing weapons, menacing, capable of almost anything. It was composed of Negroes ordinarily kindly, good-humored, obliging, but at the moment inflamed by carpetbag oratory and crazed by free whisky dispensed by scalawag politicians.

In a small house that the mob was nearing, a mother looked anxiously at her four young sons, whose father was away on an emergency sick call.

Grimly she opened the cupboard door, took out two ancient single-barreled shotguns, which she handed to the two oldest boys, and led the boys to the second-floor porch.

"Let them see the guns," she said, "but don't shoot unless I say so."

There was scarcely a Negro in the crowd who did not know and like Miss Belle, the mother. There were few of them whom the doctor, her husband, had not taken care of when sick or who had not been furnished with food and medicine when in need. Many of them knew the little boys, now standing guard so brave without and so fearful within. Some of the Negroes even knew that the boys were pretty fair shots for their age. They had hunted wild turkeys and ducks and quail with them.

Maybe the mob would never have bothered the house, anyway. Maybe the guns prevented trouble. But had those guns been fired this book would never have been written. The guns were muzzle-loaders. It took time to reload them, and the Negroes were temporarily insane.

But Miss Belle was not taking any chances of an unnecessary shot. When she said, "Don't shoot unless I say so," she knew she would be obeyed. All her orders were obeyed by her sons in those days, and, with rare exception, to the end of her life, whether the boys liked them or not, whether the mature and successful men they became liked them or not.

The younger of those little boys with the guns was Bernard Mannes Baruch. The older was Hartwig, Bernard's boyhood idol, a natural shot, a born fighter, a ballplayer—everything that little Bernie, chubby, inept with his fists, and given to violent tempers, wanted to be.

Not long afterward occurred an event that may surprise many persons who think of the Ku Klux Klan as a bigoted organization opposed to Catholics, Jews, and Negroes. They forget that a generation earlier there was another Klan, from which the Klan of the present century stole the name, and that the objectives of the earlier Klan, while quite without the sanction of law, were scarcely comparable.

Bernard and Hartwig were rummaging in their attic at Camden. Opening an old trunk they found the regalia of a Knight of the Ku Klux Klan. It belonged to their father, in whose veins, according to family records, flowed nothing but Jewish blood.

Their mother, who had followed the boys up the attic steps to see what they were doing, froze with fear when she saw them unearth the regalia. Dr. Baruch would certainly pay with his life if his membership in the Klan should be disclosed. She swore them to secrecy, and, as usual, they obeyed her commands.

In telling this story, years later, Baruch remarked that, so far as he had ever heard, no member of the Klan was ever betrayed. Who were members of that organization of Reconstruction days was one of the best kept secrets in all history.

Bernard M. Baruch was born in Camden, South Carolina, on August 19, 1870, the second child of Dr. Simon Baruch and Belle Wolfe Baruch. Dr. Baruch was an immigrant from Prussia; Miss Belle was the seventh generation of her family in America.

Camden was a sleepy, small town some twenty-five miles northeast of Columbia, the state capital. It is low country, with occasional swamps that furnished fine cover for game birds. It is still great shooting country; in those days it was a sportsman's paradise. This was fortunate, for the country was desperately poor when Bernard was a small boy. The Civil War ended shortly after Sherman had marched through with what is today called the "scorched-earth" policy, his object being to prevent food being raised to keep Lee's soldiers fighting. Then came Reconstruction, the blighting economic effects of which were to be in full sway during the first 6 years of Bernard's life and the repercussions of which continued long thereafter.

So it was not surprising that the two oldest Baruch boys knew how to shoot those old muzzle-loaders. Shooting was not only great fun for little boys, it was essential to provide meat.

The boys were not permitted to think of hunting in that connection, however. Quite the contrary. They had to do odd chores here and there, for their father, for their grandfather, for anyone who would employ them, to earn money to buy powder and shot for their hunting expeditions. They carried their shot in a leather pouch and their powder in a cow's horn, which they had scraped so thin that they could see through it. Loading one of these old muzzle-loaders required skill, especially when speed was necessary.

Among the chores by which they earned powder-and-shot money was picking cotton. They worked in the fields of Dr.

Baruch's experimental farm, right along with the Negroes, and Bernie became rather adept. Dr. Baruch seemed to be more interested in his agricultural experiments, or at least so Miss Belle thought, than in his medical practice. He was continually winning prizes at state fairs with his products and astonishing the neighbors by such experiments as planting alternate rows of sugar cane and cotton. This was but one of the many experiments he tried on the little 3-acre farm adjoining the rambling frame house in which his sons passed their early boyhood. One time he actually bought some bottom land for the purpose of finding out whether draining it by tile would make it productive.

This experimental farming was of absorbing interest to the doctor and provided Hartwig and Bernie—the other brothers were too young—with many dimes for powder and shot, but it was by no means profitable; in fact, it took some of the doctor's medical fees to finance it.

These fees were not lavish, either, by any standard. So Miss Belle supplemented the income by giving piano and singing lessons. Nevertheless, she always had breakfast in bed, a "befo' de wah" luxury she would not relinquish. This was no strain on the budget. If physicians' fees were small, so were servants' wages.

Sometimes the boys earned a few handfuls of brown sugar—they were never to see white sugar until they moved to New York—by doing some chores for Grandfather Saling Wolfe. Miss Belle's father had been a fairly rich man when the War between the States broke out, but now everything save the land was gone, and Sherman had burned his house.

At the time the Baruch boys were helping out by distributing the weekly rations of sugar, coffee, prunes, bacon, and rice to the Negroes, for a brown-sugar wage, Saling was trying to rebuild his fortune. He looked like an English squire, Baruch said in later years, as he rode his horse, Morgan, around the place.

Incidentally he did a fairly good job rebuilding that fortune until he lost a lawsuit over a lot of cotton that Sherman had burned. As a result he died poor.

So there was no money on Miss Belle's side of the family, she being one of Grandfather Saling's thirteen children, while on Dr. Baruch's side there was only the part of a country doctor's earnings that was not poured into experimental farming.

But, poor as the Baruchs were, there were servants, and the most important of these was Minerva. It may be that Minerva had something to do with the extraordinary unswerving obedience to their mother's commands which characterized all four of the Baruch boys and which was to overrule Bernard's choice of a college, change his intended profession, and even interrupt his stock-market operations when millions of dollars were at stake.

Minerva was black as coal, as broad as she was tall, swung a very heavy hand on very slight provocation, and made the children's blood run cold with a wealth of supernatural stories, which she told with the terrifying, conviction-carrying power of a fanatical believer.

There was nothing amusing to Minerva about a hant or a plat eye. They were real and greatly to be feared. To this day there are Negroes in the South Carolina coast country who will not have glass windows in their houses, insisting on shutters instead. They are afraid the hants and plat eyes might look in!

Minerva's recollections of the boyhood of Mr. Bernie seemed to give her great satisfaction later. She loved to tell of his misdeeds and of her terrific punishments of him therefor. But there was plenty of pride over her success in having inclined the twig as it should grow and a broad inference that, if it had not been for her corrective influence, particularly the heavy hand, Bernie might have come to a bad end.

The first school Bernie attended was kept by a Mr. and Mrs. Wallace. Mrs. Wallace taught the younger children in her home, often nursing her baby during the lessons. The older children were taught by Mr. Wallace in a wooden schoolhouse near by.

Soon after he was promoted to the schoolhouse Bernie committed his first and only theft. One of the boys in his class had left on his desk a half-consumed stick of hard candy. Observing this, their mouths watering with desire for this exotic luxury, Bernie and another boy sneaked back to the schoolhouse after it had been locked, crawled underneath the little building, which, like most Negro cabins in the Carolinas to this day, was supported by piles and stood about 18 inches off the ground, pried up a loose board, took the candy stick, and divided it.

It was the unhappiest afternoon of Bernie's life up to then. There were no green-apple pains, but old General Remorse moved in on him. Memory of that afternoon's distress made an honest man of him. He never stole again.

Some children are natural show-offs, but most people remember the terror of embarrassment, shyness, and stage fright—the fear that the carefully studied lines would be forgotten—that accompanied recitations of poems before one's classmates at school.

Bernard learned by heart a famous poem. He recited it many times to his mother while he was girding himself for his ordeal. Finally he recited it at school.

A few nights later the family was visiting Mr. and Mrs. Mannes Baum, the first friends his father had made in this country, and Miss Belle suddenly decided to show off her child's latest accomplishment. She directed him to recite. Never was her power to compel obedience so severely tested, but it held. Bernie arose, struck an attitude, and began:

"On Linden when the sun was low . . ."

At this point Dr. Baruch, who had probably had all he could stand of the singsong cadence he had heard around the house during the preceding weeks, put his finger alongside his nose and emitted sounds something like this:

"Ta-dah—ta—dah—ta—dah—ta—dah."

That ended the elocution for that night and for all time. There being no way to get through the floor, the boy darted out of the room, dashed through the front door, and ran all the way home. His career as an orator was finished. Dr. Baruch was distressed at the result of his derision. He told Bernie afterward that he regretted it exceedingly. But the thing had been done; Bernie had an inhibition about public speaking so firmly planted that after sixty years it is still potent.

Near Camden was Factory Pond, whose water supplied the power for Malone's Mill. Here the Baruch boys learned to swim. The pond had the sporting element of danger: during a period of high water a boy they knew had been carried over the dam and his leg had been broken on the rocks below.

The chief feature of the pond was that it had natural markers to determine swimming prowess. There was First Stump, Second Stump, Third Stump, and Flat Stump. What a thrill when Bernie first swam fearfully out to First Stump and hung there, triumphant, though more than a little frightened about his prospects for swimming safely back!

Hartwig easily made Flat Stump, touched it without pausing for rest or breath, and then swam back to shore. Bernie never achieved Flat Stump, but when he went north in his twelfth year, he had successfully negotiated Third Stump.

Camden, being merely a big village, contained only two small-boy gangs. That with which the Baruch boys played and waged war was called the Uptowners. The other was the Downtowners. There was a distinct line of social cleavage; the Uptowners had to wash their feet oftener than the Downtowners. In fact, there was a distinct suspicion, not unmixed with envy on the part of the Uptowners, that the Downtowners did not have to wash their feet at all!

The Uptowners and Downtowners opposed each other in various sports, as well as in battle, though the sporting events generally turned out to be merely curtain raisers for riots. In a baseball game one afternoon Bernie thought he could stretch a two-bagger to a three-base hit. Seeing the grinning Downtowner third baseman catch the ball and wait for him, Bernie ran into him full tilt, hitting him so hard that he dropped the ball. There ensued a battle royal, with all the spectators joining in.

"I got my usual licking," Baruch commented later.

There arrived in Camden about this time Joe Baruch, the youngest brother of Dr. Baruch. He came to America immediately after completing service with his Uhlan regiment. Joe fitted up a sort of outdoor gym for the boys, with parallel bars and a trapeze. He gave Bernie and the other Uptowners their first scientific physical training.

It does not seem to have been too helpful, so far as the battles with the Downtowners were concerned, for a little later a desperate military situation resulted in the employment of a "secret weapon." The Uptowners, outnumbered, were faring badly at the hands of the Downtowners. Hartwig, always the leader, shouted to Bernie to run into the barn and get some sticks. Bernie raced in, looking for barrel staves or anything that might do. None of their usual weapons were in sight. Searching frantically, for the battle alarms outside were far from reassuring, he suddenly spied some wagon-wheel spokes.

Out he ran with an armful, hastily handing one to each Uptowner. The day was saved! Soon the Downtowners fled. After that the wagon spoke was the favorite weapon of the Uptowners. The barrel stave was as obsolete as the muzzle-loader. Later the Baruch boys were to astonish hostile gangs of small boys in New York with the efficiency of the new weapon.

Summer evenings on the porch in front of Dr. Baruch's office, which was the front room of their home, and winter nights round a log fire, there was nothing the boys liked better than to have their father tell stories about his boyhood in East Prussia and his experiences in the Confederate army during the Civil War.

Dr. Baruch was born in Schwersenz, East Prussia, on July 29, 1840, and came to this country when only fifteen, hating Prussian militarism. The only person his parents knew in America was Mannes Baum, who kept a small store in Camden. So to Baum young Simon Baruch went. Baum and his wife took a great fancy to the young immigrant, who was soon keeping the books of the store as well as doing other chores. Young Simon knew no English when he arrived, but he learned it, while at the Baum store, by reading American history with a translating dictionary beside him. Mrs. Baum insisted that his talents justified higher education, and it was at her urging that Mannes Baum sent Simon to the South Carolina Medical College at Charleston and later to the Medical College of Virginia at Richmond.

Here he was graduated in 1862, and he immediately joined the Confederate army as a surgeon, without "ever having lanced a boil," as he afterward said. Incidentally Mannes Baum, whose first name Bernard Baruch was later to be given, presented Simon with his Confederate uniform and a sword. He was wearing this uniform, but, one hopes, without the sword, when he performed his first operation, at the Second Battle of Manassas (Bull Run in Northern histories). His superiors commended him for his skill in this operation, he would tell the boys slyly, making no mention that it was his first.

Surgeon Baruch served with the Third South Carolina Battalion, commanded by George S. James, who was killed at South Mountain, just before Antietam. The Third was a part of Kershaw's brigade and had been recruited in Laurens County, South Carolina.

In charge of the Antietam wounded, Dr. Baruch was working in a churchyard in Boonsboro, Maryland, when the Union forces, advancing, surrounded that town. Somebody once remarked that the War between the States, as the Southerners insist on calling it, was truly a "civil" war, because everybody was so polite except when fighting. On this occasion a Union surgeon, J. P. Daly, seeing that Dr. Baruch had more than he could do, proceeded to help with the operations and dressings.

Dr. Baruch was taken to Baltimore, where, with other Southern prisoners, he was lavishly entertained. In telling of this he would show the boys a photograph of himself in his Confederate uniform, taken at Baltimore between parties during his "imprisonment."

It was the practice of the considerate generals in this 1861-1865 war to exchange doctors as speedily as possible, so that the sick and wounded might not lack for medical attention; so Dr. Baruch was soon back with his command.

How the boys thrilled when he told them of watching Pickett's charge at Gettysburg! Again he was in charge of the wounded when advancing Federals surrounded his casualties. This time considerate Union surgeons not only gave him medical supplies and a wagon to haul them to his field hospital, but presented him with eggs and wine for his patients.

Again he was taken to Baltimore, but this time his treatment was drastic, for those "civil" war days. He was actually interned at Fort McHenry, where the flag that had inspired Francis Scott Key years before had flown. Of course, he was allowed out any time he wished to go to any entertainment the hospitable Baltimoreans were giving, but only on his solemn promise to come back as soon as the entertainment was over!

It was really tough, but there was an explanation for it. It seems that the wife of a Union surgeon had been arrested on a civil charge in West Virginia and was actually being kept in jail. So this was by way of retaliation.

While he was thus imprisoned, Dr. Baruch wrote *Bayonet*

Wounds of the Chest. During the First World War Surgeon General Ireland told Bernard Baruch that this work was still of value to military surgeons.

Eventually the Union surgeon in West Virginia escaped so the cruel restrictions were relaxed, and Dr. Baruch was exchanged again.

In July, 1864, Dr. Baruch was transferred to the 13th Mississippi Infantry, which was futilely trying, with what was left of Joseph E. Johnston's army, to resist Sherman. The doctor organized a temporary hospital in several churches, two small factories, and a hotel at Thomasville, right in the path of Sherman's army. There he performed operations all night long by the light of pine torches.

This was the last of his war experiences. He collapsed with a fever brought on by his round-the-clock operating schedule. When he regained consciousness the war was over.

Turning northward meanwhile, in pursuit of General Joseph E. Johnston's Confederate army, Sherman's men put Dr. Baruch in a danger he knew nothing about until after Lee's surrender. On his occasional furloughs during the war, the doctor had been paying court to Miss Belle. She had painted a picture of him which hung on a wall in the Wolfe home. When Sherman's men burned the house Belle rushed in and rescued this picture. As she dashed from the house a Union soldier stopped her, tore the picture from her arms, and destroyed it before her eyes. What she said to him is not recorded, but it caused the soldier in fury to slap her face.

Then came the menace to Dr. Baruch's happiness. A young Union officer, Captain Cantine, rushed up and proceeded to beat the soldier with the flat of his sword. This acquaintance, so theatrically begun, ripened rapidly. The captain wrote to Belle and she to him, with what warmth we do not know. Despite her northern correspondent, however, Miss Belle married Dr.

Baruch in 1867, and Bernie was born in 1870. More than fifty years later, when Bernard Baruch was chairman of the War Industries Board, a young man came into his office with a letter in Miss Belle's handwriting.

"The bearer of this," she wrote, "is a son of Captain Cantine. I know you will do what you can for him."

CHAPTER . . TWO

Experimenting in medicine as well as agriculture, Dr. Baruch, early in 1881, became very much interested in hydrotherapy—treatment by the internal and external use of water—and decided that New York would offer a better field for study. Perhaps Miss Belle had something to do with the decision to move to the big city; many young southerners of that time moved to various northern cities where financial opportunity seemed to beckon. Educational advantages for the children may also have entered into Miss Belle's calculations. The boys were growing up. Bernie was in his twelfth year. Dr. Baruch went ahead to locate a home and make plans, Miss Belle following with the four boys. It was the first long trip the boys had taken, yet what they remembered most vividly in later years was the marvelous meals they had had in Richmond.

At Camden, Bernie had listened to Civil War stories. In New York he and his brothers were thrilled by stories that stretched back not only to the Revolution, but to Colonial days. In New York they met their great-grandmother, who had danced with Lafayette in Charleston, South Carolina, when that great Frenchman was touring the United States he had helped create.

This old lady, wearing neat shawls the boys were always to remember, and "half hands," as they called fingerless gloves in those days, also had a host of stories from her mother, Bernard's great-great-grandmother, who had been a young girl in New

York City during the British occupation. She was born Sarah Harris, in London, and came to New York as a child. She had seen British officers swaggering about New York, using gold to buy food and delicacies when the patriots were almost starving, since Continental paper money had little buying power.

She went to theatrical performances, notably those of the Garrison Dramatic Club, of which Major John André, later to be executed as a spy in connection with the Benedict Arnold treason, was a leading spirit. She knew about the horse racing, cockfighting, and even bullbaiting for the amusement of the British officers.

Sarah Harris also told her daughter, who told the Baruch boys, of their first ancestor to come to America, in 1696 or 1697. This was Isaac Rodriquez Marques. In old records the name was also spelled Marquis, Marquiz, and Marquise. Marques is favored because it eventually became Marks, pronounced the same way as Marques probably was.

Marques was a Spanish-Portuguese Jew whose people had been expelled after the reconquest of the Iberian Peninsula by the Christians. The Spanish and Portuguese Jews were perhaps the most cultured group in Europe and included many famous artists, scholars, surgeons, mathematicians, poets, merchants, and navigators. Just before the first voyage of Columbus they were exiled, threatened with death if they remained.

For this reason the family never took seriously one legend that a Marques had been court physician to Ferdinand and Isabella. They regarded it as possible, but highly improbable, since he would have died at the stake if his ancestry had been discovered.

Maybe Isaac Rodriquez Marques was a pirate. If so, he probably reformed after coming to New York. He sailed ships, and later sent them, to Africa for slaves and ivory. Usually his slave ships unloaded the slaves in the West Indies and then took on rum for New York, but sometimes they brought Negroes directly to New York.

On at least one voyage his ship, the *Dolphin*, carried a surgeon, which for those times was so unusual as to be a matter of widespread comment. That Marques was not a pirate, at least not after settling in New York, is indicated by the fact that when a reform governor, the Earl of Bellamont, was trying to clean up the port he left Marques alone.

The port of New York needed a bit of reform at that time, incidentally, since previous administrations had been so hospitable to skippers who did not have proper manifests for their cargoes that New York had become a perfect haven for the skull-and-crossbone gentry.

It was on September 17, 1697, that Marques became a "freeman," or voting citizen, of New York, taking the oath on the steps of the City Hall, flanked by a pillory, cage, whipping post, and ducking stool. He paid £5 for the privilege.

The mayor of New York who conferred the dignity of freeman on Marques was William Merritt, who himself had sailed his ship into port only 6 years before, and whose store, on Broad Street, was reported to stock its shelves largely from pirates' loot.

New York was then a bustling town of 3,000, but only two or three suburban streets extended beyond the wooden wall, whence Wall Street got its name. Marques' first New York home was a house in Dock Street, now 64 Pearl Street, which he rented from Adolphus Flypse—a name that became Phillipse, as Marques became Marks. Next he bought, for £550, from John Burrow, a "large brick house" in Queen Street, the grounds of which ran through to the East River.

Diagonally across from the Marques home lived the widow and children of Captain William Kidd, who had a short time before been hanged in London on the charge of piracy and whose name to this day, strangely enough, is the one most associated with buccaneering. Strangely, because evidence tends to show that Captain Kidd was not a pirate at all but was executed on charges made up out of whole cloth. One of Marques's friends, William Emott, a vestryman of Trinity Church, was the defending lawyer for Captain Kidd.

Nicholas Roosevelt, a sugar importer, was alderman of Marques' ward. Abraham De Peyster lived only a block away. Night watchmen patrolled these streets, ringing bells and announcing the hour and weather, as in the days of ancient London. Chimneys and hearths were frequently inspected by city officers to guard against fire hazards.

Another associate of Marques, the records show, was Rip Van Dam, who had a shipyard on North River in the rear of Trinity Church. Van Dam was the first native-born American to serve as governor of New York. Still another associate was William Peartree, who was also in the slave trade. Peartree had run away to sea as a boy, become master of his ship, established a plantation in Jamaica, and then moved to New York. As mayor of New York, Peartree established the first free school in Manhattan.

Marques made his will, in which he requested Rabbi Abraham de Lucena, of the Beaver Street Synagogue, and Luiz Gomez to aid his wife in the management of her estate, and sailed away. He was never heard from again. Shipwreck and piracy took a heavy toll in the early days of the eighteenth century.

Marques' grandson, Isaac Marks, fled from New York when the British entered during the Revolution, taking his son, Samuel Mendez Marks, to Albany. There Isaac joined Colonel Kilian van Rensselaer's 4th Albany County Regiment of militia.

Samuel returned to New York with his father after the Revolution and married the great-great-grandmother of Baruch. A short time later he moved to Charleston, South Carolina. At that time he was a shipowner, but he seems to have fallen on evil days, financially, for the Charleston City Directory of 1802 records him as the proprietor of a small store.

Samuel's daughter, Deborah, married the Reverend Hartwig Cohen, and their daughter, also Deborah, married Saling Wolfe, who "looked like an English squire" and was the father of Miss Belle.

The engagement of Miss Belle's parents was contracted in the old Jewish manner, with stipulations as to dowry and what the groom should bring to the household in the way of worldly wealth. It was dated: "70th year of Independence of the United States and month of Cheshvan 5606."

They had a pleasant home, even "after Sherman." There was boxwood in their garden and apricot trees and flowers. There was a vegetable garden and apple and fig trees. Most important of all to small Bernard Baruch, when he visited his grandparents, was a railroad that ran behind the house. It was the old Charlotte, Columbia and Augusta line. Bernie often threw stones at the trains and dreamed of growing up to be a railroad man, of owning a railroad, *that* railroad! Years later he almost got it.

When he arrived in New York with his parents in 1881, Bernard Baruch was still short and fat. His face was covered with freckles, and the nickname Bunch seemed a "natural" to his playmates. His chief ambition at the time was to become more adept at the art of self-defense. Not that he would have put it in those words, then—he was interested in avoiding the beatings he had to take, some from bigger boys, some from stronger boys, but lots from boys who were better boxers.

He began going to Wood's gymnasium, on 28th Street, and he continued his boxing lessons and general athletic training until long after he had left college. Bernard felt that it made him conciliatory, tolerant, and patient, just to know that if tolerance and patience no longer served he was there with the punch. When he learned to fight he lost the ungovernable temper of his early childhood.

The first New York home of the Baruchs was the boarding-house of Mrs. or Miss (no one remembers whether she was a widow or a spinster) Jacobs, 144 West 57th Street. The father and mother and the two younger boys, Herman and Sailing, all slept in one room; Hartwig and Bernie had a small hall room. On cold nights of their first northern winter they found it pleasant to lie up against the wall, because the chimney was there.

Dr. Baruch did not build up a practice quickly. He grew sick, and his ailment was diagnosed as heart disease. The family was in despair. They came very close to moving south again, thinking that the climate would be better for the doctor's health. A specialist relieved this worry by telling Dr. Baruch that his heart was sound, that his trouble was nervous indigestion. Pretty soon patients began to come, and, more important, to pay their bills, whereupon the worry that had brought about the supposed heart trouble disappeared.

Bernie attended Public School No. 69, on 54th Street, between Sixth and Seventh Avenues. The principal was Matthew J. Elgas. Bernie's first teacher was Katherine Blake, and she must have been very sweet, or perhaps Bernie, exerting some foreshadowing of the charm he could so easily turn on in later years, became teacher's pet. Certainly he would wax almost sentimental when talking about her in after years. She gave him the first prize he ever won, a copy of *Oliver Twist,* with the inscription "Awarded to Bernard Baruch for Gentlemanly Deportment and General Excellence, June, 1881." This volume is still on the shelves at Baruch's New York home, 1055 Fifth Avenue, as this is written, more than sixty-two years later.

The first few days Baruch attended school the teachers were worried about whether he, and some other new boys, could find their way home. Volunteers were called for to show the youngsters. His guide the first day was Clarence Housman, later to be his partner in Wall Street. Another of the guides was Frederick B. Sondern, who nearly forty years later was to be called in when one of Bernard's children was sick.

Where the Plaza now stands lived a squatter who owned a bad-tempered little dog. This dog used to chase a girl named Annie Griffen, who lived in a brownstone house at 41 West 58th Street. Annie Griffen was to become Mrs. Bernard M. Baruch, but he didn't know her then but admired her from a distance safely out of squelching range and was bitter about the nasty dog that made this lovely creature run. Miss Griffen at the time attended Mrs. Sylvanus Reed's school on East 53rd Street.

One of Bernie's classmates was the son of a blacksmith named Gardner, who pounded his anvil on the north side of 57th Street and whose bulging muscles were the pattern of the goal for which he was striving.

The most dreaded of boy gangs in that neighborhood was the 52nd Streeters, led by one McNally, for whom Bernie had great admiration, mixed with gratitude because McNally never gave him a beating. A lieutenant of McNally named Johnston, however, attended to this thoroughly.

About this time the new weapon served its purpose. One day four of the enemy cornered Hartwig near the Baruch home. Hartwig yelled to Bernie to get the wagon spoke. While Bernie was running for it Hartwig played for time by offering to fight any two of them at once. This touched the sporting instinct of one of them, who offered to take Hartwig on by himself. Hartwig gave him a thorough beating.

Maybe it was Hartwig's fighting ability, thus demonstrated or maybe it was the wagon spoke so menacingly produced by Bernie. At any rate, a lasting peace ensued. After that the 52nd Streeters conducted no more raids in the Baruch country. The lads in that vicinity were able even to play marbles without risk of having them snatched.

During the summers of that period Dr. Baruch substituted for Dr. William Frothingham, and, to be nearer the Frothingham patients, lived during the hot months in the Frothingham house at 157th Street and St. Nicholas Avenue. From the house thick woods, where blackberries and honeysuckle, and plenty of poison ivy, grew, stretched back toward the Harlem River. The marshy stretches of the Harlem were fine for crabbing, as the boys soon learned, but what they liked best was to hire boats and go on cruises of adventure. On one of these voyages they encountered some strange boys in another boat and at once began to tell them wild tales about their journeys to the South Seas, putting into the stories, as though it were gospel truth, everything they had read in adventure books and everything they had been imagining as they rowed their small boat from cove to cove.

When almost home there was a collision "at sea"—nearly 30 feet, as a matter of fact, from the nearest land. Bernie was knocked overboard and, though a fair swimmer by that time, became so entangled in ropes and weeds that he was sure he would drown.

Fifty years later he could still remember what he had thought during those dreadful moments. He was sure that it was punishment for having been such a dreadful liar, but then he remembered that he had killed a black cat, which everyone knew was bad luck. Finally he worried over how grief-stricken his mother would be. At about that stage Hartwig, aided by boys in the other boat, pulled him, gasping, into the fresh air.

CHAPTER . . . THREE

Now that Dr. Baruch's practice was producing an income sufficient to permit her a little leisure, Mrs. Baruch was finding a new vocation. She had a flair for charity entertainments and in planning them became associated with Mrs. J. Hood Wright, wife of a member of the firm of Drexel, Morgan & Co. When the J. Hood Wright Hospital was established, later, Dr. Baruch was appointed a visiting physician for that institution.

Mrs. Baruch was happy for another reason. At Camden there had been no synagogue. In fact, save for their immediate families (even Mrs. Mannes Baum was a relative of Miss Belle) there were few of their faith near by. She had always insisted that the children dress up on Saturdays, and this was the only day the little boys wore shoes. They also dressed up on Sundays to conform with local custom, but not to the extent of wearing shoes. But she had longed for regular religious services, and these the Baruchs now had.

Bernard studied German under a professor named Hofstadt, who amused his students by taking snuff and startled them by "blowing his nose mightily" in a big red handkerchief. He studied Hebrew under Dr. Mendes, a Portuguese rabbi. By the time he was eighteen he could speak and read German and French fairly well and could read Latin well and Greek "with a little difficulty." This "little difficulty" must have been slight indeed, for he was to insist that he had read most of the old Greek plays and epics in the original!

"What, no Sanskrit?" jeered Hugh Johnson once when this subject came up.

Baruch's attitude as he has looked back over his student days has been one of gratitude to his parents for the self-discipline, application, and hard work that they forced on him. Dr. Baruch justified the rigorous study on which he insisted by quoting a French proverb to the effect that if application is not genius, it is a good substitute for it.

With her sons' musical education, however, Miss Belle was not satisfied. Herself a musician, she had hoped for great things from them. Actually only two ever played any musical instrument at all, Hartwig and Sailing plucking the banjo. Apparently she thought this very little better than the musical zeros registered by Bernie and Herman.

In the fall of 1884 Baruch entered the College of the City of New York. This was not his choice. He had made up his mind to go to Yale. He had obtained literature about Yale, and had studied the prospects of working his way through, which he had decided to do by being a waiter. Miss Belle, however, didn't want her boys going away from home, so she decided on City College, and City College it was. Mrs. Baruch's word was still law!

Bernie's course stressed science and modern languages, but he later switched to a classical course, being obliged to use a tutor to catch up on the new studies. City College was not only good economy in that it enabled Bernard to live at home, but it was a poor man's college in other ways. There was no tuition fee. Books and even notebooks and pencils were free.

City College did require its students to study. Twice each term came examinations, and those who did not pass had to leave. Baruch's class started with about three hundred, but fewer than sixty were graduated. Some of these, however, were economic casualties; the boys had had to go to work to help support their families.

The college building was then at Lexington Avenue and 23rd Street, to which Bernie walked from 49 East 60th Street. His allowance was 25 cents a week until his fifth, or senior year, when it was raised to 50 cents. However, on very bad days he was allowed 10 cents extra for carfare, and by walking in the rain he could have more to spend. Even in the blizzard of 1888 Bernard staggered through snowdrifts to get there, though most of the students and some of the professors did not show up.

Many of the boys at City College worked at night. Gano Dunn, one of Baruch's friends, was the night-shift telegraph operator at the old Park Avenue Hotel. Bernard worked on his father's books and helped collect the accounts.

Often Baruch spent his entire weekly allowance to buy admission to "nigger heaven," as the boys called the second gallery in theaters. There were no reserved seats, of course, so the lads would be on hand before the doors opened in order to race upstairs and get places in the front row.

To have seen *The Black Crook* gave a lad a sophisticated standing. In that show Bernie first saw women in tights. His parents liked Shakespeare and took him to see all the best actors of the day, but somehow his recollections of *The Black Crook* were more vivid.

Bernie's particular chum at college was Richard P. Lydon, later a justice of the Supreme Court of New York. When Dick's sister Marie was to make her debut, Dick saw to it that Bernie got an invitation. Not content with that, Dick told Mrs. Baruch that he particularly wanted Bernie to come. He knew perfectly well that Bernie would not come unless Miss Belle forced him.

Bernard pleaded with his mother. He said he had no clothes. But Father's dress suit would do, said Miss Belle. It was brought forth, and everything was wrong. The pants were too short and so were the sleeves. The waistcoat bucked up at the slightest movement, displaying a wide gap above the trousers.

All this discouraged Mrs. Baruch not at all. She produced a lot of safety pins, and let out the suspenders so that the pants were only a few inches above Bernie's shoe tops. When the shy, embarrassed, and thoroughly ashamed kid was finally pinned up, his face, ears, and neck found to be clean, his shoes shined, and a clean handkerchief in his pocket, Mrs. Baruch saw that a little improvement in his morale was necessary, or the boy still might not be able to force himself to go to the party.

So she made him a little speech, which went something like this:

"You are the handsomest boy in the world. Remember, the blood of princes flows through your veins [an allusion to her claim to be descended from King David]. No one is any better than you, but you are no better than anyone else until you prove it."

The flush of pride this produced lasted until Bernie got inside the doors of the Lydon home. As he slipped upstairs to the room set aside for gentlemen's hats and coats, the last particle of it evaporated, so he just stayed up there. He could not screw up enough courage to go downstairs, where sounds of merriment foretold scores of boys and girls who he imagined would laugh at his clothes, his awkwardness, his utter lack of social graces.

Just why, after what seemed hours of torture, Bessie Lydon, a younger sister of the debutante, should peer into the gentlemen's coatroom, Baruch cannot explain. But she did, and spotted him. She dragged him downstairs and insisted on his dancing with her.

Safety pins popped as he danced, falling all over the floor, but fortunately the suspenders held. Bernie forgot his shabby and ill-fitting attire, forgot his lack of social grace, forgot even that he was an awkward dancer, as he cavorted over the floor with Bessie in his arms, for she told him he was a good dancer.

In fact, he had the time of his life and ate such a prodigious supper of foods delightful to his boyish palate that for many years its memory would make his mouth water.

That party was a turning point in Baruch's life. He has said that if it had not been for the kindness of people like the Lydons he might easily have become a recluse. This seems a bit far-fetched, because he was a good teammate in athletics, a quality not often found in unsocial people. In more ways than one, however, this was a very important episode in its effect upon his character as well as the course of his life. His friends certainly dragged him out of his shell, and his safety pins, that night!

Despite the lad's interest in languages, the professor who seems to have had the most influence on his mental processes taught political economy. This was George B. Newcomb, who insisted that two and two always make four and that you can't lift yourself by your own bootstraps.

"When prices go up," Professor Newcomb said to the boys, "two processes will set in—increased production and decreased consumption. The effect will be a gradual fall in prices. If prices get too low, two processes will set in: (1) decreased production, because a man will not continue to produce at a loss, and (2) increased consumption. These two forces will tend to establish the normal balance."

"Simple and true," Baruch often said afterward, "and yet how often forgotten."

Once, when particularly disturbed by an economic proposal of a left-winger who at the moment seemed to have the inside track with Franklin D. Roosevelt, Baruch said, "Professor Newcomb would never have agreed with the popular present-day economic theories. For he plugged away at the law of supply and demand and taught us to believe in it."

In their senior year at City College Dick Lydon and Baruch virtually ran the politics of their class. Lydon was president of the class and Baruch the chairman of the class-day exercises. Both played on the lacrosse team. Neither, however, joined a Greek-letter fraternity. Lydon was often invited to do so, and by several of them, but always declined. Baruch was never invited. Every year they were at college some of his friends put up a fight in one or another of the fraternities, but they always lost the battle.

This was to have a profound effect on Baruch's life. He often commented on how miserable this type of discrimination made many men, but he would add, with a little pride, that under such a system the strong were apt to grow stronger.

Feeling on this subject was to result in the first interest he took in Woodrow Wilson. This was when Wilson, as president of Princeton University, made his fight for the democratization of the student body. Dr. Wilson opposed any special privileges, such as sites around the campus for the fraternity houses.

There was enormous public interest in this fight, not only because of the issue itself, but because it was one more episode in a long warfare between the president of Princeton and the trustees. The battle became more spectacular later because one of the trustees, always on the opposite side of each engagement from Dr. Wilson, was Grover Cleveland.

When William F. McCombs brought Wilson around to see Baruch, years afterward, in the hope of interesting this generous giver to Democratic campaign funds in Wilson's presidential aspirations, he found a door already pushed wide open by Baruch's enthusiasm for Wilson's course with respect to college fraternities.

Baruch became a member of two senior societies in his final year at City College, the Eiponia and the Kappa Beta Sigma. After the First World War he wore a Phi Beta Kappa key, not for any scholastic attainment, but for the work he had done during the war. He was childishly proud of this, but even more proud of his brother Herman, the scholar of the family, who had won his key while in college.

He was not the class orator; he made no attempt to win this honor. His embarrassment over the thought of public speaking had not abated since his humiliation that terrible night when he started "On Linden when the sun was low." But in college he noticed that some of the boys who seemed most intelligent in their conversations became tongue-tied, and therefore ineffective, in class meetings.

"I have never learned to speak well in public," he said later, "and this may not be a public loss. Yet I have known so many who could have enriched the lives of their fellows had they not been tongueless outside their own intimate circle. On the other hand, shallow people seldom seem to be troubled that way and demagogues *never*."

CHAPTER . . . FOUR

A BASEBALL game thwarted Bernard's ambitions as to his career, and a phrenologist changed his mother's determination that he should be a doctor. In their early boyhood Mrs. Baruch had picked professions for three of the four boys, and Dr. Baruch had agreed. Hartwig should be a rabbi, Bernard a doctor, Herman a lawyer, with decision as to Sailing, the baby, reserved.

While he was at City College, however, Bernard was offered an appointment to West Point. His boyish enthusiasm, perhaps reinforced by Miss Belle's recollection of military heroes in the Civil War, won over the projected career in medicine. Bernard was allowed to take the examination.

It developed that he was almost totally deaf in one ear, and he was rejected. He was injured when he was first baseman on a club team that played Manhattan College, on a lot at about 119th Street, on what is now Morningside Heights. In the ninth inning the score was 3 to 0 against Bernie's team. They had the bases full, enough prospective runs to tie, but two hands were out. Bernie, like the mighty Casey about whom De Wolf Hopper recited, came to bat.

"Home run, Shorty," yelled the boys on his side. He had attained his 6 feet 3 by that time, so Shorty had succeeded the Bunch of his younger days.

Baruch hit the first ball pitched with the best wallop he ever delivered. The three men on bases got home easily. The score was now tied, but Baruch was not satisfied to stay on third; he tried to beat the ball home and win the game. He arrived at the plate just as the ball hit the catcher's glove, ran full speed right into that player, and both fell to the ground, the ball rolling from the catcher's glove as they fell.

There was a riot. In the mêlée someone hit Bernie on the left ear with a baseball bat. Neither the blow at the time nor the subsequent wrecking of his military career ever diminished in retrospect the thrill that that achievement for his team gave him. It was what a hole in one is to a golfer, plus what an end run that scores the winning touchdown is to a football star.

In the days of the First World War, however, he was often to speculate on how different his life might have been but for that particular ball game. He thought he might have been a major general, with a chance to distinguish himself under Pershing. Many generals of the First World War were in the class that Baruch would have entered had it not been for that bad ear.

The other episode that changed the course of Bernard's life occurred during a visit to New York by Samuel Wittkowsky, a partner of his Uncle Herman Baruch, at Charlotte, North Carolina. This was a glorious occasion for the boys, because their uncle's partner took them on the iron steamboat to Coney Island.

Wittkowsky persuaded Mrs. Baruch to have the boys examined by a Dr. Fowler, a phrenologist whose office was approximately across the street from where the store of A. T. Stewart, now Wanamaker's, was located. Dr. Fowler was very impressive, with a fine head, a stately beard, and gold-rimmed eyeglasses.

"What do you propose to do with this young man?" he asked, as he moved his fingers through the mop of hair that protected Bernie's skull.

"I am thinking of making him a doctor," said Mrs. Baruch.

"He will make a good doctor," said Dr. Fowler. "He will

make a good lawyer, but"—here there was more scientific appraisal of the bumps—"my advice to you is to take him where they are doing big things, in finance or politics."

The words "big things" struck a responsive chord in Miss Belle in her plans for the future of her boys. Then and there the plan to have Bernie study medicine was discarded. She admitted afterward that she never forgot Dr. Fowler's words and that they were potent in her decision that Bernie should go into business. Politics had no great appeal to her. She still had a distaste for politicians that dated back to Reconstruction days in South Carolina.

After he was graduated from City College young Baruch's first efforts to get into business resulted in a long series of rejections. Nobody seemed to be willing to give him a job. At last one day he took a list of his father's patients and studied it with a view to finding a possible employer or someone who, because of friendship for his father, might at least give him a friendly hearing. His first call then was on Daniel Guggenheim.

Meyer Guggenheim, having made a fortune in the lace business, had just come to New York from Philadelphia with his seven sons, seeking new worlds to conquer. Bernard had met Meyer at Long Branch, New Jersey, where Dr. Baruch was now spending each summer as house physician at the West End Hotel. Meyer was "as big as a pint of cider," as Baruch described him, but he always wore a frock coat. He stroked his sideburn whiskers as he spoke, had a thick German accent, and spiked his conversation heavily with German phrases.

Son Dan, whom Bernard approached regarding a job, was no larger than his father. He already liked the nineteen-year-old boy, had appraised his keenness and judgment, and, to Baruch's astonishment, offered him a job as ore buyer in Mexico.

Could Miss Belle have foreseen what brilliant success the mining ventures of the Guggenheims were to reach, the decision might have been different, but, difficult as it had seemed for Bernard to get any job at all, this one did not appeal to her. It involved his going far away from home. The same desire to keep the family together that had prevented Bernard from going to Yale now kept him from going with the Guggenheims.

Mrs. Baruch consoled her son that night as they walked up Fifth Avenue. "You see that house?" she said, pointing to the mansion of William C. Whitney, on Fifth Avenue at 57th Street. "You will be living there some day."

His first job, acquired shortly after Miss Belle's disapproval of the Guggenheim offer, did not seem to promise a Fifth Avenue palace. It was with Whitall, Tatum & Co. at 86 Barclay Street, wholesale dealers in glassware for druggists. This was in the autumn of 1889. Baruch ran errands, made copies of letters by wetting them and putting them in an old-fashioned letterpress, indexed the letter book, and took invoices to different consular agents. The firm shipped goods all over the world, and on sailing nights there was such a press of business that he had to stay after supper. The pay was $3 a week.

Not long after Bernie went to work the son of the Samuel Wittkowsky who had taken the boys to Coney Island and to the phrenologist became ill in New York. It was obviously the trouble that at the time was called "inflammation of the bowels." Dr. Baruch called in Dr. Sands, who had as his assistant Dr. William T. Bull, later to become one of the most famous surgeons in the country.

As the boy grew worse despite every treatment then recognized as orthodox, Dr. Baruch proposed that his appendix be removed.

"He will die if we do," said one of the surgeons.

"He will die if we don't," said Dr. Baruch.

The operation was performed, and the patient recovered. Naturally the Baruch boys were proud of this part their father played in a medical advance of such magnitude.

On week ends, during the summer of Bernie's first job, he and Hartwig slept on cots in their father's office in the West End Hotel, at Long Branch. Sometimes, however, Bernard and his friend Ed Kaminski put up at the boardinghouse of a man known to everybody thereabouts as Uncle Dick Borden, at Little Silver, New Jersey. The town was within long walking distance of the race track at Monmouth. The boys always walked, so as to save the 50 cents round-trip fare, and thus have more with which to bet. Garrison, of "Garrison Finish" fame, was riding horses at the track then, as were many other famous figures of the racing world of that period.

Small-boat sailing was another of the pleasures during the summers Dr. Baruch held the Long Branch post. Bernie grew proud of his ability to maneuver and went in for cutting his boat far too close to a pier to impress any girls that might be watching, as some generally were. One of these times he nearly came to grief. He was standing in the stern, attired in duck trousers and nothing else whatever. His athletic training must have developed him a bit by that time, and he was not averse to its being noted. Suddenly he saw on the pier, not a young girl, but a lady who impressed him as the most beautiful woman he had ever seen. She made a remark about the young yachtsman so complimentary that, in his embarrassment, he nearly rammed the pier on which she stood. He learned later that this was Lily Langtry, the famous Jersey Lily.

Bernie's love of gambling manifested itself this summer, not only by his visits to the Monmouth track, but by envious and futile watching of the gamblers at Phil Daly's place at Long Branch.

He could not afford chips there, but one night he learned that chips could be bought at John Daly's for only 50 cents. Pretty soon Bernie was $2 ahead, feeling not only like a man of the world, but with that "how long has this been going on" notion that comes to so many novices who experience beginner's luck.

There was a little hush in the room, and Bernie, turning round, saw his father. The doctor was not so tall as Bernie now. He was only 6 feet, but he was drawn up like a ramrod, his blue eyes stern and unwavering, as they always were when he was serious, his beard adding to the awe-inspiring quality he always had for Bernie.

"Son," said Dr. Baruch quietly, "when you are ready we will go home."

Bernie was ready. If he had been caught stealing he could not have felt more guilty. He did not feel any better after a few well-chosen words from his father on arriving home. In fact, he decided to run away. Actually, Dr. Baruch and everyone else in the family had been terribly worried while Bernard was in the gambling hall. They had concluded, after a search, that he had been drowned. Bernie did not realize that it was the natural reaction from this anxiety that accounted for his father's attitude. He thought his disgrace was much more serious than did his parents.

So he slipped back to New York. There he ran into some boys who wanted to play poker and, knowing the Baruch house was empty, took them there for a game. Only a few hands had been played when the front door opened.

"It's Miss Belle," said one of the alarmed guests. Bernie's mother was not angry, however. She had grown so worried over his reaction to his father's scolding that she had been afraid he might do himself some harm. She was much relieved to find him enjoying himself.

But although tolerant of Bernie's card playing Mrs. Baruch was by no means satisfied with his first job. The wholesale druggists' glass business did not seem to her to fit in with the phrenologist's recommendation that he should be placed where there were "big things" in finance and politics.

Therefore, as the result of a casual meeting with Julius A. Kohn, a retired wholesale clothing merchant who had gone into Wall Street, she wangled a job for him there. Mr. Kohn impressed on Bernie that, as an apprentice, he was not worth any pay, but it was not long before he gave the lad the same pay he had been getting in the glass establishment, $3 a week.

This job was much better training for the life Baruch was to follow later. The chief interest of the firm was in arbitrage—the trade in securities between cities and nations—and in the purchase of old securities about to be retired and the sale of new securities issued in their place. The same bond would be quoted at slightly different prices in New York, Baltimore, Amsterdam, and London. By buying where it could be obtained cheaply and selling in a higher market, a small profit could be made.

It was Baruch's first insight into exchange, and he was fascinated. He practiced until he could instantly turn any given sum from guilders into sterling, sterling into francs, francs into dollars, or dollars into marks. He also learned to beware of certain market dangers; for instance, sometimes the firm would purchase old bonds expecting reorganization, the reorganization would not go through, and the firm would be stuck for the time being at least with the old bonds.

In this job Bernie had a bleacher seat for observation of arbitrage, exchange, reorganization, and speculation—a very sound foundation for the career he was to follow.

That summer, 1890, Dr. Baruch made his first trip to Europe since he had come to America as an immigrant boy of fifteen. Uncle Herman and Bernie went down to see him off and were standing on the deck of the old *Columbia,* of the Hamburg line, when Uncle Herman suddenly said, "Why don't you take Bernie with you?"

It had not occurred to anyone before, but Dr. Baruch, after a moment's thought, said he would if Bernie could get home, put some clothes in a bag, and be back before the boat sailed. In those days transit in New York City was not so rapid as today, but Bernie made it.

A berth was found for him in a cabin with three Cubans, but, as he was seasick all the way over, he did not remember much about his first transatlantic crossing. It was on this trip that he met his grandfather and grandmother, who still lived at his father's birthplace, Schwersenz, East Prussia.

Grandfather Baruch, according to legend, was descended from Baruch the Scribe and from an earlier Baruch who helped King Nehemiah rebuild Jerusalem.

Bernie asked his father about this Baruch the Scribe story after his grandfather had told him about it, showing the boy a skull on which was the genealogy of the family. The skull showed that Grandfather Baruch was, like Miss Belle's family, from Spain and Portugal. Dr. Baruch was certain of this. As to descent from Baruch the Scribe, he said it was not so important where you came from as where you were going.

The boy talked in German to his grandfather, who could not speak English, though he spoke many other languages, including Sanskrit. The old man's chief pleasure was to sit in a beer garden, smoking and talking.

Bernie's grandmother, Theresa Gruen, was short and stocky and had very blue eyes. Baruch had the impression that she was of Polish or Russian Jewish blood. He attributed his own and his father's blue eyes to this strain.

The strutting of German officers made the lad see red, especially when he was pushed aside if he did not get out of their way quickly enough. After a few of these experiences he told his father—he had considerable confidence in his boxing ability by this time—that he was going to knock the next one down. Dr.

Baruch dissuaded him, pointing out that the consequences might be serious.

Bernie was not bragging to his father when he offered to knock down an officer. He probably could have done it. He had kept up his boxing at the 28th Street gym and had been coached and complimented by no less pugilistic figures than Bob Fitzsimmons and Joe Choynski, not to mention Billy Smith, Sailor Sharkey, and Tommy Ryan, all of whom occasionally boxed with the amateurs who trained at Wood's gym.

Fitzsimmons had told Bernie that his trouble was that he did not hit hard enough. "When you hit a man in the jaw," Fitz said to Baruch, "try to knock his block off. When you hit him in the belly, try to drive that glove clean through him."

"Watch your man," Joe Choynski told him after a brief sparring match one day. "If he pulls back like this"—here Joe circled his hand away from his body, striking without the weight of body and shoulders behind the blow—"walk in and sock him, because he can't hit hard enough to hurt. But when you see a man keep his hands in close and use his shoulders, look out, for that fellow may hit you like a mule."

Not long after that advice from Fitz, Bernie had a bout in the gym with a policeman. He kept getting the worst of it, taking a pretty bad beating. He kept on taking it, however, and just as he had made up his mind he had to quit his opponent suddenly gave him an opening. Bernie stepped in and knocked the policeman cold.

Fitz had been watching.

"The ring lost a good man when it lost you," he said, obviously pleased that his advice had been so aptly followed.

Some of Bernie's amusements at this time were not so commendable. One night he was nearly caught when the police raided a cockfight!

C H A P T E R . . . F I V E

Some time after returning from his first European trip, Bernie and his friend Dick Lydon decided to take Horace Greeley's advice. They went west to make their fortunes. Cripple Creek seemed like a good place, from what they had heard about it; so there they went. Bernie got a job as a mucker, in a shaft next to what was then the well-known San Francisco mine.

This was hard work. A mucker follows the blasting crew, putting rock in buckets to be hauled to the surface. Soon Bernie was promoted to the blasting crew, his job being to hold the drill while another man pounded it into the rock to make a hole for the explosive.

It wasn't all work, however. The boys became regular attendants at the local gambling hell. Bernie worked out a system. He had noted that the house won most of the time, so whenever he saw some prospectors making big bets he would make small bets against them, with the house. This proved fairly profitable, for a while. Then he was told by the proprietor that his patronage was not wanted.

"The owner of the place seemed very much in earnest," said Bernie, "so we left."

Enthusiastic about the prospects of the San Francisco mine, they put into its stock all their cash—hard-earned wages and easily earned bets with the house. They lost every cent.

Home began to seem very attractive to the young men about this time, so they returned to New York, and Miss Belle again got Bernie a job. At her suggestion A. B. de Freece, who was active in some of the charitable affairs in which Mrs. Baruch was taking an interest, introduced Bernie to Arthur A. Housman, of A. A. Housman & Co., brokers. Housman gave him a job at $5 a week.

At once he started night-school courses in bookkeeping and contract law. This was just a little chore compared to his studies at City College, however, so he devoted his spare time to that encyclopedia of corporation fiscal affairs, *Poor's Manual*, and read the *Financial Chronicle* religiously.

Perhaps because of his boyhood dream about the railroad whose trains he had stoned, he learned the routes of all the important railroads and studied how their possibilities might be affected by droughts, floods, the discovery of new mines, or the settlement of the country they served.

Soon he could draw from memory a fairly accurate map of the United States, showing industries, railroads, and political divisions. His constant reading of *Poor's Manual* enabled him to rattle off the financial structures of many corporations, particularly the railroads, like an overgrown Quiz Kid.

He did not hide all this knowledge under a bushel. In fact he must have been a bit of a show-off, because pretty soon employees and brokers from other houses were asking him for the answers instead of looking them up.

One of his daily errands was to Jewett Brothers. There the clerks were behind a counter with wire above it, very much like an old-fashioned country bank. Bernard's desire for more time to study made him impatient of any delay, so on one occasion when things seemed too slow he began demanding service in no uncertain terms.

"Get down off that stool," said a bored clerk behind the counter.

Bernie was not on a stool, but from the other side of the counter his 6 feet 3 made it look as if he were.

One word led to another, and the clerk came out to settle the matter. When he saw all of Baruch he burst out laughing and called the partners to look at the elongated errand boy. Years afterward, on the floor of the stock exchange, one of the Jewett partners would yell at Baruch, "Get down off that stool!"

In his studies of the financial structure of the railroads, Baruch became interested in the possibilities of some of their underlying bonds, which seemed to him to be selling too low. At every opportunity he would deliver sales talks about them, hoping to find a purchaser and thus make a commission for his employers.

For a long time he had no success. He selected a man whom he did not know but who he thought should be a likely prospect. Day after day he visited this man's office but never could get past the protecting clerks.

One day he waited outside until the prospect came out. Joining him at once as he walked along, Bernie delivered his often-practiced sales talk.

The gentleman seemed very bored, as though resisting a persistent beggar or peddler but eventually started to listen, for Baruch was talking language he understood. He surprised young Baruch at the end of their walk by giving him an order for one Oregon and Transcontinental 6 per cent bond, selling at about 78.

This first customer was James Talcott. The commission on the sale was small, but the bond turned out well, and Talcott became a good customer for A. A. Housman & Co. In fact, this sale actually resulted in Baruch's being recognized, from the beginning of Talcott's patronage, as a full-fledged customers' man.

A friend he made in that capacity was Middleton Schoolbred Burrill, one of the few successful "amateur" stock-market operators Baruch was ever to know. Burrill introduced Baruch one day to James R. Keene, at that time a big operator in shares of the

American Sugar Refining Company. Baruch was operating in this stock too, betting a dollar once in a while on whether the next quotation would be the same or different!

Keene sent the young man down to the Coney Island race track to place some bets on a horse he was backing. Keene didn't want anybody to know he was backing this horse lest a mob of his would-be followers tilt the odds. Baruch managed to get all the money down without anyone's suspecting that he was representing a big operator and returned to New York with his pockets bulging with money. Keene was highly pleased.

Raises having followed his success as a customers' man, Baruch with a salary of $25 a week now began to speculate in earnest. He did this not through his own office, but through Henigman and Prince, on Broadway. There he bought and sold ten-share lots on the Consolidated Stock Exchange. He would win a few times, pile up a stake of two or three hundred dollars, and then be wiped out.

Asking for a raise to $50 a week, Bernie was told by Mr. Housman that he could not have that much salary, but he could have a one-eighth interest in the firm. Housman pointed out that in the previous year the firm had made $14,000; thus a one-eighth interest would be slightly more than $33 a week, and if the firm made more, his share would be larger.

This arrangement turned out to be much better than the young man had expected. The first year of his partnership the firm made $48,000, and Baruch's share was $6,000.

Along about this time Baruch learned a bitter lesson about advising friends and loved ones on speculations. On his advice Dr. Baruch put $8,000 of his savings in a trolley venture on Put-in-Bay Island in Lake Erie. Every penny of it was lost!

Dr. Baruch made no comment then or later. Some time afterward, however, Bernard told his mother that if he dared he would advise his father to invest $500 in another speculation.

Next day Dr. Baruch handed $500 to Bernie and told him to go ahead with it. That gamble turned out better.

The reason Baruch had demanded such a big raise was that he wanted to get married. The little girl the squatter's dog had chased a few years before had made an impression. He could not forget her.

Courtship had not been easy. In the first place, it seemed almost impossible for him to get an introduction. Despairing of formal methods, Bernie waylaid the girl one day and, raising his hat politely, asked if he had the privilege of addressing Miss Annie Griffen.

"No, indeed!" said the girl, with a toss of her head.

But Bernie was as persistent in this campaign as he had been in trying to find his first customer for an underlying bond. After some weeks he was able, through the aid of his friend Dave Schenck, to obtain a proper introduction.

Now apparently the sailing was smooth so far as Miss Griffen was concerned, but trouble occurred on two other fronts. One was money. The Griffen family was well-to-do. They had their own carriage, which for city people in the 1890's was a much greater symbol of comfortable means than even an expensive automobile was to be later. Bernie, however, kept making a little pile by speculating and then going broke.

The other difficulty was the opposition of Annie's parents because of the difference in religion. Her father was Benjamin Griffen, a Phi Beta Kappa man of City College and the grandson of a Methodist minister. Miss Griffen's mother was the daughter of W. J. Wilcox, a lard merchant.

Mr. Griffen was sure that a marriage with Baruch would not lead to permanent happiness for his daughter. He had strong views about religion, and thought the possibilities for friction were much too great. Bernie talked this over with the girl many times, and they decided that, while it might be difficult for other couples, it would not be for them. Moreover, the young people realized that, despite Mr. Griffen's convictions, he personally liked his daughter's beau and could be won over in time.

But in the spring of 1897, when this decision was reached, Bernie was broke. He did not reform. On the contrary, he scraped together enough money to take a margin flier on American Sugar Refining, then selling at about 110. Brokerage houses did not require big margins then, protecting themselves by selling out the customers the moment their accounts seemed in danger, unless they hastily put up more margin.

Sugar Refining began to go up. Baruch parlayed. It went up more. Then it hung, with dealers waiting to see what Congress would do about the sugar tariff. Baruch decided that Congress would not reduce the tariff (the administration of William McKinley had just come into power, following Grover Cleveland). The final tariff action helped the stock, and Baruch closed out with a profit of $60,000.

So Baruch and Miss Griffen were married on October 20, 1897, the Episcopal ritual being read by Rev. Dr. Richard Van Horne, a relative of the bride's father. Dr. Van Horne offered to omit the reference to the "Father, Son, and Holy Ghost," but Baruch told him by all means to include it. Mr. Griffen withheld his consent to the very last, but finally yielded to the inevitable despite his fears. Years afterward he told Baruch that his fears had been unfounded, for the marriage was certainly a success.

Shortly after his marriage Baruch bought a seat on the New York Stock Exchange for $19,000. His success story had reached what seemed to him a climax. He was eager to tell his mother all about it. But he found his mother terribly concerned about Hartwig. Instead of becoming a rabbi, as Miss Belle had planned, Hartwig had become an actor.

Some time before, Hartwig had met a lady who admitted being a very great actress, though out of a job. Hartwig had been studying acting under Dion Boucicault and thought himself a good judge of such things. Bernie happened to be at the top of one of his stock-market cycles and agreed to back a show in which the great actress would be starred and Hartwig would play her lead.

There was nothing wrong with the vehicle. They selected the tried and tested *East Lynne.* However, stage management and producing directorship seemed not weak but missing; for the lady had decided that no rehearsals were necessary!

One of the actors was smarter than the rest. He insisted on some pretext that unless Bernie gave him $10 he would not go on. He got the ten. The production opened at Centerville, New Jersey. It lasted for two acts, after which the entire company hurried out the stage door and rushed for the train, leaving the audience doubtless planning a little assault and battery. Bernie was broke again, but he was about due for his regular wiping out in the market, so that was not very important.

John Golden loved to tell this story. He would inquire if his auditors knew about Baruch's "spectacular if not dramatic career" and then tell the tale of the flop that ensued the first time Bernie tried being a theatrical angel. Golden told it to Woodrow Wilson, and the President delighted Admiral Cary T. Grayson and others with it one night at dinner.

Hartwig at the time was disillusioned about the lady but not about the theater. He kept on, playing with Robert Mantell, Marie Wainwright, and Olga Nethersole. To the teen-age boys of the nineties Olga Nethersole was what Frank Sinatra is to the young girls of the Second World War, so when Hartwig, as her leading man, assisted in the famous "Nethersole kiss," sometimes called the "soul kiss," he was an object of widespread envy.

Miss Belle didn't like it, particularly the running around the country that a theatrical life involved. She wanted her boys to stay home. At the depth of her depression about Hartwig, Bernie came to tell her about his purchase of the seat on the stock exchange.

But first he had to listen to her worries about Hartwig, and before she had concluded Hartwig himself appeared, almost as depressed as his mother, though for another reason. He had just had some difference of opinion with the fair Olga, and life looked very dark. He was in a receptive mood, therefore, when his mother and Bernie argued that he should seek some other means of livelihood, especially when Bernie offered him, as an inducement to leave the theater, his newly acquired stock-exchange seat.

Hartwig accepted. Miss Belle was happy. Bernie saw his "king for a day" illusion dissipate. He would have to go back again to the first rung of the ladder.

CHAPTER . . . SIX

DIME novel thrills packed the night of July 3, 1898, for Bernie and his young brother Sailing. It was a quiet holiday eve on the Jersey coast, but things had been happening down off the southern coast of Cuba. The United States fleet had sunk the entire Spanish fleet, which had been bottled up in Santiago harbor. Not even a destroyer had escaped. Spain had no navy left. She could not reinforce her garrison in Cuba. It meant the war was virtually over, and it meant a boom in the stock market.

There was no radio. Hardly anybody knew about it. A newspaperman, Harry Alloway, ran into Arthur Housman, Baruch's senior partner, at Long Branch, and told him of the American victory. Next day was Monday, but the stock exchange would be closed because of the July 4 holiday. The London exchange, however, would be open before daylight in New York.

It was imperative, Housman and Baruch knew, to get on the cable to London and make purchases that would take advantage of the certain spurt in stocks on the New York exchange when it should open on Tuesday. No regular trains were running at that hour from Long Branch to New York.

So they hired a locomotive and tender to take them—Housman, Bernie, and Sailing, the latter taken to give the little fellow a thrill and on the slight possibility that he might be useful—from Long Branch to Jersey City.

Memories of the Rothschild coup at the first news of the battle of Waterloo and less pertinent train-robber stories flashed through Baruch's mind as they tore noisily through the night. The engineer whistled almost continuously because the truck gardeners hauling their produce to market on roads crossing the tracks at frequent intervals would not be expecting a train at that hour.

Eventually reaching their office in New York, Housman and Bernie discovered that in the excitement neither had remembered to bring a key. Little Sailing was boosted up through the transom, and before daylight they were on the cable to London, buying stocks right and left. Housman cranked the old-fashioned telephone until his arm was sore, calling up customers, telling them the news, and asking if they wanted to buy stocks on the London market.

They bought a lot more stock that night than they could get customers to take, so the firm made a fat profit, as well as a lot of commissions. Best of all, however, was the prestige this coup gave the firm throughout the financial district.

That fall Lieutenant C. W. Hazeltine, just out of the Navy, told Baruch about maneuvers that were going on in the tobacco industry. Not long before, a spectacular coup had failed to produce the expected results. James R. Keene had bought control of the American Tobacco Company simply by continuous though unspectacular buying of its shares on the stock exchange. When James B. Duke, head of American Tobacco, found out about this, he announced to Keene that he would get out. Keene could buy the company, he said, but Keene could not buy Duke's brains. Keene surrendered. He did not want American Tobacco without Duke, especially as Duke might start another company.

What Hazeltine told Baruch was that a new company, called the Union Tobacco Co., had already bought control of W. T. Blackwell & Co., which owned the famous Bull Durham brand, and that it was after several other companies.

Baruch went to see Thomas Fortune Ryan about this, and here began one of his most interesting connections. Behind Ryan in the Union Tobacco maneuvering were William C. Whitney, P. A. B. Widener, Anthony N. Brady, William L. Elkins, and some other important figures.

Ryan sent Baruch and William H. Page to St. Louis, to negotiate for the purchase of Liggett & Myers Tobacco Co. Colonel Moses Wetmore, president of this company, owned the Planters' Hotel, and there most of the negotiation occurred. American Tobacco was represented by Harrison I. Drummond and E. W. Russell.

The negotiations went on endlessly, often stretching through the night and made pleasanter by such colorful figures as Governor William J. (Gumshoe Bill) Stone, afterward chairman of the Senate Foreign Relations Committee.

"We wore Colonel Mose down with amiability," said Page, afterward.

Union won. Baruch and Page agreed to pay $6,000,000. Then came a question about who should pay the legal fees, $200,000. Stone was interested in this, talking to Page and Baruch. Finally it was agreed that this should be decided by flipping a coin. Baruch and Page lost.

Liking the job Baruch had done in St. Louis, Ryan put the young broker in charge of a raid he was conducting on Continental, a subsidiary of American Tobacco Company. Every morning Baruch would drop by Ryan's house on his way downtown. Generally he talked to Ryan while the latter, a late riser, was shaving.

Mrs. Ryan, who cared nothing about business, just as Ryan seemed to care about nothing else, became interested in the Baruch family, and that winter she knitted a little woolen jacket for Belle, Baruch's first child, then a baby.

Shares of Continental were listed on the Curb Exchange, which then really was a curb, the brokers conducting their business in the open air, come blizzard or heat wave. By this time Baruch had discovered that he was not a particularly good floor trader, a statement that may surprise many and that possibly may not be true. Perhaps the real reason for his seeming mistakes there may have been to conceal his operations.

At any rate, he engaged two brokers and within 6 weeks had driven Continental down from 45 to 30. At this stage Ryan rushed into Baruch's office one day and told him to let up.

"How much have you lost for me?" he inquired.

"I have made a little," said Baruch.

"Well," said Ryan, "I want you to annoy them, but I don't want you to ruin them." He left the office, however, in a high good humor. Baruch's method in this operation had been to sell the stock short and then, after the stock broke sharply, buy it back, waiting for any rally that might start to sell short again.

Usually a broker determined to smash the price of a particular stock will sell heavily while it is down in an effort to drive it still lower. This will often work, Baruch has pointed out, but it is also apt to be expensive.

On March 1, 1899, American Tobacco bought the Union company, thus getting its three former competitors and ending the battle. Ryan, Widener, and Brady went on the board of directors of American, the stock soared, and both Duke and Ryan made considerably more money than they had lost when fighting each other.

Housman & Co. were paid a commission of $150,000 for Baruch's work in the Liggett & Myers deal. As by this time Baruch had a third interest in the firm, his share was $50,000. With part of this he bought a seat on the New York Stock Exchange to replace the one he had given Hartwig. This cost him $39,000.

Buying a stock-exchange seat began to look like a hard-times omen. He had had it but a short time when he was told that Ryan was buying American Spirits Manufacturing Co. and thought it a good thing. This time Baruch did not go to Ryan. He merely acted on the tip and put all the money he could get his hands on into that stock.

He went broke again. He had bought his wife a cabriolet and was proud of her driving around town with two men on the box. The two men had to be dismissed, for there was no money to pay them, and the cabriolet was sold. Ryan stopped Baruch on the street and asked him if he had lost a lot of money in American Spirits. Baruch said that he had and that he had bought the stock because he had heard Ryan thought it was good. Ryan said:

"I didn't tell you to buy American Spirits. Never pay any attention to what I say to anybody else. A lot of people ask me questions who have no right to the answers."

Baruch was shy of liquor securities from that time. He decided that the whisky business did not seem to lend itself to corporate management but was more or less a personal or family business, although that opinion did not soften the blow to his own esteem.

"Nothing but my own bad judgment was responsible," he said. "My course was in violation of every sound rule of speculation. I acted on unverified information and after only superficial investigation of the properties involved and, like 10,000 other suckers before and since, I got just what my conduct deserved."

He soon recovered, however, increasing the shoestring to which he had been reduced to a sizable roll for stock-market battling. He was in around the edges of the famous collapse of Brooklyn Rapid Transit after the sudden death of Governor Roswell P. Flower, and then came one of the most curious episodes of his speculative life.

The "big fellows" of the market were launching Amalgamated Copper, and the bull tide was in full swing. Allie Wormser, son of a partner in I. & S. Wormser, bid par for two or three thousand shares. Bernie sold him the lot. They never touched that figure again, and Baruch made $60,000. But this was only the beginning.

Herman Sielcken, a coffee merchant, talked a lot to Baruch about copper. He thought the price of the metal was too high. Baruch agreed with him. President McKinley was shot on September 6, 1901. Stocks broke, but soon rallied. The moment they rallied Baruch began selling Amalgamated Copper short.

During this drive Ryan sought him out.

"Bernie," he said, "I hear you are short of Amalgamated Copper. I just want to let you know that the big fellows in it are going to twist your tail."

By then Baruch had three brokers working for him executing his orders, Harry Content, Eddie Norton, and Charlie Dewitt. On September 20 the directors of Amalgamated cut the dividend from 8 to 6 per cent. The stock broke seven points in the short session on Saturday. The crisis was expected on Monday.

Then Miss Belle intervened.

"Son," she said over the telephone, "do you know that Monday is Yom Kippur?"

Baruch tried to protect himself as best he could. He ordered Norton to carry on on Monday, to offer to sell stock whenever it rallied. Then, when liquidation came in, he was to offer the stock down and finally, after selling, to buy it back at the same price or lower. Then the operation was to be repeated. Baruch gave Content an order to buy in the stock at a certain price, to cut the loss should the whole trend go against him.

Baruch then went to South Elberon, New Jersey, for Yom Kippur. His New York office could not reach him. His brokers certainly tried, with every means then possible, but they did not succeed.

On the floor of the exchange the stock opened at 100, broke, then rallied to 97. Had he been on the floor, he admitted afterward, he would have closed out at that price. But in the afternoon the price sagged again. By December it had reached 60.

Baruch's profits on this one deal when he finally closed out were about $700,000.

Now, perhaps because he had operated against the "big fellows" who had sent him to St. Louis on the tobacco deal, Baruch was becoming known as a "lone wolf." Otto H. Kahn, of Kuhn, Loeb & Co., was telling his friends with great amusement that Baruch had said to him:

"Please do not tell me anything that is happening to Union Pacific. I do not want to have my judgment affected by anything you might say."

Baruch cashed in pretty well on the 1901 crash but was nearly caught in the Northern Pacific corner. He discovered that Northern Pacific was selling considerably lower in London than in New York. He was about to buy in London and sell in New York when, just before he placed the orders, he was stopped by Talbot J. Taylor, son-in-law of Keene. Taylor advised Baruch to stay out of Northern Pacific, telling him that it was a battle for control. Baruch explained what he had planned to do. Taylor pointed out that stock bought in London could not be delivered in time.

Northern Pacific went to over 1,000 in the frenzied corner that followed, but eventually, the battle for control between the House of Morgan and Harriman having been decided, the "shorts" were let off by being permitted to buy in the stock and settle for $125 a share.

It was soon after this that Baruch nearly realized his dream of owning the railroad that ran back of Miss Belle's girlhood home. Actually it had become part of the Atlantic Coast line, which was closely interlocked and was eventually to control the Louisville and Nashville.

It was on this latter road that Baruch began to figure. With Edwin C. Hawley and others he began to buy the stock. John W. Gates also began to buy, and pretty soon between them they would have had control had not the board of directors of Louisville and

Nashville authorized the issuance of 50,000 hitherto unlisted shares. Baruch and his associates had been buying from 95 up.

J. Pierpont Morgan sent for the conspirators. Baruch would not go but told Hawley to attend the meeting. Morgan agreed to take at 130 one-third of all the stock they had bought and secured a 6 months' option on the other two-thirds at 150. Baruch, much to Hawley's surprise, did not like this. Among other reasons he was afraid that Morgan would not exercise the option. He therefore obtained permission from Hawley to sell all but 10,000 of the shares he held.

Within months Morgan bought the Monon Railroad, pledging the credit of the Louisville and Nashville. This, it was contended, obligated him to buy all the Louisville and Nashville stock on which he had options at 150. He yielded to this argument, and at once turned all the Louisville and Nashville stock he had acquired over to the Atlantic Coast Line. This was how the Coast Line obtained control of the Louisville and Nashville.

Baruch's personal profit on this whole deal was 1½ million. Gates cleared 7½ millions. The public generally applauded Morgan's action, it being considered that Morgan had bought Monon to keep it in reputable hands, rather than let it go to Gates. Gates was delighted to have the public think he had outwitted Morgan. He was proud of being called "Bet a Million" Gates, and that was how he was best known to the public.

One night, Baruch actually saw Gates bet a million, though there is an anticlimax to that story. He laid half a million on each of two cards, won one of the bets and lost the other.

Diamond Jim Brady at that time was arousing interest in his amazing jewelry, his extraordinary gifts, and his perfectly flabbergasting ability to consume food. Some of Mrs. Bernard Baruch's friends, hearing that Bernie knew Diamond Jim, wanted to meet him, if possible to see him eat, and perhaps to look at his jewelry.

Diamond Jim was delighted when he heard about it. He told Baruch to bring twelve guests besides his wife and himself. When the guests arrived they found that Brady had arranged a display of all his jewelry, at least twenty-five or thirty sets of everything, studs, buttons, suspender clasps, card cases, belt buckles, rings, lead pencils, and removable heads for canes. All were gold and jeweled, save one set of all gun metal for funerals!

The ladies received jewelry or novelties as dinner favors and were so excited about these and about seeing Diamond Jim's jewelry that no one remembered afterward whether or not Brady had performed remarkably as a trencherman!

CHAPTER . . . SEVEN

DESPITE his Cripple Creek mining and gambling experience and his one trip to St. Louis on the sleeper, Baruch really knew very little about the United States at this time except what could be learned from books and reports. Henry C. Davis, a breezy westerner who knew this country as a farmer knows his fields but who cared nothing about anything overseas, became connected with A. A. Housman & Co. as a sort of scout to look over situations and developments in that strange country west of the Hudson River.

He persuaded Baruch to make a swing around the circle with him, during which he explained all sorts of things that most New Yorkers didn't understand about western farmers, businessmen, political upheavals, and the demagogues who took advantage of them. He was fond of quoting James G. Blaine, whom Grover Cleveland had defeated for the presidency, and especially valued Blaine's remarks about gold. When a heckler in Minnesota defied Blaine to say who had determined that gold should be the only money, Blaine had replied, solemnly: "The Lord God Almighty." Then he had quoted the Bible about gold, somewhat to the surprise of the heckler.

Baruch was impressed with the advantages of seeing the various sections of the country at first hand. From that time on, every year until 1917, he made a trip around the country, studying everything that might affect the value of any securities in which he might be interested.

Gold was not a new subject when Davis quoted Blaine to Baruch on that first trip. The Bryan campaign was only a few years behind. Folks still talked about the "crime of '73," which meant the demonetization of silver. Long afterward Baruch said: "I have paid careful attention to the theories of those who would find a substitute for gold. I have studied paper dollars, silver dollars, commodity dollars, managed dollars, and all the rest. They have not worked, and I do not think they will work. But gold has worked, from Alexander's time down. Of all things that could be used as symbols of value it has proved by practical test the best. When something holds good for two thousand years I do not believe it can be so because of prejudice or mistaken theory."

In the summer of 1902 Baruch suddenly realized that he was far from satisfied with his life. His home life was as nearly perfect as he could have hoped. His marriage had turned out beautifully, despite his father-in-law's pessimism, and he was devoted to his three children. But he thought he should be doing something more important than piling up more and more money.

He was only thirty-two, and he had, as he put it, $100,000 for every year of it. But he wanted to accomplish something that would be substantial, more or less lasting, and perhaps even beneficial to his country or mankind. Several times he had tried to be constructive, as a financier, but generally he had been shunted off, most frequently by Morgan & Co.

In short he was regarded as a success, but as a successful gambler, and he smarted under this label. He had come to be rather sensitive about the very word "gambling." He regarded his stock-market success as the result of very hard work, aided by a very capable brain, but he knew that most people, even many of his best friends, thought of it merely as luck. In fact most of them thought he had a kind of magic touch and implored him to use it for their benefit.

He went to Europe, ran into a lot of his big gambling friends in Paris, and had a fairly good time. Charles M. Schwab, on that visit, got Baruch into the Capucine Club, a de luxe gambling resort, despite the fact that Schwab could not speak a word of French. He simply kept pointing to Baruch, as the guards barred Bernie's entrance, and repeating "diplomat."

Inside Baruch found John W. Gates, who shouted, "Come on in, Bernie, and place some bets. And don't be a piker."

Gates was betting 100,000 francs (the franc was then 19½ cents) on each turn of the wheel or card. Baruch made some bets, but not enough to satisfy Gates.

He returned from Europe more dissatisfied than ever. The following May he retired from A. A. Housman & Co. and set up his own office at 111 Broadway, the first rule being that there should be no clients whatever. Whatever he was to do in the market from that time on was for himself alone.

For quite some time he actually did very little. He would sit at his office window, which commanded a view of the Hudson River, staring out. He would walk the streets, reciting to himself Gray's "Elegy Written in a Country Churchyard."

Garet Garrett, later to be assistant editor of the *New York Tribune*, and then an editor of *The Saturday Evening Post*, was at that time a financial reporter. He would drop in frequently and talk with Baruch. The two men discussed their larger hopes and aspirations, their doubts, misgivings, and occasional despair. In one of these talks Garrett said, "You know, B.M. [not only Garrett, but many of Baruch's friends call him B.M.], you are not really a Wall Street man at heart. You should go into public life, and some day you will."

Baruch thought about the phrenologist's words to his mother, and wondered.

For some time during this period he actually considered studying law and giving up the stock market altogether. He abandoned the notion reluctantly, figuring that it would take too long, in view of the fact that he was beginning to get old!

This black spell was lightened and the ambition to play a part in public affairs postponed when the Guggenheims called on him to help in one of their plans. The Guggenheims had come a long way since Miss Belle had refused to let Bernie go to Mexico for them as an ore buyer. Meyer and his seven sons would swarm all over an industry. Every one of them was an expert in some vital line or other, and it did not take them long to make an accurate appraisal of anything in which they might be interested.

At this time they were in trouble with the Rockefellers. The Guggenheims had obtained control of the American Smelting & Refining Company, but the Rockefellers had the Federal Mining & Smelting Company and had begun to dicker for the Selby Smelting & Lead Co. of California and the Tacoma Smelting Co. of Washington. The Guggenheims wanted Baruch to go after these two properties for them.

Baruch knew that the chief stockholder in Tacoma was Darius Ogden Mills and that Mills was also a big shareholder in Selby. Mills was then living in New York. Baruch went to see him.

Mills refused to give him an option on his stock, but advised him to go west and contact other stockholders in the two companies. He promised that meanwhile he would not deal with the Rockefellers. This was a great victory. Baruch went west, got the other options, returned to New York, obtained Mr. Mills's stock, and turned control of the two companies over to the Guggenheims for American Smelting.

Samuel Untermyer, attorney for the Guggenheims, came round to ask Baruch his fee.

"One million dollars," said Baruch.

Untermyer tried to beat him down, but Baruch simply refused to discuss the thing further.

When Untermyer told the Guggenheims about it, Daniel said, "If Bernie says he ought to get a million dollars that is what he will get."

Baruch paid off the legal and incidental fees involved and then sent $300,000 each to Henry C. Davis and William R. Rust, who had helped him with the western negotiations. They were probably the two most surprised men in the country the morning they received the checks. They had thought they were merely doing Baruch a favor! Incidentally, they both tried to return the money, but Baruch wouldn't take it.

His next job for the Guggenheims was to buy control of National Lead, not by negotiation, but by buying its shares on the floor of the stock exchange. Baruch again used Harry Content as his floor operator. There were so many sales, with Content first seeming to be trying to drive the stock down and then up, that by the end of one day 116,000 shares of this company had been traded, four-fifths of the entire capital. When the gong rang the Guggenheims had control, the stock closing at 64 and a fraction, up less than 8 points from the opening!

"Where is there another broker who could do that?" demanded Baruch.

Once later, when there was a tight situation, there were ugly rumors about the Guggenheims being in financial trouble. Baruch marched around to their offices and said he wanted to deposit $500,000 with them. Having done that he asked, "Is there anything else I can do?"

The grateful brothers told him that they were actually all right but that it would help if Baruch would tell people he knew they were. The Guggenheims wanted Baruch to come in with them permanently—"just like one of the brothers"—but he wanted to continue to play a lone hand.

Brown Brothers

SPECULATOR

Bernard Baruch in 1908.

On the advice of John Hays Hammond's mining engineers the Guggenheims and Baruch became interested in a porphyry, or low-grade ore, development by Daniel C. Jackling and Spencer Penrose (brother of Senator Boies Penrose) in Bingham Canyon, Utah. This concern went along all right but suddenly, in the 1907 panic, it could not get the cash for its pay rolls.

On a day when call money was 150 per cent, Jackling sent a frantic wire to Baruch for $500,000. Nothing but cash would do. That was the time when there was no cash available anywhere, and the banks were using clearinghouse certificates in lieu of currency. It was the situation that resulted in the Aldrich-Vreeland law and, after long delay, in the Federal Reserve System.

Baruch had formed the habit, after several of his early ups and downs, of keeping considerable quantities of currency in safe-deposit boxes. He shipped the $500,000 by express, for of course checks were worthless no matter what one's bank balance.

The interesting point of this is that here was a sound company, a company that was to pay $250,000,000 in dividends after Jackling started his mass-production mining of copper, and yet on the day Baruch saved it the company could not find the currency to meet its pay roll!

Shortly before this, in late December, 1906, William H. Crocker, of San Francisco, brought Senator George Nixon into Baruch's office. Crocker wanted Baruch to lend Nixon a million dollars and was willing to guarantee it. Curiously enough, although a lifelong Democrat, the only two men in high public office for whom Baruch has had accounts were both Republicans. Nixon was the first. Senator Nelson W. Aldrich, of Rhode Island, was the other.

Nixon was in a curious spot. He had agreed to buy the Combination Mines Co., whose workings adjoined his own Goldfield Consolidated. The price was $2,578,216, to be paid in three installments, the first in cash and the second and third in either cash or stock, at the option of the sellers.

All he wanted from Baruch was the money for the first payment, but Bernie saw that more help might easily be needed. First he made Nixon promise to do exactly what he was told, and then he gave Nixon a certified check for the million.

Nixon, following Baruch's directions, then went to the Waldorf men's bar, where the financial personages gathered every afternoon and where Nixon of course was well known. Several men asked him about Goldfield, the securities of which were active. Letter-perfect, Nixon replied each time: "That is all out of my hands," and waved the certified check.

Nixon went west to meet the people who were selling him the Combination Mines. Baruch watched the mining-shares market like a hawk. While Nixon was dickering, one of the group with whom he was dealing slipped out of the room. A few moments later, as Nixon and Baruch checked afterward, there was a heavy offering of Goldfield stock in New York.

Baruch had been waiting for this, thinking they would attempt to drive Goldfield down, trying either to get a better deal if they took Goldfield stock or to squeeze Nixon out altogether. Baruch bought enough Goldfield stock to hold it firm. When the sellers saw there was a demand for Goldfield shares, they agreed to take their second and third payments in Goldfield stock. The grateful Nixon gave Baruch 100,000 shares of Goldfield.

Baruch and Nixon went out to see the property together, shortly after. They met Nixon's partner, George Wingfield, who did not wear a coat but did carry five revolvers. Baruch developed a great admiration for Wingfield, who was to have many ups and downs but who took them all in good humor, neither swelling with prosperity nor shrinking overmuch in adversity. Years later he was to run one of the best known gambling halls in America, highly patronized by the divorce colony at Reno.

Just before starting on the trip Baruch yielded to the arguments of his old friend, Herman Sielcken, the coffee merchant who had proved so sound in his judgment about copper. Sielcken was sure that the price of coffee would go up, so Baruch went overboard buying that commodity. Having committed himself up to his neck he went west with Nixon.

He got some disturbing messages while out beyond the Rockies but did not realize the extent of the disaster that had befallen him until he got back east. Despite everything Sielcken had told him, and that he had heard elsewhere, the price of coffee kept dropping. His first action was to violate one of his fundamental rules of speculation—to sell the good to save the bad. He had some Canadian Pacific, which had gone up, so he sold that in order to carry on with the coffee speculation. Canadian Pacific continued to go up, coffee to go down.

When he finally tried to sell his coffee he found that he could not sell it on the regular market. It would not grade! He had learned a lot as a boy in South Carolina about the farmers' troubles in not getting so satisfactory a grade for their cotton as it merited and therefore getting a lower price than they should receive. This was another jolt down the same alley. He had a very sympathetic ear—and voice—for farmers' troubles ever after.

As soon after that as he felt financially comfortable Baruch bought his first automobile, a Panhard. As a means of transportation it was not very satisfactory. The French chauffeur could be depended on to get it running each time it stopped, but he was not so dependable if exposed to alcoholic temptation. If it was not satisfactory transportation, however, it was excellent advertising. Everybody within a mile could hear it, could not help hearing it. That was before mufflers were thought of.

The second machine, a $22,000 Mercedes, with 40 horsepower and a bright yellow body, was even better advertising. It was exactly like one acquired by William K. Vanderbilt and the *New York Herald* printed a picture of Baruch at its steering wheel, the first time his picture had ever been in a newspaper!

CHAPTER . . . EIGHT

Baruch learned about rubber the hard way. At this stage of his career he had become more interested in the development of natural resources than in stock-market operations, but his attention was first turned to rubber when he saw an opportunity for profit by buying shares in the Rubber Goods Manufacturing Co. He planned a pool to buy heavily into that company.

He suggested this to Dan Guggenheim, who listened gravely but said nothing encouraging. This was not unusual. The Guggenheim clan never did anything without a family council, and the consideration of any proposal often took a long time.

Baruch had bought a few shares himself, as a starter, this being a usual precaution when he was planning to take others into a large operation. In fairness it should be pointed out that in the dozens of times he followed this procedure he always told the men he was trying to get to join him that he would throw his own shares, purchased before he spoke to them, into the common pool, at cost. It was frequently a persuasive argument for them to join him, as there was always a pretty sweet profit in the shares Baruch already held. If the movement had not been in that direction he would never have pursued it to the extent of trying to form a combination.

But time passed, the Guggenheims said nothing, and Baruch grew tired and sold his rubber shares.

About a year after his first mention of the rubber company to Dan Guggenheim the latter asked him about it. It developed that Dan was not so much interested in a stock-market speculation as in the development of a new idea. An inventor named William A. Lawrence had worked out a process for taking rubber from guayule.

The first men Lawrence had interested seriously in this were Thomas Fortune Ryan and Nelson W. Aldrich. They formed first the Continental Rubber Co. and later the Intercontinental Rubber Co., which indicated the change of scope of the proposed operations to a world-wide sphere.

Aldrich, Ryan, Dan Guggenheim, and Baruch took equal amounts of stock, Baruch putting in $925,000. Additional shares were taken by John D. Rockefeller, Jr., Harry Payne Whitney, Jacob H. Schiff, Levi P. Morton, C. K. G. Billings, and others.

There was certainly plenty of money behind the new enterprise and fortunately so, since the 1907 panic broke shortly after the company was formed.

Neither Baruch nor any of the big names associated with him in this rubber venture, which was to spend millions in an effort to provide a rubber supply for America, foresaw a rubber shortage. They had no thought of a war in the Far East that would cut off the supply of natural rubber from the world. The profit motive was the only driving force in the whole enterprise. Baruch was particularly enthusiastic because he was sure that the production of rubber at that time had reached a very unsound basis. He had seen the same sort of thing happen in copper and other things, and he was sure the Far Eastern producers of rubber had become so greedy for excessive profits and were holding up the price of rubber at so high a figure that the foundation could be dug from under them—and incidentally at an excellent profit to the diggers.

One of the reasons Baruch had bought into the Utah Copper Co., for mass handling of cheap ores, and was to go into others later, was that he had been convinced by Herman Sielcken, the coffee merchant, that the price of copper was being held too high by the producers. This had the effect, he observed, of reducing consumption or at least of curtailing the possible expansion of consumption that cheaper prices would bring. He had made a small fortune applying this theory when he went short of Amalgamated Copper Co. shares. It had now become fundamental in his economic philosophy that producers should hold prices at as low a level as possible consistent with proper operation and a small profit. Holding prices too high was sure to breed competition that might easily prove ruinous.

Baruch was sure now that the price of rubber was too high, and he was sure that the new company would be able to produce rubber, if not in one way, in another; if not in this country, then somewhere else in the world. This rubber would produce dividends for the company and, eventually, a lower price of rubber for the consuming public. Meanwhile, however, his company would have become the world's low-cost producer, he figured, and hence continue to hold a financial advantage over the rubber producers of the Far East.

The first move was to try to develop guayule plantations in northern Mexico. Baruch went to that country and had a long series of conferences with President Diaz, other officials, and plantation owners in the rich part of central Mexico just south of the border.

He was enormously impressed with the aristocrats who owned the lands. For the first time in his life, though he had been raised amid poor whites and recently liberated Negroes in the South, he became conscious of a real social problem. For the contrast between the luxury and culture of the plantation owners and the peons who worked on the land was beyond anything he had ever read or dreamed.

He found the Diaz officials, from the president down, and the plantation owners as well, to be very reasonable. They had very definite ideas as to what they wanted, but from all that Baruch could see these demands were fair and equitable. Diaz seemed interested chiefly in bringing about the development of his country, particularly the increasing of its wealth.

With this development under way and a contract to take the product signed with the Rubber Goods Manufacturing Co., Baruch widened the search for cheap rubber. He sent out expeditions. One went up the Amazon, crossed the Andes, and worked down the western slopes. Others explored the Congo and its tributaries. Still others sought out the possibilities in Borneo and the Straits Settlements.

Two men were lost in Africa and a third was swept off the deck of a ship in a storm on the Caribbean. Captain William H. Stayton, one of these scouts of the Intercontinental Rubber Co., got lost in the jungles in Venezuela. He had long been thought dead when he managed to make his way to the coast. There he attracted the attention of the crew of a small schooner that happened to be passing and was taken aboard. This was fortunate not only for Stayton but for the crew, which came down, to a man, with yellow fever. Stayton, a graduate of the Naval Academy, was a good navigator and managed to bring the little vessel safely to port.

Some time after Captain Stayton returned to the United States he went to Mexico and there ran into Captain Hueneck, who had been managing the guayule plant. Stayton told Hueneck of his adventures searching for the plant in Venezuela. Hueneck listened in amazement and finally broke out laughing.

"What's so funny?" demanded Stayton.

"It just occurred to me why you were sent to South America," said Hueneck. "Just before you started, as it happened, I was sore because the people around here were boosting their prices for guayule to an unreasonable figure. So I thought it might be smart to let them think that there was plenty of the stuff in the world and that, if we had to pay too much for it here, we would operate somewhere else.

"So I put an ad in the Mexico City newspapers, offering large tracts of guayule land in South America for sale. I didn't know whether there was any guayule in South America or not, but I knew that the word would get round here in Mexico and that the people supplying us might be more reasonable."

That ad in the Mexico City papers had been duly noted in the New York office of the company, and no time had been lost trying to locate those "guayule lands."

The company eventually went into Africa in a big way on the invitation of King Leopold. The Belgian king had inquired who was the ablest Catholic capitalist in the United States and had been given the name of Thomas Fortune Ryan, who, of course, was heavily in the Intercontinental.

The operations of Leopold in the Congo Basin, Baruch told friends on his return, would have done credit, so far as business ability and intelligent management were concerned, to a Morgan, a Harriman, a Rockefeller, or a Ryan. He made it clear that he was not defending the labor conditions in the Congo, nor Leopold's private life. In fact, he said, there was a certain similarity between Ryan and Leopold, though of course there had never been a breath of scandal about Ryan. Neither, Baruch said, gave a rap for public opinion and neither hesitated at ruthlessness to attain his ends. In the negotiations Leopold proved himself a better businessman than Ryan, though Baruch always believed that Ryan was so flattered by the patronage of royalty and his unexpected association with it that he made concessions he would never have made in any ordinary business deal.

Two corporations were set up, and Leopold took a half interest in each of them as his share. Apparently his contribution to each was that he was king. But this was not all. The king insisted that some of his friends should be put into the companies on favorable terms.

"It took a smart king to put that over on Ryan," Baruch grinned, when told the terms Ryan had accepted.

So far as rubber was concerned the Congo Basin projects were disappointing. Diamonds were discovered, however, and made the whole project a sound, if not brilliantly successful, investment. For years Ryan would always have a few of the diamonds in his pocket, showing them to friends on the slightest provocation, as an excuse for telling fantastic stories about what he and King Leopold were doing in the Congo.

Meanwhile the Intercontinental was having trouble with the United States Rubber Co., which had taken over the Rubber Goods Manufacturing Co. It refused to buy the rubber being produced by the Mexican guayule development of the Intercontinental. Baruch was all for suing United States Rubber, but J. P. Morgan and George F. Baker persuaded the company not to do so.

The guayule development was successful. It found other customers and was paying dividends when the Madero revolution overthrew Dictator Diaz and put things economic in Mexico on the "indefinitely postponed" calendar. This turn of politics was to make a very great difference in the economy of the United States some thirty years later!

Perhaps the enterprise with which Baruch's name has been most associated in Wall Street is Alaska Juneau. This was a mass-production gold mine, which curiously enough grew out of his interest in Utah Copper and, particularly, his friendship for Jackling.

In the spring of 1915, after Frederick Bradley, J. H. Mackenzie, and Mark Requa had, with Jackling, made a glowing report, an offering of stock was made. This was for 400,000 shares and included the statement: "All stock not taken by public subscription will be taken by Eugene Meyer, Junior, and B. M. Baruch."

Baruch was to regret that statement—as giving a personal endorsement to the gamble that all mining ventures must be—bitterly, so bitterly that he was to resolve never to repeat it.

Shortly after operations began the word got round that the ore was of unexpectedly low grade. The end of 1916 found the stock at 7¾, the end of 1917 at 2, and in 1920 it closed at 1⅛.

William H. Crocker, Ogden Mills, Fred Bradley, Meyer, and Baruch together put up $3,000,000 to carry on. In the depression of 1921 the stock fell to ⅝. Beginning in September of that year the tide turned. The mills made an operating profit of $24,000, not enough to pay fixed charges but helpful.

Actually the mills began handling, at a profit, ore that only yielded 80 cents' worth of gold to the ton! By 1930 all debts were paid off and the company began to pay dividends. For years it was to be, both literally and figuratively, a gold mine.

Not long after the rubber episode Baruch figured in a fight over the reorganization of the Wabash Railroad. Up to that time he had maintained very friendly relations with Kuhn, Loeb & Co. In this fight there were two separate reorganization committees, plenty of lawyers, and the bankers in the background.

As Baruch saw the situation, no one was willing to do anything with a view to helping the company and its security holders. There were wires and cross wires, with always some power to prevent any beneficial action. He finally gave up in disgust but not before he had so antagonized the House of Morgan that Kuhn, Loeb & Co., fearing repercussions in other directions, dropped him like a hot potato, as he put it afterward.

He was a lone wolf again.

CHAPTER . . . NINE

I NEVER gamble."

J. Pierpont Morgan bit the words out angrily, a little contemptuously. His great tawny eyes, which had been fixed on his visitor with cold disapproval, turned deliberately away. The interview was over.

Morgan was to die without knowing that his objection to Bernard M. Baruch's use of the word "gamble" was to cost Morgan & Co. millions. But to Baruch his own loss seemed incalculable, and he was never to change this view.

Morgan's rejection meant, not financial destruction, as it had meant to so many men over the years, but the frustration of an ambition that Baruch had nurtured steadily since, as a young office boy, he had had his first glimpse of and word with Morgan the Magnificent.

Association with the House of Morgan was the one thing that Baruch had craved. He wanted it more and more as the years went by, and he came to think of his own financial operations as mere moneymaking. He dreamed of doing big things, accomplishments of permanent value to business, to the country, perhaps even to the world, doing them in association with Morgan.

His turndown this day revived sharply the black spell through which he had gone in 1902, when the mere making of money first lost its savor, and he yearned to do something more constructive.

Moreover, in offending Morgan by the use of the word the great financier hated Baruch realized that he had been extraordinarily stupid, because he knew perfectly well what Morgan thought of the word, what Morgan wanted the world to think he thought of the act of gambling. He knew that he ought to have suggested his proposal as a "sound investment, calculated to aid business generally, provide employment, and make the country bigger and stronger." Baruch could have said that accurately and truthfully. He really was convinced of it.

Instead he had been flippant to the "King," and the "King" had resented it by a royal veto, which amounted not only to a rejection of his immediate proposal but to a refusal of any association, ever, under any circumstances, with Baruch. And all because Baruch, perhaps because of a subconscious contempt for Morgan's stodgy persistence in calling a spade an agricultural implement, had tried to make Morgan swallow the hated word —and like it. He had thought, in the back of his head, that Morgan would permit Baruch to force the word on him because it was sugar-coated with the prospect of an enormous profit!

The occasion of the interview was this. Charles Steele of Morgan & Co. had asked Baruch, in 1909, to investigate a sulfur dome in Brazoria County, Texas, about 40 miles west of Galveston. Baruch looked into it, thought extremely well of it, and came back to report. Taken in to see the senior partner himself, Baruch said he had options to buy all the necessary property at $500,000 and that he, Baruch, was willing to "gamble half that sum." Morgan was not.

Years passed and Baruch and his friends held on to the property. By 1916, the Freeport Sulphur Company, operating a similar property, had paid something like 200 per cent on the investment, and the prospects looked bright for opening up Bryan Mound, as the Brazoria County deposit was called. At the insistence of Seeley W. Mudd, a former Guggenheim engineer,

Baruch planned to do this. Before taking action, however, and remembering that his first interest in the property had come at the suggestion of the House of Morgan, he decided to offer Morgan & Co. a chance to participate.

The Elder Morgan had long since passed on, but Baruch felt an obligation to the firm and perhaps a belated hope that it might welcome him. So he called on Henry P. Davison at Morgan & Co., who turned him over to Thomas W. Lamont. As a result Morgan & Co. called in Colonel William Boyce Thompson. So enthusiastic was Thompson's report that Morgan & Co. actually purchased a 60 per cent interest.

Before the development had gone very far, however, the House of Morgan, perhaps chilled by a recollection that the Senior Partner had turned this very proposition down, sold the entire 60 per cent of stock in the company to Colonel Thompson at a small profit.

Baruch marched into the famous "house on the corner" and told some of the Morgan partners just what he thought of them, or at least part of it. He told them that he considered it "unfair" (a terribly strong word for Baruch to use with respect to a business deal) and that Morgan & Co. should have offered the stock to him. This did not improve their relations.

Had Morgan & Co. held the stock Baruch allotted to them at $10 a share their original investment of $3,600,000 would have grown to $45,000,000, and meanwhile they would have received close to $25,000,000 in dividends!

The first time the name of Morgan had meant anything to Baruch was when, as a newcomer to New York, Miss Belle had become a friend of Mrs. J. Hood Wright, whose husband was then a member of Drexel, Morgan & Co. He was nineteen years old when he first actually saw the Elder Morgan himself. At the time he was running errands in his first job, with the druggists' glass concern. He could never remember afterward why he, a young errand boy, should have been ushered into the presence of the great man, but he was.

Baruch often talked afterward about that first sight of Morgan. He came away convinced that Morgan deserved his reputation. Boylike, he noticed the famous nose; boxerlike, he thought Morgan would be a formidable figure in the prize ring; and studentlike, he imagined him as Charlemagne, sitting on a horse, with a battle ax in his hand, ready to strike down his enemies. Through the years, whether he was temporarily on Morgan's side or against him, Baruch never uttered a word of disrespect for the great financier. On the contrary, whenever he spoke of him it was with great admiration.

Baruch said many times that he regarded Morgan as the first figure of finance in the United States since the Civil War. When the book *Morgan the Magnificent* came out he commented that the title did not exaggerate, that Morgan was also courageous and usually magnanimous.

Baruch's position on social and economic questions was considerably to the left of Morgan. He agreed much more, during the first 8 years of this century, with the ideals of Theodore Roosevelt. This does not mean that he ever supported T.R. in a campaign. During the couple of months ending with election day every campaign year Baruch was always a fanatical Democrat, but for the rest of the time T.R. had few more sincere admirers.

But Morgan, Baruch thought, had character and solidity which those who followed him felt, even though he lacked the brilliance and swiftness to act possessed by some of the more spectacular figures of his day. Hence he was able to dominate the economic situation during that period of our history when industry was emulating the beanstalk in the fairy tale. The big mergers Morgan engineered, Baruch thought, restrained a tendency of our business structure to run wild, and Morgan saw to it that the combinations made for order instead of chaos. Morgan did not always succeed, Baruch would point out. For instance, he took beatings on International Mercantile Marine and New Haven Railroad.

Baruch resented, however, Morgan's holier-than-thou attitude about the stock market. Also he resented Morgan's ability, in a brief interview, to change completely the minds of Baruch's associates, often, or so Baruch thought, to Baruch's disadvantage. He was far from amused when Morgan talked Edwin C. Hawley into the deal that smashed Baruch's hope of controlling the Louisville and Nashville and the Atlantic Coast line. Somehow the same royal hypnotism, when exerted on Thomas Fortune Ryan by King Leopold, he found humorous. Yet strangely enough the Leopold-Ryan episode cost him money, whereas the Morgan-Hawley deal put money in his pocket.

"I see you have come back with a little gold dust in your eyes," he would say to an associate fresh from a visit at the House of Morgan.

One friend of Baruch was to use the same phrase to him after Baruch returned from a talk with Woodrow Wilson.

Actually, there is no certainty that Morgan & Co. would not have permitted Baruch to achieve his boyhood ambition about railroad ownership had it not been that John W. Gates injected himself into the picture. Gates had acquired more Louisville and Nashville stock in that deal than Baruch, though not coming into the operation until after Baruch, Hawley, and some others had started. Then, when the visit was made to Morgan & Co., Baruch, as has been told, would not go.

Now Morgan detested Gates. He kept Gates off the board of directors of the United States Steel Corporation. Gates was very bitter about this. He went to Morgan to beard the lion in his den.

As Gates told the story afterward, he demanded to know what Morgan had against him.

"I don't like your relations with women," Morgan said.

"That from *you?*" sneered Gates.

"The trouble with you, Mr. Gates," Morgan was said to have replied, "is that you do not know what doors are for."

No verification whatever is obtainable for this allegation that Morgan ended a sentence with a preposition.

Be that as it may, Morgan turned the control of the Atlantic Coast line and the Louisville and Nashville over to three Baltimoreans, Henry Walters, Michael Jenkins, and B. F. Newcomer (father of Waldo Newcomer).

In the panic of 1907, when currency went into hiding, Morgan & Co. arranged a fund to take care of banks that might be crippled by runs, despite their fundamental soundness. Baruch procured $1,500,000 for this fund from his safe-deposit boxes (this, added to what he sent Utah Copper, as already told, makes $2,000,000 at least he had in boxes when that crash came).

Why he did not carry out his original intention and hand it to Morgan personally he could never explain satisfactorily, even to himself. This was two full years before the "I never gamble" interview. He was in no doubt whatever that he wanted to put this money into the pool Morgan was raising to help distressed banks. His only doubt was as to whether he would walk into the "house on the corner" and be put in the light of showing off.

All through his life he was to be as sensitive about anything pertaining to Morgan & Co. as he was about speaking in public after his childish embarrassment. Whoever first said that a man is only a little boy grown up certainly put the finger on two curious kinks in Baruch's make-up.

After considerable mental wobbling, Baruch gave the $1,500,000 to Stephen Baker, of the Bank of the Manhattan Co., and it went into the Morgan fund through that channel, without Morgan's knowing whence it came.

He had hardly done this when he began to be sorry that he had not gone directly to Morgan with the money. He was to regret it mildly for years and wonder whether, if he had done so, it would have made any difference in their relations.

When Morgan dismissed Baruch with the plain implication that he regarded Baruch as nothing but a gambler, he was far more brutal than he could possibly have realized. In addition, he was a bit unfair. This sulfur proposition *was* of course a gamble—any such business is—but it was a development of the type that has made this country rich, a development such as Morgan usually approved heartily, and a development, furthermore, to which Baruch's attention had been drawn by none other than the Morgan firm.

The scolding rankled for another reason. Much as Baruch admired Morgan, he did not think that Morgan's methods of bringing about movements in stock prices (anybody but Baruch might use the words "rigging the market") were above criticism. Baruch felt that Morgan often used the prestige of his name and his banking house to bring about advances in prices that sometimes were not justified.

On one occasion, Baruch told friends, Morgan was angry because Baruch thought United States Steel was worth more than it was selling for. So when Baruch kept buying, after a pontifical warning from the "house on the corner," Morgan began selling Steel on a scale-up. That particular maneuver resulted profitably for Baruch and his friends, unprofitably for the House of Morgan.

When talking of Morgan afterward Baruch would quote Sir Ernest Cassel as saying, "When as a young and unknown man I started to be successful I was referred to as a gambler. My operations increased in scope. Then I was a speculator. The sphere of my activities continued to expand and presently I was known as a banker. Actually I had been doing the same thing all the time."

That comes pretty close to being Baruch's favorite quotation. He was sure it would not appeal to Morgan. Moreover, Morgan did not play cards for sizable stakes and did not, so far as the public knew, bet on horse races. Baruch would talk about this and then comment on Morgan's talks on returning from Europe from time to time, giving out interviews about "sound conditions" that could be expected to affect stock prices.

Baruch seldom used sarcasm. As a matter of fact, he seldom said an unkind thing about anybody, unless that somebody had said or done something against Woodrow Wilson. There is little doubt, however, that Baruch resented Morgan's frequent condemnation of gambling.

Baruch always puzzled his friends by his remarks about gambling. The word had plenty of unpleasant connotations for him, as has been told. He disliked the idea that people thought of him, up until 1917, only as a stock-market gambler. But the plain truth is that Baruch *loved* gambling, loved it for its own sake. He likes to bet, on a horse race, on an election, on almost anything. He loves to own race horses and to back them when they run. He could hardly keep away from gambling halls when a boy. When he had more money he liked to go to parties where there was big gambling, even though he would not compete with such friends as Gates and Harriman.

As he grew older, and richer, the stakes became less important. One summer in Vittel, in France, he spent his evenings playing backgammon with Frank R. Kent, of the *Baltimore Sun*, for a few francs a game.

The stake might not be important, but "he would never let you quit if he was behind," Kent said.

Just after the Hoover election Charles Michelson, then Washington correspondent of the *New York World*, and I were in South Carolina with Baruch. He made a series of bets with each of us as to whom Hoover would put in his cabinet. Michelson and I both thought we were pretty good political reporters, but we both had to send him checks.

CHAPTER . . . TEN

HERE is the Baruch formula for making millions in the stock market. It seems very simple, if one will only follow the rules. Baruch freely admits that he often violated them and not only took some bad beatings, but, in the early days, went broke several times in consequence. But of course the thing to do is *not* to violate them. It is as easy as that.

Following are the rules, not in Baruch's language, but boiled down from many conversations:

1. Don't speculate at all unless you give all your time to it and make it your life work. Amateurs always go broke. In all his experience Baruch knew precisely one amateur who succeeded in making money over a period of years.

2. Never play tips or what you believe to be inside information. Suppose you do get it "straight from the horse's mouth"? So what? The "insiders" are more apt to lose their shirts than the outsiders. They can't see the forest for the trees, so why should their information be any good?

3. Always keep a strong cash reserve, both to protect yourself and to be able to take advantage of opportunities—this in addition to buying all stocks outright. Under no circumstances trade on margins.

4. Never buy any stock unless you have studied and know *everything* possible about the company, about its officers and directors, about its bankers, about its competitors, about condi-

tions that may affect its profits (for instance, new processes in the offing, new arts that may curtail the company's business, political moves that may hurt the company).

5. Be sure your facts are up to date and that you have taken every possible precaution to peer into the future as to possibilities.

6. Don't buy without going into the whole situation with some good investment counsel. (Baruch regards the growth of the investment-counsel business as one of the healthiest developments in recent years.)

7. Never hesitate to admit that you are wrong. Don't let pride of opinion, regardless of how much investigation the opinion was based on, prevent you from getting out—cutting your losses—as quickly as possible. Pay no attention to that old slogan, "Sell and be sorry." If the judgment of the whole market is the other way, get out and wait for another time. The strong probability is you were wrong. You overlooked something in your investigation, or the tide was running too strongly.

For example, a speculator who sold stocks he owned in August, 1929, as a result of his investigation indicating that a break was coming, did right. But if he sold short, at the same time, his being right would not have saved him from a bad beating in the subsequent advance of the market before the break came, unless, seeing his error quickly, he covered and thus got out of the market.

8. Don't talk much about what you are doing. If you do, pride of opinion may make you stubborn and hence may make you violate rule 7.

(For example, if you tell Friend Smith that you are buying Steel, and then comes a nose dive by Steel, you have to a certain extent frozen your opinion that it will rise, and also you will not like Friend Smith to know you sold and took a loss.)

9. Don't let bargain hunting affect your judgment. The stock

that has resisted a decline more stubbornly than certain others, and hence is *not* apparently so good a bargain, is probably better than the others. Don't sell that one. Sell the weak ones. Good stocks are worth more than cats and dogs. Hence they sell at a higher price.

10. By the same token, when the market is too high, don't be fooled by cats and dogs leaping up after the good stocks have hesitated or begun to sag. That is the time to sell.

11. Never try to buy at the bottom and sell at the top. Successful operators never do it. We have the testimony of the Rothschilds as well as Baruch on this. You are courting losses if you try it.

12. The time to buy is when the market is low, everybody talking pessimistically, and no hope in sight. Then, if you are *sure* of the *facts* about a stock, applying rules 4, 5, and 6 meticulously, make the purchase and hold on without worrying. This, of course, is on the assumption that your investigation has convinced you that the real value of the stock considered is much greater than its market price at the time of the proposed purchase.

13. The time to sell is when the market has had a long rise and seems hesitating, and everybody seems to be in a frenzy of optimism—again, however, only with strict regard to rules 4, 5, and 6 plus your conclusion that the real value of the stock you propose to sell is much less than the market price.

14. Be patient. Never yield to an impulse to plunge because it seems to be the last chance of the day. There is always another day.

15. Don't buy stocks on a scale-down. Nothing is so likely to lead to overextension of your resources. Besides, this type of operation calls for a virtuoso. Certainly it requires a talent that most people lack.

16. Don't forget that 2 and 2 make 4. Get the *facts* and be

sure they *are* facts, not rumors, not whispers, not opinions. This is harder than it sounds.

Solemn warning: there is positively no guaranty that operation on the basis of these rules will produce riches.

Two young men, during the Hoover administration, were in trouble. Their life savings were about to be wiped out. One of them was a friend of Andrew W. Mellon. The other was a friend of Baruch. Each appealed to his financially powerful friend for help. Both financiers tried to help their unfortunate friends.

The man who appealed to Mellon was running an up-to-then fairly successful business letter from Washington. He was brilliant but no businessman, so he found himself in difficulties.

"How much do you need?" asked Mellon, on hearing his story.

"A little more than $14,000," he replied.

Mellon had the check made out for the amount requested and handed it to his friend. A few minutes after the friend had left Mellon's office, however, Mellon remarked to his secretary: "I hope so and so uses that money for himself and does not put it into that business of his. If he does he will surely lose it."

The man *did* put the money in the business and lost every cent of it.

The other man told Baruch that his brokers were calling him for more margin, which he could not raise.

"What do you want me to do?" asked Baruch.

"I would like you to lend me $15,000," the applicant said.

"Tell me just what stocks you have in this account," said Baruch, and then, when he had this fact, asked, "How much do you owe the broker, altogether?" It was just under $15,000.

"I'll tell you what I would rather do, instead of lending you $15,000," said Baruch. "Have your broker deliver such and such stocks from your account to me tomorrow, at today's closing prices. I will hold them for you as long as necessary."

This was done. The stock market kept receding. There came a time when the particular stocks of that margin account were selling at less than half the figure Baruch had advanced to take them over. If Baruch had lent his friend the $15,000 he requested, the friend would have lost every cent of it, along with every other dollar he had, precisely as Mellon's friend did. Incidentally Baruch would have lost the money he lent, just as Mellon did.

Years later Baruch returned the stocks, when their price was far in excess of the amount of the loan. It proved a bonanza to his friend.

Neither Mellon nor Baruch read their friends any moral lessons. Baruch would have given no advice at all if his friend had not inquired, after the return of the stocks, what he had better do.

"Don't you think," inquired Baruch mildly, "that it would be a good idea if you got out of debt?"

Several keen students of the market have expressed doubt that even Baruch could repeat his financial success, on the theory that since he has stopped operating in the market the house rules have been so drastically changed. The take by the government, for instance, has become formidable. This includes the heavy tax now imposed on all stock transfers, stiffly boosted income taxes, and the capital gains tax. Present tax laws, of course, make the building up of a new fortune in *any* line of business far more difficult than it was just a few years ago. There are many who are sure that even Henry Ford could not repeat.

Baruch himself is impressed with this line of thought. He thinks the day of big fortunes quickly made is past. Tramping along one of the bridle paths at Hobcaw with the writer, shortly after Mrs. Baruch died, he talked of the difficulty of finding a purchaser for his huge Fifth Avenue home.

"You know," he said, pointing around the deer park we were

crossing, "nobody is going to be able to afford places like this any more or big houses such as mine in New York."

It must not be assumed, therefore, that B. M. Baruch is giving any guarantee of success to anyone following the rules laid down in this chapter.

The one amateur Baruch knew who succeeded, over a period of years, in making money in the stock market was Middleton Schoolbred Burrill, whose father, John Burrill, was an attorney for the Vanderbilts. Baruch was extravagant in his praise of Burrill as an operator. He combined the ability to think clearly and reach a sound conclusion with the courage for speedy action on that conclusion. So many people, Baruch often said, lack the latter. They may be able to investigate and to arrive at the right answer, but they falter when it comes to translating their thoughts into the action necessary to win.

Perhaps a note of warning should be sounded here lest some amateur think he, like Burrill, is another exception to prove the rule. Baruch always used the term "amateur" in speaking of Burrill, but what he said convinced many of his listeners that actually Burrill gave more time, work, and thinking to speculation than a great many professionals.

For one thing he was born in it, so to speak, his father being an attorney for the Vanderbilts. Much of his leisure time, judging from Baruch's stories, seems to have been spent with the great stock-market operators of the day. The time he spent on commuter trains may have been relaxation, but it was spent in conversation with the big plungers, who liked him personally. And it just may be that Baruch looks at Burrill through rose-colored glasses anyhow, for gratitude is a highly developed trait of Baruch, and Burrill introduced Baruch to some of the big figures and thus opened the door to some of his early profitable contacts. Therefore it would be wise not to be misled by Burrill's "amateurish" success!

Baruch's prejudice against amateurs playing the market resulted in his giving a spanking to Hugh Johnson on one occasion, from which the tough-skinned general smarted for days, though this last may be news to the financier.

Johnson was working as a special investigator on various subjects in which Baruch was interested during the boom period in the late twenties. He was beginning to feel prosperous. Baruch was paying him $25,000 a year, and by playing a few stock-market tips he was doing pretty well on the side. One day he made $17,000.

He was gazing intently at the ticker tape one afternoon when Baruch walked into the office.

"I want you to stay away from that ticker," said Baruch firmly. "I want you to direct all your attention to these investigations you are making for me. You cannot do your best on your job if you are worrying about the movements of stock prices."

Johnson was furious for a few days but did not let Baruch know how he felt. Long afterward he realized that Baruch was right. He has told of the small fortune he had made through Baruch's assigning him shares in new developments, notably Alaska Juneau and Getchell Mine, and of how he lost practically all his money, later on, in business propositions with which Baruch had no connection.

Johnson stayed on Baruch's pay roll, incidentally, for two months after he became head of NRA, at less than a quarter of what Baruch had been paying him. Publicity about his being "Baruch's man" made the financier think it wise to avoid the possibility of criticism, so the pay-roll connection was severed.

It is not of record that Baruch was ever as forceful in dissuading amateurs from stock-market operations as he was in the case of Hugh Johnson. Indeed if he had not loved Johnson so much he would have been much less peremptory. Through the years, however, the financier was constantly warning his friends, a great deal of the time unsuccessfully.

"I have done what you told me never to do," said a friend of the family to Baruch. "I played a stock on margin and have been wiped out."

Actually the friend had played the stock in violation of nearly all Baruch's rules.

Anyone attempting to digest these rules may be struck by an apparent inconsistency. He is told not to buy unless he is sure, within the scope of rules 4, 5, and 6, that the *value* of the stock he proposes to buy is greater than the market price. Yet he is also told, in rule 7, that it is unwise to buck the market.

For instance, many who bought stocks in 1930, convinced that their value was greater than their market price, were wiped out in 1932 and early 1933. But if one is *sure* of the value, he will come out all right later on, and too much emphasis cannot be put on the fact that buying at the bottom, like selling at the top, is a dream that even Rothschilds and Baruchs have not been able to achieve in real life.

In talking to the annual reunion of his War Industries Board associates on November 12, 1931, Baruch said: "There now lie before all of us, in my opinion, greater chances in every field of endeavor than have existed in my lifetime. The very things from which we have suffered have created these opportunities. It is for each one to look around and pick his opportunity and then make it his job, to nurse and grow with it. The rewards will be rich in profit and service."

Now suppose one of those present, believing in Baruch as a financial wizard, had decided to buy heavily in the stock market. He would have seen the price of any security he bought go sharply down after that. It would have been years before the slow recovery of prices would have given him a chance for a profit.

But Baruch was really talking about business rather than stock-market opportunities. These there certainly were. A number of enterprises that were started about that time have been spectacularly successful, though most of them had hard sledding for the first few years.

We must remember also that Baruch, even in his last few years in the stock market, had become more interested in development than in the mere buying and selling of securities.

One of the facts that an investor should have, Baruch contended, is whether the price of the article produced or sold by the company or development under consideration is right. One of Baruch's most serious differences of opinion with the Guggenheims was over the price of copper. He thought it was being held too high. He thought the American copper interests were actually holding an umbrella over the development of competition.

Holding the price of a product too high also encourages the development of substitutes, he contends, and sometimes invites governmental interference that will hurt the stockholders. The chief objection is that it prevents the use of that product from expanding and thus deprives the producer of the wider market such increased use would provide.

Baruch liked gold mines. There is always a market, he pointed out, for their product, and at a satisfactory price. Gold, he insisted, is one of the very few things in the world that approaches the status of a permanent investment.

Bonds, he admitted, may be a better investment for the average person than stocks, but one has to apply rules 4, 5, and 6 here just as in the case of stocks. He illustrated this point, and the difficulty of obtaining a permanent investment, by a story of one of the Rothschilds, who, in trying to set up a permanent trust fund put the money into German, Austrian, and French bonds and British consols. At the time Baruch heard about this the original investment had shrunk to about one-fifth of its original value. Later on it shrunk still more!

"But gold doesn't yield any interest," a friend protested after listening to this story.

"True," replied Baruch, "but consider the fabulous wealth of some of the Indian princes and rajahs. I had dinner with the Maharajah of Kapurthala on one occasion in Vittel, France. Several of us talked afterward about his wealth, and someone said that among the treasures of these Indian moguls were gold coins brought to the East by Alexander the Great hundreds of years before Christ.

"Their gold and jewels had earned no interest during these more than 2,000 years. But they still had their capital! Suppose they had attempted to provide income from it. They might have been no more farseeing than the Rothschild I mentioned. If they had tried speculation there have been many times in each century that has elapsed that they might have gone broke.

"No, save for gold, jewels, works of art, perhaps good agricultural land, and a very few others things, there ain't no such animal as a permanent investment."

Even in agricultural land, Baruch pointed out, there is some risk. Lands that made men rich in rice cultivation years ago, in his own state of South Carolina, are not nearly so valuable now that rice is produced more economically in other sections. What used to be good cotton land in the southeastern states is no longer so valuable since the development of cotton raising in Texas, Oklahoma, and Brazil.

City real estate is subject to all sorts of hazards, as he learned when he no longer needed his big Fifth Avenue mansion.

So, like the Red Queen, one may have to run as fast as one can in order to stay where one is, but, in the running, one must be sure to observe rules 4, 5, and 6.

CHAPTER . . . ELEVEN

THE whole course of Baruch's life was changed by his contacts with Woodrow Wilson. Not only was Wilson to become his idol—a god who could do no wrong—but he was to afford Baruch opportunities for accomplishment that cured the black spells from which the successful financier suffered. He was to point the way to the big things of which he and Miss Belle had dreamed.

All of this, and much else that was to happen, was made possible because Baruch was a stanch member of the Democratic Party, not just a regular Democrat, but a passionate approver of the party label and an almost fanatical hater of the Republican label.

Baruch was not a Democrat on specific issues. On the contrary, he had made a fortune at least once because the Republican view on the tariff had prevailed. Incidentally he was much more enthusiastic about the gold standard when McKinley was the Republican nominee than McKinley himself.

But a little thing like differing with the candidate of his party on the paramount issues in a campaign never caused Baruch to hesitate a second in his allegiance. He was a Democrat and would contribute generously to a Democratic Party campaign regardless of what he thought about the issues or, for that matter, about the candidates. And he would vote the Democratic ticket—straight.

Because this known record of his political actions affected his life so greatly it is necessary to understand it. The cause of Baruch's unswerving devotion to the Democratic Party had nothing to do with the ambition it was so effectively to serve. Baruch had no political ambitions up until Wilson's time. He had no desire for office, before or after that eventful period. In fact, he declined a Cabinet post, even when his idol, Woodrow Wilson, urged him to become Secretary of the Treasury.

The party regularity dated back to his childhood. He had been raised on Confederate war stories and his whole family was devoted to the Southern cause. Years after the Baruchs moved to New York Dr. Baruch had embarrassed Miss Belle frightfully by giving the rebel yell in the crowded Metropolitan Opera House.

But it was not the war or even his mother's story of how her home had been burnt by Sherman's men so much as it was Reconstruction that turned Baruch and thousands of other Southerners into such fervid partisan Democrats that the "solid South" has been at once a conundrum and a problem to most residents of other parts of the country ever since.

Imagine the indelible impression on the mind of a small boy that the Camden mob scene made! That was not the Civil War, the War between the States. That was Reconstruction, and Reconstruction, with all its terrible connotations, bred hatred for the Republican Party.

The terrors of Reconstruction lasted from shortly after the close of the war until 1877, when Baruch was seven years old. In that year Federal troops were withdrawn from the South. Then came the struggle to turn the rascals out, now that they were no longer protected by Federal bayonets—followed by the long uphill battle to work order out of the chaos they had left. Not much of this progress was made by the time the Baruchs moved to New York.

In those first eleven years of his life Baruch heard constantly

Wide World

FATHER AND SON

With Bernard Baruch, Jr.

of Republican misrule of his town and county and state, misrule seemingly directed and certainly protected by soldiers sent by a Republican administration at Washington. The stories told of how the Republican carpetbaggers looted the state and local treasuries, of how they prevented the Confederate veterans from voting while the Negroes, directed by Republicans from the North and local scalawags who had turned Republican for the easy graft involved, elected officials whose only thought was to line their pockets.

Money was extorted from the helpless local whites, and more was obtained by the sale of bonds, some of which were later repudiated, to innocent investors, not only in the North, but abroad! All this left the South not only in unspeakable poverty and want, but under a mountain of debt. Those states and communities which sought to get from under this burden by repudiation of the debts had to pay through the nose in the higher interest rates this brought about by impairing their credit in Northern and foreign sources of capital.

This last phase was impressed on Baruch in his financial dealings in Wall Street. The other parts had been dinned into his ears during the formative years of his life. Even the final withdrawal of the Federal troops did not cause him to feel any gratitude; nor did it mitigate his hatred of the Republican Party, though it was a Republican president who did it.

Baruch knew, as did nearly all Southerners at the time and as few Northerners have ever known, that it was a stolen presidential election that brought this about, the election of 1876. When the South realized that Rutherford B. Hayes was to be counted in after that election, although Samuel J. Tilden had been elected, Colonel Henry Watterson, editor of the *Louisville Courier Journal,* called for 75,000 volunteers to put Tilden in the White House.

The South was prostrate but feeling was high. Certain shrewd

Republicans sent for a number of Southern leaders. They promised that if the Southerners would lie down and take it, Hayes would withdraw the Federal troops from the South as soon as he got in office. Cool heads among the Southerners prevailed. Colonel Watterson and other indignant leaders suddenly discovered that they had no following. Hayes kept the promise that had been made.

The Klan, of which Dr. Baruch was a member, had little trouble after that, even in those sections where the newly enfranchised Negroes outnumbered the whites. The carpetbaggers and the scalawags disappeared.

Much as it may mystify and sometimes irritate Northerners, Baruch's attitude toward the Republican Party is actually typical of most Southerners brought up during Reconstruction. His close friend Thomas Fortune Ryan, who was so vilified by William Jennings Bryan at the Baltimore Democratic convention, came from Virginia, a state that was troubled far less by Reconstruction than most of the Southern states. Yet he remarked before he died that he would like to live to see another Democratic president!

Bryan's economic views were anathema to Ryan and to Baruch. Actually it would seem that the views of Ryan and Baruch were much more in accord with those of Calvin Coolidge.

Many Southern Democrats, up until the late twenties, would occasionally get so disgusted with some particular Democratic candidate that they would stay at home on election day. Of course it never occurred to them to vote for the Republican candidate!

In the three decades I have known Baruch, only once have I seen him give anything approaching a display of anger. This was at the Houston convention of the Democrats in 1928. I showed him a statement by Daniel C. Roper, of his own state of South Carolina. This statement said that maybe the convention would nominate Alfred E. Smith, but if it did the country would smash Smith in the November election.

Baruch read the statement, which had already gone over the news wires, with mounting rage. It was a plain threat of a bolt, and a bolt meant of course a Republican victory. For a South Carolinian who had lived through Reconstruction to advocate a course that would elect a Republican was something beyond the pale. As a reporter I followed the angry Baruch, who had inquired where Roper could be found, rather expecting an even better story for my "black" Republican newspaper than Roper's statement had already made.

No blows were struck, but it was years before the two men spoke to each other. Even then there was a distinct chill in the air. A little more than four years later, when the appointment of Roper to the first Franklin D. Roosevelt Cabinet was announced, Baruch managed to prevent his state pride from producing an unseemly display of enthusiasm.

One day Baruch was holding forth to a friend about the mistakes and blunders a certain Democratic officeholder had made. This Democrat was running for reelection; the name of his Republican opponent was mentioned, and Baruch said he was a very able man.

"Are you going to vote for the Republican?" his friend asked.

"Why, no," said Baruch, in obvious surprise. "I am a Democrat."

"You remind me," the friend said, "of Colonel George Harvey's mythical Mr. O'Tutt, about whom he wrote to the editor of the *New York Times,* back in the 1916 campaign."

"What was that?" asked Baruch.

"Colonel Harvey," replied the friend, "said that years before he had advised an immigrant to read the *New York Times* every day, particularly the editorials. Just before the 1916 election the immigrant came to Colonel Harvey in some perplexity. He quoted editorial after editorial from the *Times,* condemning nearly everything Wilson had done in his first term.

"Then he quoted an editorial calling for the reelection of Wilson. So Mr. O'Tutt's problem, Colonel Harvey said, was whether he 'should vote for your principles or your candidate.' "

Baruch gave a sheepish smile.

"You know," he said, "I am afraid that all my servants are going to vote for this Republican. Yes, I am afraid my vote is the only one in this house that Blank [the Democratic candidate] will receive."

The little group present when Baruch made that statement knew that Baruch had contributed handsomely to the campaign fund of this candidate, whose record he did not like. They knew that he had contributed to the fund of nearly every Democratic campaign since he had possessed anything to give.

Some cynics, speaking of Baruch, have quoted the quip of Senator Henry F. Ashurst, of Arizona, that "there are times when a man must rise above principles." Others have said that early environment had produced prejudices that were too strong to be overcome by facts, no matter how obvious.

I think it more accurate to lay this "my party, right or wrong" policy to another trait that Baruch acquired as a small boy in South Carolina and a larger boy in New York City, loyalty to his gang. The word "gang" is used deliberately because Baruch literally played his part in these small-boy gangs and thought of them as such.

The gang might not always be right. Indeed, its temporary objectives might be deplorable from the viewpoint of any individual member. But for the ultimate good of each and every member it is far better for the gang to win its fights even on those occasions when it is temporarily in the wrong.

It is what would be called, among investment counsel, the "long view." To Baruch it is true of each group of which he is a member, starting with the family, then the gang, then the town, the state, the country, and finally something approaching a League of Nations.

Whether that is the correct explanation or not, it is certain that loyalty to the *n*th degree has characterized all Baruch's life—loyalty to the Democratic Party, loyalty to the President of the United States—of whatever party he might be—loyalty to his friends, loyalty to his business associates—whether in temporary deal or long-term arrangement—and loyalty to his principles if this did not clash too harshly with the other loyalties just stated.

All that most politicians in 1912 knew about Baruch, however, was that he was a generous giver to Democratic campaign funds, and it was because of this knowledge that William F. McCombs, then promoting the candidacy of Governor Woodrow Wilson of New Jersey for the presidency, brought the Governor to see Baruch.

As has been told, Baruch had long been interested in Wilson, because of Wilson's stand about special privileges for Greek-letter fraternities, and he had friends who wished to see Wilson become president. One of these was William G. McAdoo, and there was Cleveland H. Dodge, also a generous giver to Democratic campaign funds.

Thomas Fortune Ryan, a much closer friend of Baruch, was making no statements, but he was a member of the New York delegation to the Baltimore convention, and that delegation started off for Judson Harmon, of Ohio. It was when the New York delegation switched to Champ Clark that William Jennings Bryan, whose delegation had been committed to Clark, used this manifestation of the real desires of the "vested interests" as an excuse to bolt Clark.

Clark had been the choice of Democratic voters over Wilson in most of the primaries, but Bryan's bolt killed Clark off, and Ryan had the pleasure of seeing Woodrow Wilson, who had written that he would like to see Bryan "knocked into a cocked hat," elected President. Baruch had the pleasure of seeing not only a Democrat, but a Democrat who had objected to college fraternities, in the White House.

As a boy of fourteen Baruch had thrilled, as did hundreds of thousands of other Southern-born boys, when Grover Cleveland was elected, the first Democratic President since the Civil War. He thrilled again in 1892, when Cleveland defeated President Harrison for reelection. He was twenty-two then, but thrilled is not too strong a word. Remember that rebel yell by his father at the Metropolitan!

Unlike most other Wall Street men Baruch agreed with the economic and social-welfare views of Theodore Roosevelt. But Roosevelt wore the hated Republican label, so while Baruch approved, he was not thrilled. It must not be construed from this that Baruch disliked people because they were Republicans. He has been very fond of hundreds of individual members of the GOP. It is only when they are banded together for an election, with that name which opens vistas back into Reconstruction, that he becomes their enemy.

Some friends of Baruch have wondered what would have been the course of his life had that terribly close election in 1916 gone the other way—if Charles E. Hughes had been elected. Having watched both men operate for a great many years, my personal view is that Baruch would have been tremendously important in the Hughes administration, both in the conduct of the war and in the making of the peace.

This might not have occurred without the opening wedge into public affairs that Baruch obtained through his friendship with Woodrow Wilson. But Baruch was in the national-defense picture well *before* the 1916 election. It is inconceivable that he would have refused to serve Hughes, whom he greatly admired, and it is almost as inconceivable that Hughes would have deprived himself of Baruch's service just because Baruch was a Democrat.

At any rate Baruch had the greatest political satisfaction of his life, up to then, when Wilson was elected in 1912, though he surely did not dream how radically it was to affect his life.

CHAPTER . . . TWELVE

MARCH 4, 1913, was a great day for the Democrats. They trooped into Washington from far and near, but particularly from the South, for the inauguration of their second president since "the War." Baruch trooped with them. He had all the thrills of the most enthusiastic and none of the worries that tempered the enjoyment of so many of them. He didn't want a job or even a title. He didn't want any favors, or believed he didn't. He had thoughts about legislation—quite a number—but was utterly serene in his confidence that Wilson would do the right thing.

The war in Europe was more than two years in the future. It cast no shadow on the day's gaiety. Bands in the inaugural parade played "Dixie" and "Bonnie Blue Flag" and "My Maryland." Southerners cheered the West Point cadets not only because they marched so true, but because they wore the Confederate gray. The crowds nearly went crazy over the gray-clad Fifth Maryland Infantry, the Richmond Light Infantry Blues, and dozens of other historic Southern military organizations.

The Taft inauguration, 4 years before, had been held in a blizzard. Now the sun was shining. The South was in the saddle. Woodrow Wilson had been born in Virginia!

Thousands of Democrats in Washington that day looked forward, joyously, to a glorious administration in which they would play prominent parts. Most of them were to be disappointed.

Many of them were to hate Wilson bitterly by the time he left the White House, 8 years later. Some of the most prominent were to be cast into outer darkness by presidential repudiation.

There had already been signs and portents. The very man who brought Wilson and Baruch together, William F. McCombs, was slipping. Another of Wilson's early backers, Colonel George Harvey, had walked the plank amid a fanfare of publicity. The monetary views of William Jennings Bryan, who had been chosen as Secretary of State, the first place in the Cabinet, shocked Baruch.

Baruch, however, moved serenely into the inner circle and stayed there, never in danger, never ruffled, never repudiated, one of the barest handful Wilson was to love until he died. He was to see Bryan virtually kicked out. He was to see Lindley M. Garrison resign in disgust. He was to see James C. McReynolds kicked upstairs. He was to see McAdoo grow to enormous stature and then decline in Wilson's regard.

He was to see Colonel E. M. House and Secretary of State Robert Lansing *personæ non gratæ*, to put it very mildly. He was to see loyal, devoted Joseph P. Tumulty denounced.

This mutual and enduring devotion of Wilson and Baruch was an enigma. It puzzled Wall Street. It was a mystery to businessmen. It baffled other would-be insiders and made politicians of both parties wonder. The form of the enigma changed. The seeming impossibilities were of one variety during Wilson's first term, of quite another during the war, of still a different character during the peace conference at Versailles and during Wilson's fight with the Senate. They changed again while Wilson was a caged lion at his S Street home, furiously anxious to regain his strength so that he could smite his enemies.

Looking back, it seems as though there may have been just one person who knew all the answers during all these periods. This was Rear Admiral Cary T. Grayson, the President's physician. He adored Wilson. He loved Baruch. Like the financier, Grayson wanted nothing of Wilson save the privilege of serving him and being near him.

For one thing, Wilson not only loved Baruch, he *admired* him. We have testimony on this point. Mrs. Wilson makes the specific statement in her memoirs. It is fairly easy to see why. Wilson was a schoolmaster at heart; he had spent his life at it until he became involved first in college politics and then in Democratic Party politics, first in the race for governorship of New Jersey and then for President.

As an educator he admired Baruch's learning. Very few of Baruch's friends in Wall Street, for example, realized that Baruch had read most of the great Greek and Latin classics in the original. Few of them knew of his knowledge of history.

Here was a man who could talk Wilson's own language—another scholar! This, combined with a pleasing personality, a loyal devotion, and generous contributions to the Wilson campaign fund, produced ground precisely adapted for ripening the seed to produce that enigmatic flower.

Like most educators, Wilson was not too practical. Like most people, he admired extravagantly in others qualities he himself lacked. In Baruch he found not only an equal in education, but a man who in the rough and tumble of business had proved himself an outstanding success. Put this together with his speedy discovery that Baruch saw eye to eye with him on economic and social reform, on the need for a greater measure of control by government over business and finance (remember that this was in 1913), and the desirability of improving the lot of the common man, and you have nearly everything that is needed for a working personal and political alliance.

But there was another element, one not so easy to understand, one almost incomprehensible to scores of men I have known who admired Baruch extravagantly but could never fathom his attitude toward Wilson.

When his relationship with Wilson began, Baruch gave Wilson, at once, the same unswerving, unquestioning, and absolute obedience that all his life he gave Miss Belle. It simply never occurred to him to question any decision of or command from Wilson. The President became a superbeing to Baruch. The Baruch brain, so active and so relentless in pursuit of every fact in connection with every other situation and every other person, had a different formula when it came to Miss Belle and Woodrow Wilson. This was to start on the premise that his mother or the President, as the case might be, was absolutely right—and then go on from there!

Senator John Sharp Williams, of Mississippi, and Carter Glass, of Virginia, then a Representative, later Secretary of the Treasury and then Senator, were under the same sort of spell. They *understood* Baruch's feeling for the President, but probably even they did not appreciate and understand the President's feeling for Baruch as did Cary Grayson.

Mr. Wilson had not been in office long before he had various opportunities to determine just how selfless was Baruch's devotion to the President and to Wilson's ideas of what was best for the United States. The first big legislative problem was the tariff. Every President in whose administration there has been a general revision of the tariff law has experienced a lot of grief. It was in the tariff revision that enmities grew up between President Cleveland and a powerful group of senators headed by Arthur Pue Gorman, of Maryland. Theodore Roosevelt did not have a general tariff revision. Neither did Calvin Coolidge. In Franklin D. Roosevelt's administration this was avoided by the reciprocal trade-agreement plan.

Taft never recovered from the effects of his signature of the Payne-Aldrich tariff bill in 1909. "Schedule K" became a term of opprobrium. Hoover never recovered from the effects of signing the Smoot-Hawley bill.

In the Wilson revision, which was to correct the highly unpopular Payne-Aldrich bill, Wilson alienated many powerful Democrats, for example, the "sugar senators," notably those from Louisiana and the beet-sugar-producing states. Every special interest in the country brought all the influence it could to bear. Wilson found out that Democrats did not really mean their old slogan "a tariff for revenue only," unless the words "except on the products of our section" were added.

Here was Baruch, with money invested in industries that were crying to be spared from the ruin they alleged would come upon them if the Wilson schedules were put into effect, with friends in almost every possible line that might be hurt. Here was a big campaign contributor, who had the right, as most politicians saw it, to ask for favors. He asked nothing, either of Wilson direct or of the growing number of his friends on Capitol Hill.

Then came the Hetch-Hetchy bill, which provided a water- and electric-power supply for San Francisco and in which left-wingers of the day had inserted a provision that none of the power could ever be sold to any private corporation—a long step toward forcing government operation on the California city. Again close friends of Baruch were aghast, were sure that he would use his influence with Wilson and with Congress to prevent this outrage. As far as Baruch's talks with Wilson at the time were concerned, however, Baruch might have been a professor of economics from Columbia—a professor who had actually had practical experience.

Next came an even more searching test, the Alaska railroad bill. It should be remembered that the clamor for the Alaska railroad was primarily based on the thought that the natural resources of the country should be available for development by *all* the people, or perhaps *any* who should desire to try. If there was one word more than another that figured at the time it was "Guggenheims." At that time the Guggenheims were busy developing mines in Alaska. They had built the Copper River Railroad to reach some properties.

This aroused a torrent of abuse from the followers of Gifford Pinchot. The picture painted was that by controlling the means of transportation to these riches the big interests were preventing the little fellows from having a chance. Baruch had been perhaps more closely associated with the Guggenheims than with any other group in the development of natural resources. Surely, some folks thought, and perhaps Wilson thought, he would intervene *this* time.

There have been cynics since who said of course the Guggenheims would not even have asked Baruch to intervene—that the Alaska railroad was far from the Guggenheim development, was a stupid thing economically, and that the people who were crying out against the Guggenheims were hitting a pillow that did not even belong to that great mining group.

This may or may not be true. It is of no importance so far as the relation between Wilson and Baruch is concerned. What is important is that Wilson, and most people, *thought* the Alaska railroad would be a severe blow to the Guggenheims, *thought* that it would lead to the development of Alaska and to the opening of the door of opportunity for less privileged persons to develop its riches.

George White, later chairman of the Democratic National Committee and still later governor of Ohio, was a member of the House at the time. He said afterward that just before the final passage of the bill he had been called to the White House. Wilson wanted to know why he had voted against the bill. White told the President that he had been in the Klondike rush, that he thought he knew something about Alaska and went on to give reasons why he thought the railroad was an economic mistake.

According to White, President Wilson said that if he had had this presentation of the case earlier he would not have fought for the Alaska railroad but that it was too late to change then.

Actually the Alaska railroad, exclusive of its spur to the navy-owned coal field, is 471 miles long, longer than the distance from Washington to Boston. The total population along its route, including Eskimos and inhabitants at both terminals, was about 6,000 at the time the road was built. It was still about 6,000 when President Harding rode over the line in the summer of 1923, and the project was costing the government about a million dollars a year to operate, exclusive of interest on the fifty millions it cost.

Next on the Wilson legislative schedule was the Federal Reserve Act, and this was to afford Baruch his first opportunity to be constructively helpful, while continuing to demonstrate his disinterested devotion to the Wilson reform policies.

It will be recalled that in the panic of 1907 Baruch had seen a distressing demonstration of the inadequacy of our currency system. Cash could not be obtained anywhere; clearinghouse certificates circulated in lieu of money in most cities. He had found it necessary to ship by express $500,000 in currency to his friends in Utah Copper to meet their pay roll and had produced another $1,500,000 in currency from his strongboxes to supplement the Morgan pool for the protection of banks.

During the 7 years that followed, Senator Aldrich and other big Republican leaders had tried to work out some plan for a strong governmental bank that would make such a crisis impossible. They had worked out, as a matter of fact, a bill that experts have since said was pretty sound, but they could not pass it. Filibustering always stopped the measure in its tracks in the Senate.

The elder La Follette literally talked the bill to death every time it had a chance to pass. There was no popular clamor for the bill. The people had lost confidence in the Taft administration, which had come into power before the details of the bill were perfected. The idea of a central bank was unpopular.

Meanwhile, opponents of the Aldrich central-bank plan had permitted an emergency measure, called the Aldrich-Vreeland bill, to become law, and it was this law that was invoked at the outbreak of the First World War, in August, 1914, although the Federal Reserve Act was already on the statute books.

When the Democrats came into power with Wilson they at once went into a brown study on the situation. Wilson himself knew approximately what he wanted to accomplish but was not stubborn about details that did not obstruct his purposes. Under Carter Glass the House Banking and Currency Committee brought forth a bill. Wilson expressed approval. The House adopted some amendments. Wilson still liked it. The Senate Banking and Currency Committee, under Senator Robert L. Owen, of Oklahoma, revised it some more. Wilson had no objection to the changes. Finally the Senate Republicans, and particularly Senator Theodore Burton, of Ohio, forced a lot more changes.

It was charged afterward that President Wilson bought off the opposition of Senator James A. Reed, of Missouri, by promising him two of the twelve regional banks for Missouri. At any rate, Senator Gilbert M. Hitchcock, of Nebraska, who thought the Kansas City bank should have been located in Omaha, was very bitter about it.

The chief interest today in reviewing this battle was in seeing how differently Wilson acted then from the way he conducted his fight for ratification of the Versailles Treaty. It is interesting because Baruch was at his elbow then, and Baruch, when defeat on the League of Nations was looming in that later battle, urged the President to do a little compromising, to accept ratification with reservations if he could not get Senate approval without. It is interesting because the Federal Reserve System was changed considerably after the passage of the original bill and, incidentally, always in a way to make it more like the old Aldrich plan, whereas Lord Robert Cecil was to tell friends later that the Lodge reservations to the Versailles Treaty would not have made any difference, if Wilson had been willing to accept them.

Through all this period, while Baruch was proving himself with Wilson and was advising with Carter Glass and Democratic senators about the Federal Reserve Act and other legislation, he was still known to the country almost entirely because of his stock-market reputation. When he saw Wilson and the newspapermen found it out, it was assumed that Wilson was simply paying off, with a little White House hospitality, a generous campaign contributor. His visits to senators and representatives were not regarded by the newspapermen as of much importance and hence were not called to the attention of the public.

There was far more interest in the mysterious Colonel E. M. House, who couldn't have breakfast with the President without provoking columns of speculation as to the subject of their discussion. There was more drama in Postmaster General Burleson, who stormed up to the Capitol and marched on the Senate floor with his umbrella, trying to dragoon the solons into voting as the White House directed. There was the forceful and likable William G. McAdoo, even then courting the President's daughter, whose press conferences produced first-page news. And we must not forget Bryan, who, a fish out of water as Wilson's Secretary of State, was providing the newspapers with an almost continuous flow of copy. He wept on the shoulders of the reporters about the inadequacy of his cabinet salary, and the need, therefore, for him to earn lecture fees on the Chautauqua circuit. He preached prohibition and advocated the use of grape juice to such an extent that cartoonists usually depicted him clasping a bottle of that beverage no matter what the chief point of the cartoon was. His lack of geographical and historical information provided many

Brown Brothers

SPORTSMAN

With Harry Payne Whitney at a race meeting.

front-page items, for instance, when he referred to the Central American republic of Honduras as an "island," and when he referred to the navy of land-locked Switzerland. Probably more columns of type he didn't like were printed about Bryan in this period than about any cabinet member since Washington's time.

However, there was plenty of publicity about Bryan that he really liked. His crusade for world peace, his treaties providing for a cooling-off period after any dispute between nations, the so-called "Breathing Spell" treaties, won lots of front-page space, not only when first proposed and approved by many nations, but later, when critics thought it amusing that Bryan should fight for treaties while Germany was making "scraps of paper" of them. Bryan was a great help to anybody who wanted to keep his own name out of the papers in the first Wilson administration.

Baruch has never been accused of having a passion for anonymity, but looking back over those days it almost seems as though he had. In fact, if a newspaperman had had a chance for a heart-to-heart talk with Baruch in those first few years of Wilson's regime he would probably have been hoping for a stock-market tip!

CHAPTER . . . THIRTEEN

UNDER this curious cloak of anonymity Baruch exercised a very unusual type of political power in those early Wilson days. He was cultivated by most of the Wilson lieutenants, who speedily found out that he could do more for them in certain quarters than they could do either directly or by appealing to Wilson.

This power of Baruch was utterly unsuspected on the outside and, quite possibly, by President Wilson, yet the fact that Baruch was important to a number of the insiders was due to a very definite Wilson policy. The President would permit the men he trusted, once he assigned them to particular jobs, to run those jobs with very little interference from the White House.

Thus if *Y* was running a job, and had Wilson's confidence, and *X* wanted to get a man appointed under him or to induce *Y* to do something different from what he was obviously about to do, there was little use for *X* to appeal to Wilson. This was true even if *X* were sure that Wilson would agree as to the merits of his proposed candidate or suggested policy. In most instances Wilson would not even listen, once he realized what *X* was after.

"That is entirely up to *Y*," he would say. "I will not interfere with his organization or policies so long as he is doing a good job."

This does not mean that Wilson took no interest in seeing what happened on that particular job. He took an almost schoolmasterly interest in watching his appointees to important positions.

But he was also schoolmasterly in hoping that his "pupils" would work out their own problems without help from other pupils.

"I like to watch men I appoint to office," he said once, "to see whether they grow or merely swell."

This was the reason, the newspapermen soon discovered, that Bryan spent almost as much time trying to land jobs for his host of followers in other government departments as he did on State Department business. That was the only way he could do it, and Bryan had a tremendous army of supporters who, having fought for him since 1896 without reward, thought they were entitled to get on the pay roll now that Bryan was in office. Wilson wouldn't help Bryan on this, and the State Department did not offer much in the way of patronage. So Bryan had to pester his fellow Cabinet members.

But if *X* could not get action out of *Y* by appealing to Wilson or by appealing to *Y* direct, he very soon found out that if he could only persuade Baruch to go to *Y* the chances for success were enormously improved. This curious situation continued as long as Wilson was in the White House.

Naturally there was no publicity for all this. If *X* telephoned Baruch and asked Baruch to telephone *Y* and recommend some person or policy, there was no way for the newspapermen to get a story about it. *X* did not want the public in general, or Wilson in particular, to know what he was doing. Sometimes he did not even want *Y* to know that he had originated the idea. Baruch had learned on the stock market to be one of the best secret keepers alive.

This sort of thing had been going on for 4 years before it was suddenly forced out into the light of day, but so much else happened that day that this little ray of light attracted no attention.

Baruch, on the stand before the House Rules Committee, was

asked if he had talked with Secretary of the Treasury McAdoo on the telephone on a certain day in December, 1916.

Baruch admitted that he had but insisted that it had nothing to do with the "peace leak" the committee was investigating.

Hot on the trail of what looked like the first break, committee members pressed Baruch. What was this telephone conversation about?

"A friend of mine suggested a certain man for the Federal Reserve Board," said Baruch, "and asked me if I would speak to McAdoo about it."

(Next day the *New York Times* suggested that Baruch meant the Federal Reserve Bank of New York board instead of Federal Reserve Board.)

"Who was this person who wanted you to talk to McAdoo?" demanded a committee member.

"Colonel E. M. House," said Baruch.

The committee, the press tables, and the audience in the packed room in the House Office Building sat stunned. There was a long pause, and then the committee went on to something else. Even the Republican members saw little point in going into that. Wilson had been reelected less than 3 months before. The newspapers did not think it was important, next day. In the *New York Times* you were forced to read several thousand words about that committee hearing before you came to this item.

For reasons having nothing to do with this disclosure that day's committee hearing was another of the important turning points in Baruch's life.

Thomas W. Lawson, of "frenzied finance" fame, charged in December, 1916, that there had been a leak about a peace note President Wilson had written and that as a result of this leak millions had been made on Wall Street. Lawson gave the impression he knew all about it but used no names in his early statements. Ounces of facts and pounds of rumors combined to build up what looked to Congress and the press as though it might make the biggest scandal since Grant's administration.

We have to look back a little to understand what happened. On November 20, 1916, a front-page headline in the *New York Times* said: "Wilson Mediation Rumor Stirs Berlin." The next day the death of Franz Joseph was recorded. On November 24 the headline was: "Hostile to Urge Peace on Britain, Northcliffe Says." On November 26 a "peace drive" in which Jacob H. Schiff, David Starr Jordan, Hamilton Holt, and Oswald Garrison Villard were interested was on the front page.

On December 3 the big headline was "Peace Can Come Only with Liberty, Not While Destinies Are Ruled by Small Selfish Groups, Says Wilson." This was the report of a speech at the Hotel Waldorf-Astoria, in New York.

On December 6 the headline was that Asquith was out as British Premier, and another was "Victories Revive Berlin Peace Talk."

On December 7: "Lloyd George to Be Premier."

December 13: "Germany and Her Allies Offer to Negotiate for Peace." This an eight-column screamer.

December 14: "Germany Plans a Round Table Conference at The Hague to Decide Whether Peace at This Time Is Practicable. England Will Not Lightly Disregard Germany's Note."

December 15: "Attack by Bears Upsets Wall Street, 4 to 10 Points Drop in 2,412,000 Share Day."

December 16: "President to Offer No Mediation in Forwarding Peace Notes Today."

December 19: "Berlin Now Hopes for Wilson's Aid."

December 20: "Lloyd George Demands; Premier's Speech Upsets Wall Street. Rumors of Manipulation."

December 21: "Wilson Calls upon All Warring Nations to State Terms upon Which War May Be Ended. Stocks Fall Again on Peace Efforts."

December 22: "Peace and War Talk Hit Stocks. Most Violent Slump Known in 15 Years. Some Issues Off 30 Points. Entire List Down 5 to 15 Points."

In the issue of December 31 it was reported that Chairman Robert L. Henry, of the House Rules Committee, which was considering whether to have an investigation, called the whole Lawson business a "mirage" after talking with the Boston speculator.

The United States at the time was flourishing on war industries—"War Babies" the leading munition stocks were called. Led by United States Steel and Bethlehem, hundreds of stocks had soared to unheard-of prices, dragging the whole market up, so that every time there was a whisper of peace there was unloading *and* short selling.

It was known that Baruch had been a heavy short seller during this series of drops. Pretty soon his name was connected with the idea of a leak. It was mentioned by a Republican Congressman on the floor of the House, thus giving the newspapers a chance to print it without fear of libel. Then a Congressman charged, again on the floor, that Joe Tumulty, the President's secretary, had talked to Baruch. He also mentioned the name of Otto H. Kahn.

After stalling for weeks, Lawson finally mentioned the name of the Cabinet member he had been hinting about. He meant William G. McAdoo. On January 4 the *Times* headline was, "Hears Baruch Sold on Peace Note Talk," quoting Representative William S. Bennet of New York and tying Baruch into the administration by pointing out that he was a member of the Council of National Defense.

The thing was getting too hot to handle. Chairman Henry had tried to end the investigation in December, but it would not die. Lawson kept pouring oil on the fire. He fanfared: "Canceling a Trip to Europe" so as to be available to testify.

The country was wild with suspicion. Many people honestly believed that a member of Wilson's household had given the information, in advance, to Baruch, that Baruch had made millions, and split them.

Administration leaders on Capitol Hill were worried. Baruch had frankly admitted, in December, that he had made half a million dollars in one day on the stock market by short sales. His name was now coupled with that of McAdoo, a Cabinet member and the son-in-law of the President.

That was the situation when Baruch appeared before the committee in late January, 1917. He had produced the records of all his transactions for December for Sherman L. Whipple, special counsel for the committee. They were terribly complicated, for a layman. He had followed his old practice of buying in the stock and then selling heavily on the rallies.

Whipple contemplated presenting the whole record to the committee but decided to try to simplify it for the committee by confining the whole inquiry into the dealings in one stock, United States Steel common.

Baruch, it appeared, had begun selling Steel on December 11. Before the close of the exchange on December 15 he had sold the 30,000 shares that he already had, and 25,000 to 26,000 in addition, selling these last short. On and on went the review of his operations.

The climax of the testimony was when Baruch was describing his operations on December 18, the day of the Lloyd George speech. He was following the speech carefully as it came over the news ticker, he said, the first part of the speech bristling with the idea that Britain would fight on until victory. Suddenly the word "but" came over the ticker, as it reported Lloyd George's speech.

When he saw that word, Baruch said, he knew that what followed would have to be softer, that it would leave the door open for peace moves. So he rushed to sell. That was the day he admitted making half a million dollars.

He had no information from Washington or the administration at any time, he insisted. He had taken his short position in the market because he knew that the country was enjoying an utterly false prosperity, owing to war orders, and that a terrible collapse was due the moment peace came. He said further that he had known that the technical position of the market was bad, that it would not take much to knock it down.

Incidentally, Baruch was not a very good prophet that day. He said that peace was certain to come because "everybody wanted it." He was a better prophet when he predicted that when peace did come this country would be in for very serious trouble indeed in the adjustment of the war industries and in the unemployment that would ensue. But that was not to come for years.

The amazing part of this whole picture is that there was not a member of the committee, Democrat or Republican, or a newspaperman, no matter what the political complexion of his newspaper, in that room who was not utterly convinced, when Baruch completed his testimony, that he had told the truth, the whole truth, and nothing but the truth.

There was just one feeble attempt to hit him. One of the Republican members inquired why it was, if he were not expecting some important tip from Washington, that he had a locomotive attached to his private car at Georgetown, South Carolina, on the night of December 6, so that he could leave for the North 1 hour ahead of the regular train.

Baruch said that "southern trains are frequently late, and so are northern ones" and that he had been very anxious to get to Washington on time the morning of December 7, because there was to be a meeting of the Council of National Defense that day and he wanted to be on schedule!

Perhaps nothing could better demonstrate the conviction Baruch carried to everyone present than the fact that no Republican member of the committee attempted to cast any doubt on this, that no Republican in Congress afterward attempted to make any political capital out of the leak and the stock-market killing, even though the stock-market killing was admitted. In 30 years' experience as a Washington correspondent I have never seen anything like it.

There were lighter touches. Baruch was asked how much he had contributed to the Wilson 1916 campaign fund. It had been printed that he had given $35,000.

"Fifty thousand dollars," said Baruch simply.

"I wish we had a lot more like him," said Representative Garrett, earnestly.

"I hope you gentlemen will inject no politics into this hearing," said Chairman Henry, piously.

The hearings did not end. They dragged on, with attempts to snare R. W. Bolling, brother of Mrs. Woodrow Wilson, and others. It developed that several newspapermen had sent dispatches to brokers giving hints as to the peace move. One of them was obtained and read to the committee with a remarkably accurate forecast of just what the Wilson note said.

Several newspapermen were fired by their papers. The Press Gallery changed its rules, to bar any member working for a broker.

The leak inquiry was over. Even Tom Lawson, who admitted on the stand that he was merely trying to force an investigation of the stock exchange, didn't get what he wanted.

Actually, Baruch had ambushed the committee. When he was asked, after giving his name and address, what his occupation was, he said, "I am a speculator."

The committee, Baruch thought, had expected him to say he was a banker.

"If I had," he said a few days later, "they would have torn me to pieces. When I admitted I was a speculator, there remained no point in proving it."

"There was no occasion," Baruch added to newspaper friends, "for me to explain what I meant when I used the word 'speculator.' The word comes from the Latin *speculari,* which means 'to observe.' I observe."

In fact he observed so much, and so intently, that President Wilson called him Dr. Facts.

CHAPTER . . . FOURTEEN

BARUCH had been sowing seed in an entirely new type of political garden since Wilson entered the White House. This was the development of strong personal friendships with important personalities in the Democratic Party, with most of the beds carefully spaded and fertilized for the cultivation of senators.

It was not so deliberate as this sounds. In fact I am fairly sure that it was not deliberate at all. The best evidence of this is that he seldom bothered with any Democratic figure, even a senator, who did not appeal to him personally, and he *never* bothered to ingratiate himself with anyone, senator or otherwise, who in his opinion had been unfair or personally critical of Woodrow Wilson. Baruch liked people easily, however, so these restrictions did not make the number small.

It should be noted here that if Baruch had entertained some thought of political accomplishment, when he embarked on this course of building unusual political influence, he would have been much more catholic in his application of the tenets of Dale Carnegie. He has always rather prided himself on his ability to bring hostile persons together, make them forget their animosities, at least for the time being, and work together on the immediate task. He discovered this ability in his college days and applied it frequently in Wall Street and in his development of natural resources, long before he started his political garden.

To use a more recent illustration of this faculty, on one occasion, after some particularly blistering utterances by Harold L. Ickes about the Aluminum Company of America, Baruch managed to get a high official of that company into a room with Honest Harold. Under his ministrations their snarls gradually changed to purrs, and they parted like conspirators on some scheme for mutual profit! Actually this cooperation was aimed at benefiting the war effort.

It would seem a fair assumption, therefore, that Baruch *could* have cultivated a much larger political garden, could have brought *more* senators, representatives, and public figures generally under his spell. It might have been enormously helpful to Woodrow Wilson in 1919, during the League of Nations fight in the Senate, had he done so.

Could he have foreseen that, he would cheerfully have sacrificed his personal choice of companions better to serve the ultimate needs of his idol. Of that there can be little doubt. It tends to prove that Baruch had no particular idea of any actual political purpose the edifice he was erecting could serve.

Baruch was a tyro in politics in 1913. He was never to wade very deeply into that realm, with one exception, which did not turn out too happily. (This one exception was the result of his great personal friendship for William G. McAdoo.) Numerous other opportunities to wade were to come. On one occasion many political reporters believe he could have changed the course of history if he had waded, but that was much later.

The beginnings of his activity in politics were simple enough. He found himself much in Washington, tremendously interested in the legislation Woodrow Wilson was planning and eager to do what he could to make the Wilson program function smoothly, to eliminate as many obstacles both to its enactment and to its later functioning as possible.

He came to Washington with just a few close friends who were important in politics, but these few were very important; they were the survivors of the group that had started out to make Wilson President and had enlisted Baruch's financial aid for that purpose. Closest of these friends, probably, was William G. McAdoo, for Baruch had known him previously. As Secretary of the Treasury and as the victor in his row with McCombs, McAdoo was a prodigious figure. Many in the new Democratic Congress knew him slightly. All wanted to know him better because of his obvious closeness to the new President.

Many congressmen were also very eager to cultivate Baruch. There were very few generous contributors to Democratic campaign funds in those days. Most of the rich men of the country were in the North, and most of them were Republicans. This was not merely because of sectionalism, but because most people who made substantial campaign contributions did not do so for mere love of party—they wanted something. The Republican Party was the high-tariff party, the special-privilege party, if you please, so that heavy contributors could reasonably expect consideration when the tariff duties of schedules in which they were interested came before Congress.

There was another reason that inclined generous givers to the GOP. Many rich men, especially those with ambitious wives, coveted diplomatic appointments. The simplest way to put oneself in line for one of these plums was to make a heavy campaign contribution. Obviously this would not pay the hoped-for dividend unless the party to which the contribution had been made should be successful. There is no minority patronage in diplomatic appointments. And from the Civil War until Franklin D. Roosevelt's time the Republican Party has been traditionally the majority party. So the socially and diplomatically ambitious campaign contributors would naturally lay their wagers—contributions—on the Republican side.

We must remember another point, because it restricted drastically the number of rich and generous Democrats whom ambitious political figures in the House and Senate could afford to cultivate. In order to have enough money to make big contributions a man must either have made it himself or have inherited it. As a result of the Civil War and Reconstruction, few Southerners had inherited fortunes.

We must remember that for the 16 years ending with Wilson's first campaign the Democratic Party had been dominated by William Jennings Bryan, from his first nomination, in 1896, to 1912, and that Bryan was still potent.

No Southerner hoping to get financial support for a campaign to elect himself to the Senate would have dared take a contribution from Thomas Fortune Ryan, Bryan's avowed enemy. There was too strong a Bryan following all through the South—all through the country, for that matter.

I had been at the Baltimore convention in 1912 and was startled at the ferocity with which Bryan attacked Ryan, heedless of a Tammany spokesman's bitter: "Three times you have led us to defeat—for God's sake give us a chance."

During the first Wilson administration I was standing outside the door of the Senate Finance Committee room, where the conferees of the House and Senate were trying to straighten out differences in the Senate and House drafts of the tax bill. Claude Kitchin, of North Carolina, chairman of the House Ways and Means Committee, burst out of the door, red with anger. I walked with him through the long corridor to the House side of the Capitol, and he talked, furiously.

His anger was directed at the senators, who refused to approve the House proposal to tax copper, and he blamed the political influence of Cleveland H. Dodge for this Senate stand, Dodge having been a big contributor to the Wilson campaign.

"Is it all right to quote you on that, Mr. Kitchin?" I asked.

Kitchin stopped short. He had been so mad that he had not

realized what political murder was contained in his words. A sly grin came over his face.

"You didn't think I meant that?" he asked, with strong emphasis on the "I."

"I *know* you meant it," I retorted, "but whether you want it printed is something else again."

"Oh," said Kitchin, "I meant that is what the dirty Republicans will be saying."

This gives at least a hint of how few big contributors there were at that time from whom an ambitious Democrat might take a contribution.

It may be asked why Baruch's money, having been made in Wall Street and in exploitation of natural resources, was not "tainted."

The answer is that the reform wave that eventually resulted in the Securities and Exchange Commission, under Franklin Roosevelt, was only a ripple then. There was a little scattered prejudice against stock-market operation and against short selling in particular, but it did not command much political support, so there was no important *political* prejudice against Baruch's money.

Early in the first Wilson administration Senator Robert L. Owen, of Oklahoma, as chairman of the Senate Banking and Currency Committee, conducted an investigation of the New York Stock Exchange. The committee had as counsel Samuel Untermyer, who made, as Owen had expected, not only a brilliant attack on the stock exchange, its methods, and its practices, but a report that might be expected to rally all the reform elements, from Secretary of State Bryan down, to the support of legislation to correct the situation.

Nothing happened. All Senator Owen's zeal—he had been nursing a presidential boom that Bryan's ambition blanketed—and all Samuel Untermyer's brilliance were to no avail. The investigation started off with flourish of trumpets, but it did not live up to newspaper expectations. The number of newspapermen present to cover it dwindled, until few but the New York morning newspapers were printing anything.

There was interest at first because the country expected more of the sort of revelations produced by the Pujo Money Trust investigation and the Mullhall Investigation, which had immediately preceded it, with millionaires branded as crooks and officials as bribe takers. All the cream had been skimmed. Neither the public nor Congress was interested in a discussion of practices, no matter how bad, or theories for their reform, no matter how sound.

Further, Senator Owen was a little unfortunate in the personnel of his committee. Most of the intelligent members were quietly opposed to the Owen-Untermyer objectives. Some of the would-be reformers were not overly endowed with stock-market wisdom. One of them went to his grave without ever being able to understand just what a short sale is!

All this happened just 3 years before Baruch's revelation on the stand, before the House Rules Committee, that he had made half a million dollars in one day by short selling. In that 3 years there had not been manifested any strong desire on the part of any considerable fraction of the electorate to reform the stock exchange. Statesmen are usually callous to reforms for which their constituents do not pant, especially when the reforms might eliminate political or financial support.

Baruch has long insisted, in private conversations, that the stock exchange needed reforming. He has always expressed a high regard for the membership and the officers of the exchange and approval for many of the reforms that the exchange itself initiated, but he said many times, in the years between the Owen-Untermyer fiasco and the enactment of the Securities and Exchange Commission law, that the exchange authorities did not move fast enough in correcting abuses.

Untermyer was also a friend of President Wilson. He had been born in Wilson's own state of Virginia, at Lynchburg. At the time of the stock-exchange investigation he seemed to think he was carrying out a Wilson policy. Certainly the newspapermen covering that investigation, of whom I was one, somehow got that impression.

But neither Wilson nor Baruch moved a hand to help write the Owen proposals into law. In fact there was considerable disappointment at the lack of White House pressure for it. As Baruch has always contended that to prohibit short sales would have a harmful instead of a salutary effect on the movement of stock prices, it is possible that his opinion may have influenced Wilson against Owen's objectives.

This is pure supposition. It is more likely that Baruch and McAdoo agreed on this one particular, though Baruch had far less of the reformer in him than McAdoo. Baruch simply does not talk about advice that *he* gave Wilson. He has never said so, to my knowledge, but my impression is that he would regard such statements, coming from him, as presumptuous. There was considerable surprise, for instance, when Mrs. Woodrow Wilson revealed that Baruch had advised the President to compromise with the Senate on the Versailles Treaty.

The probability would seem to be that Wilson, McAdoo, and Baruch were in agreement that it would be very difficult to put through stock-exchange reform legislation, as Senator Owen wished, without including a prohibition of short sales. There was a popular prejudice against short sales, especially by people who did not understand them, which might have forced support for such a ban, whereas popular interest in the other changes desired by Senator Owen was practically nil.

Most of Baruch's new friends on Capitol Hill cared little about this battle to reform the New York Stock Exchange. They quickly realized that no harm could come to them, back home, from a friendship with this Wall Street operator. On the contrary, Baruch's friendship might be an important asset. He not only had influence, they soon recognized, but might prove very helpful in their individual problems from time to time. All of them knew, of course, that he was a generous contributor to Democratic campaign funds, so, meeting him through McAdoo and others, Democratic legislators did their best to be agreeable.

Many did not know, at first, that Baruch was from South Carolina, a Southern boy who had gone to New York and outsmarted the Yankees. They did not know, some of them, that his father had fought with Robert E. Lee. When they learned this, from other South Carolinians, they began to take great pride in him. A successful stock-market operator was one thing, a son of a Confederate soldier making good in New York was something to boast to the home folks about!

As they gradually grew to know him better, they found unexpected reasons to value his friendship. They came to realize that he had but one objective—to help in any way he could to make the Wilson administration a success. Now to an experienced member of the House and Senate this was something almost unbelievable. The man did not want anything!

They found him always interested in any problem that was bothering them. As those with whom he thus fraternized were all Democrats, their common objective was to glorify and build up Wilson. This was especially true in the first four years of Wilson, before he acquired so many enemies in his own party. Every senator and representative, when the President is a member of his party, is selfishly inclined to make that President as important as possible to his constituency. Unless the President *is* very strong in that senator's state or that representative's district, the voters may vote the straight ticket of the opposition party next time, which in turn may make it very difficult for that senator or representative to be reelected. There is also the little matter of patronage. Minority Congressmen do not enjoy much of that.

Some of the Democrats soon found that nobody in Washington, or anywhere else for that matter, was so skillful as Baruch in eliminating the faults from their legislative proposals, whether these were aimed at improving the conditions of the farmers or proposing social reforms or were merely of local interest.

CHAPTER . . . FIFTEEN

SOON Baruch began inviting some of his new political friends down to his estate near Georgetown, South Carolina. Little groups would accompany him in his private car and come back boasting about how many ducks or quail or wild turkeys they had shot. These parties were nothing new for Baruch. He had been giving them for years, but until 1913 most of his guests had been business friends, largely from New York.

The shooting was of course the main attraction. However, many of these guests, who loved to hunt, found the contact with Baruch so stimulating mentally that, when they accepted invitations, they came to look forward more eagerly to conversations with the financier than to the sport the visits promised.

I have never known any man who loved to hunt as much as Joseph T. Robinson, senator from Arkansas during all this period and Democratic leader for many years. Robinson had a terrific temper, and it was of the hair-trigger variety.

If on the golf course he topped his ball, what followed was something to see. He usually played with a senatorial foursome whose slowness was the bane of the existence of other golfers in the club, and if any other players wanted to go through them Robinson was fit to be tied. But Robinson would wait in a duck blind with the patience of Job. He would wallow in mud, be torn by thorns, undergo any hardships or annoyance in high good humor—if he were just hunting. Yet Robinson said to me on one occasion that if he had to choose between "talking with Bernie" or shooting on a trip to Hobcaw, as the plantation was called, he would choose talking. Senator Key Pittman, of Nevada, who as a former prospector in the Klondike rush found a community of interest with Baruch on mining experiences, told me practically the same thing.

Baruch actually bought the Hobcaw Barony in 1905, but he had been dreaming about this sportman's paradise since he was eight years old. At that time Miss Belle had taken him to Charleston and thence by boat to Georgetown, and in the course of that visit he had heard tales of the ducks, the quail, the wild turkeys, the deer, that abounded on the big peninsula opposite the sleepy old Southern port. Locally the Barony was called Waccamaw Neck, but it had been known as the Hobcaw Barony ever since the original grant, to Lord Carteret, by the King of England.

This tract, comprising about 23,000 acres, has magnificent sandy beaches on the Atlantic side, behind which are huge salt marshes, threaded with little estuaries in which the tide rises and falls, where crabs and tiny oysters of delicious flavor abound and where the ducks seek shelter at night. Behind these marshes the ground is low and swampy, with an ancient growth of live oaks overhung with Spanish moss, and it is there that the deer abound.

Four tiny Negro villages, dating back to the days when Hobcaw was a great rice plantation, still exist, and though there was no attempt by the plantation manager to grow crops for sale, there was still the feudal custom of providing work for the Negroes, at the regular wages, whenever they wanted some money. This was surprisingly infrequent, the Negroes being able to provide for their immediate needs by what they grew on their little patches and being supplied with milk and medical care free of charge.

Whenever the cabins ran down too badly the occupants were

paid for the work of putting them in good condition. Baruch always accepted the Southern tradition that the Negroes go with the land, and his one inflexible injunction to his superintendents was that no Negro could be put off the place save by Baruch's own orders.

It was an unforgettable experience to hear one or more of these Negroes bring their troubles to the Boss, as they invariably referred to him behind his back. He listened patiently and seemed to give as much study to what was bothering them as though this were a gigantic industrial proposal involving millions, or an international situation that might produce war. After many questions to bring out all the facts he finally gave his opinion as to what should be done. This was virtually law, not so much perhaps because they recognized its soundness as because they were sure that whatever the Boss said must be right.

Scientific poultry raising was definitely not a success at Hobcaw. Several times Baruch persuaded the Negroes to try modern methods, but invariably, though apparently they tried their best to carry out the instructions, the turkeys and chickens died of the pip or some other ailment. When the Negroes followed their usual routine, simply letting the birds run about as they liked, all went well. Baruch was often philosophical to visitors about this, after getting the Negroes to tell him, before the visitors, of the calamities that followed strict Department of Agriculture methods. "Drowned in the rains of paternalistic benefits" was one of his favorite expressions in commenting on the deaths of pampered turkeys when they get caught in a rain.

Another treat for visitors was a visit to the Negro church, particularly if the parson, Moses Jenkins, happened to deliver his favorite sermon. This concerned the crossing of the Red Sea by the Children of Israel. There was nothing reactionary about the Reverend Jenkins. After the First World War he introduced machine guns and airplanes and tanks in that classic flight.

If Baruch was in the congregation the Reverend was likely to cut his sermon short, informing his listeners that the Boss was going to get up early for duck shooting next morning. But if his imagination was running riot, Reverend Jenkins would thrill everybody with new episodes of the flight from Pharaoh.

Beginning in 1913 there came to be a more political and less financial tone to the guests who came down to Hobcaw to enjoy the shooting and Baruch's hospitality. McAdoo and Dr. Grayson spread the word in Washington, and it was seldom that an invitation was declined, especially if Baruch commented that he heard "a lot of birds were flying."

There was little formality about the invitations. Baruch, in New York, would suddenly make up his mind to go. He would get Grayson, or Senator Joe Robinson, on the telephone, and ask them to get aboard his car when it passed through Washington and to pick up this or that senator if possible.

In the old days, when Baruch used a private car it would run on the Atlantic Coast line to Lane and then be switched to a branch line of the Seaboard that ran down to Georgetown. There a launch would be waiting to carry the party across the Winyah Bay to the Baruch wharf. It is easy for visitors to see why, in Colonial days, it was thought Georgetown would become a great port. River transportation was king, in those days, and old rice plantations lined the Sampit, Black, Waccamaw, and Peedee rivers, all of which flow into Winyah Bay, while the Santee River is near by.

The house faces on the bay, looking across to where Georgetown dreams, in the sun, of its ancient grandeur, while south of the town a new plant, belching factory smoke, seems an anachronism.

In recent years a new bridge, just north of the Barony, has somewhat impaired its isolation, for by road the house is now only 7 miles from Georgetown. But the Cabinet members and senators cut their cables to Washington and to pestering constituents when they stepped aboard that launch, just as Baruch cut his wires to Wall Street, for there never was a telephone in Hobcaw or a semaphore system across the bay.

Once or twice a day a man drove over to the little telegraph office and brought back wires with the mail and newspapers. If some wire was urgent enough, Baruch or the visitor thus harried would make the trip over to town. The difficulty of communication gradually became known, however, and tended to discourage all but the most vital messages.

After a dinner featuring Hobcaw oysters, of which the guest was expected to consume two helpings of thirteen each, early bed was advised for duck hunters. One had to be in the blind before light, and reaching the blind took time. First there was a hearty breakfast, to help guard against the cold, then there was a 6-mile ride through the live-oak swamps, over narrow winding roads across which deer, frightened by the car lights, bounded. The car bounced and splashed in the ruts of the dirt roads, while eerie shadows in the Spanish moss added to the fantasy. The scene changed abruptly as the car stopped at the landing and took on a piratical note, as the guides in long boots and windbreakers moved about with lanterns, carrying guns and decoys and gear aboard a huge power boat.

Still in complete darkness, the big boat started on its journey around the little estuaries, pausing every mile or so as it neared some particular stand. At each of these one guest and one guide were discharged into a small boat, and the big boat proceeded on to other locations known from experience to be well chosen.

The guide rowed the small boat up into a still smaller estuary until he came to the right spot. There he jumped into the slightly higher ground, built up by thousands of years of oyster growth, and pulled the boat, with the guest in it, up into the reeds. It was a matter of moments for the guide to have the boat, which thus became a blind, concealed behind artificial fronds which he planted in the mud and shells. Then the decoys were thrown out into the estuary on which the improvised blind faced, and the hunter was ready. It was still dark—and cold. But if the hunter was not wearing long woolies he had ignored plenty of advice given the night before.

Then came the ducks, attracted partly by the decoys and partly by the guide's call. When they came the discomfort was forgotten. By and by, one had his limit, if he could shoot at all well, and was off for the return trip and a second breakfast!

Quail shooting was much more civilized for those who were used to bankers' hours. One ate breakfast at a normal hour and was driven to the huge tracts, some 50 miles inland, where Baruch had some holdings and more land on which he had rented the shooting rights. There again the rule of one hunter in a party was observed. Baruch didn't like to risk accidents. For each hunter there was a guide and a Negro to tend the horses, so there were three horses and two or three well-trained dogs for each guest.

The dogs dashed about the countryside, through thick briar-studded underbrush, into little swamps, over cotton fields, through patches of woods. Every now and then the riders, following the dogs leisurely, passed cabins from whose windows or yards pickaninnies and half-grown Negroes watched in apparent wonder this elaborate sortie of the Boss's guests. Just as the riding threatened to become monotonous one of the dogs would point. The guide and hunter dismounted and hurried up behind the dog, the guide loading the double-barreled shotgun and handing it to the guest at the last possible moment (another rule to prevent accidents). The Negro would ride off with the three horses. The dog was urged forward by the guide. He had been trained so severely not to scare up the birds that he seemed afraid to follow them as they scurried, unseen, through the underbrush. Finally there would be a terrific noise as the wings of the quail beat the air for a quick start. And, if the guest remembered to take the safety catch off and to lead the bird at which he was trying to aim, he had the tremendous thrill of seeing the bird fall.

The tyro shooting as Baruch's guest need not have been too embarrassed. No one ever denied the story he told when he got back home. He had game to "prove" his marksmanship. No wonder the senators liked it!

Novices do not show up well, as a rule, in wild-turkey shooting. Poor Admiral Grayson, always shooting, always missing, and always coming back for more, said time and again that he certainly wanted to shoot a wild turkey.

One day the Admiral, with a guide, was walking through the woods, hopefully, when the guide grasped his arm.

"In that tree, right over there," whispered the guide. Grayson looked and saw a lovely gobbler, within easy range.

"Bang," went Grayson's gun. Down tumbled the gobbler. Grayson stepped proudly forward, savoring the size of the bird his marksmanship had brought down.

But as he bent down over the turkey he noticed that it had a string round its neck. A card was attached, which read, "With the compliments of Bernard M. Baruch." Grayson was never to hear the end of that one.

Then there was the time Joe Robinson located a real wild turkey, a beauty, with what looked to the Arkansas statesman like long whiskers. The guide came back to the house in astonishment afterward.

"The senator," he said, "kept inching up nearer the tree, whispering all the time: 'Here's where I knock down Mister Secretary Hughes.' "

Secretary Hughes probably had a bite of that turkey, for it was sent to President Harding with Robinson's compliments, and the President had a little dinner party. But the joke was on Robinson; no Democrats were invited.

Some of the guides have a salty humor that delights visitors. During the early days of prohibition Senator A. O. Stanley, of Kentucky, a noted hunter and fisherman, convulsed friends in Washington with a story of how he and three other senators, all from states that were politically very dry indeed, talked over national affairs with Hucks Cains. Introducing Pat Harrison, of Mississippi, Robinson, of Arkansas, and Key Pittman, of Nevada, as they were coming back from duck hunting one morning when the ducks had not been flying close enough, Senator Stanley told Cains they were the men who made the laws up in Washington.

"Kin I say sumpin?" inquired Cains.

"The sky is the limit," said Stanley.

"Well, if you-all don't know no more about other things than you do about ducks and whisky this country is in a hell of a fix."

CHAPTER . . . SIXTEEN

THE Underwood-Simmons tariff law—into the framing of which Baruch had refused to inject himself—had been followed by unemployment in certain industries, chiefly in politically doubtful states. When war broke out, in August, 1914, there was such a crash on the stock market that it was deemed necessary to close the New York Stock Exchange. Many stocks fell to half of their prices earlier in the year.

The boom that war orders was to bring was not in sight. The Republicans were jubilant. The country, they thought, had been taught a lesson. It would not soon forget that Republican administrations always meant a full dinner pail.

In the November election many of the Old Guard Republicans who had been defeated in the Wilson 1912 landslide came back in triumph—Uncle Joe Cannon, Nicholas Longworth, William A. Rodenberg, and a host of others. There was a black cloud on the Democratic horizon, which was to continue to be menacing for a long time.

When Belgium was invaded, most of the country seemed to be strongly pro-Ally, but gradually there came rifts in this, some of them most embarrassing. For instance, there was the British interference with our export trade. Senator Hoke Smith, of Georgia, was one of the most powerful rabble rousers of the period, a man who carried great prestige, having been a Cabinet member under Cleveland. He made a powerful speech in the

Senate one day denouncing the British, who he said were depriving the cotton farmers of the South of a market for their "innocent" product, cotton.

In white-faced fury Senator Henry Cabot Lodge, of Massachusetts, replied extemporaneously, in what some of the reporters thought was the best speech of his career. Alluding to a recent submarine sinking, in which many lives had been lost, Lodge said, "A dead baby floating on the water is a more poignant sight to me than an unsold bale of cotton."

Lodge got the headlines the next day, to the great annoyance of Smith, but the situation was serious. All the cotton-raising states were torn between what might be termed their normal sentiments and their pocketbooks. Cotton dropped so low that a "Buy a bale of cotton" movement was started, President Wilson dutifully purchasing one and storing it in the White House.

At the suggestion of Festus J. Wade, of St. Louis, a fund of $135,000,000 was being raised under McAdoo's supervision, to be used in financing surplus cotton until market conditions should improve. At first subscriptions from the big banks poured in, but after a while there was a lag.

Baruch heard about this and one day walked into McAdoo's office.

"How much more money do you need to put over this cotton fund?" he inquired.

"We are short $3,000,000," said McAdoo.

"I will subscribe $1,000,000," said Baruch.

McAdoo said afterward that he was so surprised that he did not say anything and that apparently Baruch misunderstood his silence.

"I will be very glad to furnish any references you think necessary as to my ability to do this," said Baruch.

McAdoo laughed.

"I need no references about you," he said.

Within a few days Jacob H. Schiff, of Kuhn, Loeb & Co., a close friend of Baruch, pledged his firm for the remaining $2,000,000.

With the South in the saddle this discontent in the cotton states was a serious problem. The British realized it, in due time, but didn't know what to do about it. President Wilson, secretly sympathizing with the Allies, nevertheless had to write strong notes, to which Secretary Bryan's name was signed, protesting against unwarranted interferences by the British with our neutral trade rights.

One day the British Ambassador got hold of W. P. G. Harding, governor of the Federal Reserve Board. The Ambassador was terribly concerned, he told Harding. His government realized fully the feeling in the South, and its possible repercussions, but, owing to discoveries the British had made of how much American-grown cotton was getting through to Germany, where it was made into munitions, something had to be done. His government, he said, had decided to put cotton on the contraband list.

He had come to Harding for advice, not only because Harding was head of the Federal Reserve Board, but because, as an Alabama man, he would understand the cotton situation and might be able to think of some way to soften the blow. He made it clear that the British had considered every possible angle and had reached the conclusion that no matter what the public reaction in the United States they must cut off Germany's cotton supply from this country.

Harding told the British Ambassador he would do his best, and let the Embassy know as soon as he had thought of anything. He rushed to Secretary of the Treasury McAdoo with the problem.

McAdoo and Harding agreed that if some way could be found to hold up the price of cotton, so that the adding of cotton to the contraband list would not take any more money out of the farmers' pockets, no great harm would be done. But how to do it?

At this point Baruch's advice was sought. Baruch had often told his friends that he could not "feel" commodities, as he could corporations, but here was a problem that seemed to require gigantic market operations, and McAdoo was confident Baruch would have the best judgment in the entire country as to how it should be done.

A little later Harding visited the worried Ambassador. The action making cotton contraband, he advised, should be announced on Saturday, after all markets in the United States had closed. Then, when the exchange in Liverpool opened the following Monday morning, sufficient orders should be given to put the price of cotton up a small fraction.

No orders, he said, should be placed in New York at all, but orders should be given to buy cotton in the New Orleans market in sufficient quantity to make sure that the small fraction gained in Liverpool would be held.

Like the standing of an egg on its end, the idea was simple, once stated, but it had not occurred to the financiers advising the British Government. It worked out precisely as planned. The British announced their action on Saturday night. They had been highly skeptical but in such a desperate situation that anything was worth trying. The plan, they thought, might not work, but it could not do any great harm!

Early Monday morning the brokers flocked to the New York Cotton Exchange, eager to get in short selling orders in order to make a profit from the crash in the price of cotton they were sure would occur. While waiting for the gong that would start their own trading, they glanced at the tickers to see what had happened to the price of cotton in Liverpool. After an early dip, they saw, to their astonishment, that the price of cotton rallied and then moved up a small fraction above the closing on Saturday!

This gave the most venturesome pause. What had happened? There must be something to explain this utter reversal of form —the price of a product going up when a good market was cut off! The first hour was utterly inactive. They were afraid to sell, as they had planned before seeing the Liverpool quotations. They lacked the confidence to buy, without more definite knowledge as to what this unknown factor was. So they did nothing.

An hour after the New York market opened New Orleans figures began to flow over the ticker. In that primary cotton market, so to speak, it appeared that the brokers did not see anything gloomy ahead for cotton. New Orleans was *buying*, not heavily, but enough to move the price up ever so slightly. And it stayed up. There were no bear raids the next day in New York. The brokers had plenty of time to think, but it did not do them any good. There was something they could not understand about this situation, and the unknown is always menacing.

The public reaction to putting cotton on the contraband list was nil. Farmers could not be excited about something that apparently had no effect on their pocketbooks. Demagogues could not make hay where there was no increased discontent. Britain had escaped a grave danger of American disapproval. Wilson's problem was simplified.

There was a sequel to this story. Britain held the cotton she had purchased on this advice. She was probably afraid to take any chances by selling it and risking a decline in price that would bring new troubles. When the peace rumors began to come, the price of cotton rose. Everyone knew that there would be a prodigious demand for cotton the moment the war was over. Manufacturers holding cotton they had bought cheaply, it was realized, would have a big advantage in the postwar scramble for trade over those who paid inflated prices.

Britain increased her holdings. The Germans found out about

Brown Brothers

ADVISOR ON NATIONAL DEFENSE

Bernard Baruch at a joint session of the National Council of Defense and Cabinet Advisory Committee in the Wilson administrations. Seated, l. to r.: Secretary of Agriculture Houston, Secretary of War Baker, Secretary of the Interior Lane, Secretary of Labor Wilson, Secretary of the Navy Daniels. Standing, l. to r.: R. G. B. Clarkson, Julius Rosenwald, Mr. Baruch, Daniel Willard, Dr. F. H. Martin, Dr. H. H. Godfrey, Howard E. Coffin, W. S. Gifford.

this and proceeded to protect their own interests by buying cotton. They could not ship it to Germany, of course, but they could buy it and store it in this country. And that is what they did. Peace found both Britain and Germany owning large stocks of American cotton. The price of cotton never did dip seriously after the Liverpool-New Orleans manipulation coup. Actually both British and German interests benefited in the long run by the purchases started by Britain for a public-relations purpose.

One of the first close friends that Baruch made in the new Wilson setup was Cary T. Grayson, assigned by the Navy to the President as his physician and later promoted to rear admiral in the Medical Corps over the vigorous protests of ambitious naval medical officers, whose friends in the Senate were very vocal but ineffective in their attempts to prevent his confirmation.

The two men had many tastes in common. Both loved and owned race horses and loved to bet on them. Both loved hunting, though Grayson was said by the guides to be the poorest shot who ever tried to bring down a bird at Hobcaw.

A very poor shot myself, I have often said, in disgust, to the guides on the Baruch hunting grounds, "Did you ever see anybody shoot worse than I do?"

"Oh, yes," was the invariable reply, "Admiral Grayson shoots worse than you do."

Sometimes they added: "But the Admiral likes to hunt more than anybody, 'cept Senator Robinson."

It was Grayson who introduced President Wilson to Mrs. Edith Bolling Galt, a very close friend of the lady the Admiral was courting. Perhaps because they knew this, the conspirators who tried to break up the presidential match did not consult the financier.

There are several versions as to details, though the two main points are clear. Washington correspondents were driven almost crazy by hot tips and inside information the week before the engagement was announced. All were afraid of being beaten on a tremendous story, for some of the tips were that Mrs. Mary Hulbert Peck would sue the President for breach of promise if he married Mrs. Galt, and everybody knew, even then, that she had a huge portfolio of letters Wilson had written to her. (William Allen White afterward read more than a thousand of them, but all were entirely innocent.)

Mrs. Peck had been a close friend of Wilson when he was at Princeton. After the 1912 election the President-elect and Mrs. Wilson spent a short vacation in Mrs. Peck's cottage at Bermuda.

It seems clear that Colonel House went to the President, warned him of the reports, said that he had just come from consulting McAdoo about it and that both were worried. The President thought he should release Mrs. Galt from their engagement, so as to protect her from the possible publicity. Thereupon he became so ill that Dr. Grayson appealed to Mrs. Galt to come to him. Announcement of the engagement followed.

Mrs. Wilson later said that Colonel House admitted to her the rumor about Mrs. Peck threatening publicity was unfounded, that he and McAdoo had concocted it. She also said that when she questioned McAdoo he had said it was the Colonel's idea.

Years before Mrs. Wilson's story was published, House told Oswald Garrison Villard that he had been informed by someone close to Wilson that Mrs. Peck was going to bring suit, even naming the judge before whom it would be brought, and that he (House) had told the friend to watch but do nothing. House went on to say that of course there was no truth in the story.

Apparently House had no realization of how this affected Mrs. Wilson's attitude toward him. The reader of Mrs. Wilson's book is left in little doubt that she had no use for Colonel House from that moment, though the President did not turn on him till long afterward.

Whatever may be the human reaction to the "conspiracy,"

the political motives of those involved seemed very sound at the time. When Wilson's engagement was announced the Republicans were sure this meant political suicide. Politicians in that day had a lot of fixed ideas that were to be proved unsound, as that one was in the next election, for then one of the major parties nominated for President a divorced man, and the other, a man who had married a divorced woman!

The chief import of Baruch's being left out of this conspiracy, however, was that nothing happened to mar his friendship with Admiral Grayson, and there began a beautiful friendship between the new mistress of the White House and the Wilson-worshiping Baruch.

There is no thought here of intimating that Baruch *would* have taken part in the conspiracy if he had been consulted. He always had a very strong antipathy to injecting himself in affairs he did not consider his own. He had a favorite word for that and for undue familiarity with anyone who had not encouraged it.

Just after the publication of a magazine article telling much of his early days (in most respects a very accurate article) he was asked by a friend, "Did you really call John D. Rockefeller, Sr., 'Johnny'?"

"Certainly not," said Baruch impatiently. "I would have regarded it as presumptuous."

But if Baruch *had* been consulted about that conspiracy, it is very unlikely that his knowledge of it could have been kept from Mrs. Wilson's ears, in view of the quiet but determined investigation she made, so it just might have happened that he would not have been so highly regarded in the years that followed.

Women have always liked Baruch, and when he exerts himself to please, whether it be a schoolteacher giving him lessons as a boy, a queen near whose throne his path passes, or the wife of a President, "like" is an understatement. In the case of Mrs.

Wilson he had every incentive to be as charming as possible. She was not only the close friend of his chum, Admiral Grayson, and of Mrs. Grayson, but she was the wife of his idol! Nothing ever happened to mar that friendship. He was one of the few—the very few—advisers of her husband who is still her very dear friend.

Perhaps the proudest day of his life—though much more spectacular honor were to come to him—was in the summer of 1916, when the Wilsons were at Shadow Lawn, New Jersey, the summer White House of the campaign year. The two persons whose word was always law to Baruch met. Dr. Baruch and Miss Belle had tea with the President and Mrs. Wilson.

It must have been a very pleasant occasion, and Mrs. Wilson was extremely gracious, praising their son to the now aging couple in words that were music to their ears. One wonders what Miss Belle thought, to hear the President of her country and the First Lady of her land give such evidence that her ambitions for her boy had been achieved!

The shadow of United States participation in the European war was scarcely noticeable that happy afternoon at Shadow Lawn. There was plenty of talk about it in the presidential campaign then in progress, but both sides were really bending most of their efforts to make the voters believe that it was the other party whose victory might embroil us. That was the "kept us out of war" campaign.

Both Wilson and Baruch believed firmly that this country could keep out of the war. Both hoped and expected that Wilson, in less than a year, would be able to bring about peace—a peace that would not be a mere armistice, but long lasting. They hoped for the permanent outlawing of war.

They had talked over this prospect, and both had agreed that this country would be in a much stronger position to insist upon proper peace terms if our own military strength were greater.

Both Germany and the Allies, they believed, would be more likely to listen respectfully if the United States had a bigger army and a more powerful navy and was mobilizing its industries as though for war.

Wilson did not want to go to war, but he was willing to fight for peace. And to fight one had to have the weapons. He was a little tired of Bryan's "beating swords into plowshares" notions. (Bryan had actually had a lot of old swords made into small plowshares to be used as paper weights.)

Wilson was even more tired of diplomatic notes. He was irritated with the wordy diplomatic excuses of London as well as Berlin for trampling on neutral rights. He was finding out, as Baruch was to tell a Senate committee later, that "there ain't no such animal as international law," so he wanted more of the only thing Europe seemed able to understand—force.

The beginnings were small. Senators were encouraged to boost military and naval appropriations in the niggardly bills that came over from the House. The next step was to preach preparedness to the public. Wilson personally, in June of that year, marched at the head of a Preparedness Parade.

Baruch not only agreed with his chief, but thought a spending program for military purposes might be a lifesaver in the unemployment situation he expected to follow peace in Europe—a situation that he considered imminent, for he believed peace was near.

Not only were military appropriations boosted, therefore, but Secretary of the Navy Daniels was prodded into action on the naval building program. Daniels, under the influence of Bryan, had kept this program on drafting boards despite the fact that the money had long since been made available by Congress.

Franklin D. Roosevelt, then Assistant Secretary of the Navy, seeing how the wind was blowing at the White House, conspired with admirals to start things going every time Mr. Daniels went out of town.

Wilson's talks with Baruch at this time grew out of the President's respect for Baruch's knowledge of the country's war industries and natural resources. It was a knotty problem then, as later, because the President, being eager to help the Allies, did not want our own military preparations to interfere with the stream of munitions and war supplies this country was shipping to Britain and France.

Wilson had set up a Council for National Defense. Then he had appointed an Advisory Committee for the council, to which he named Baruch. Little attention was paid to either move by the public. The multiplication of new commissions and criticism of their creation by the opposition party really started during the Wilson administration. It swelled during the Hoover administration and reached a flood under Franklin D. Roosevelt.

Another new commission did not attract much attention. There was a war in Europe and a presidential campaign in America to fill the front pages, not to mention red-hot debates in Congress over whether Americans were to be warned off armed ships and whether American ships should be armed and the railroad strike, which was settled by Congress passing the Adamson act, or so-called 8-hour act.

Even for Baruch it was just a part-time job. Much of his time he still spent in Wall Street. Washington was just a break in his journeys from the money marts of New York to the hunting and plantation life of South Carolina.

CHAPTER . . . SEVENTEEN

Up until the First World War not only the peoples of the world but the army and navy officers of the various countries thought, when considering preparation for war, in terms of armies and navies. There was very little thought of *industrial* preparation.

Conversion of warships and steamships generally from coal to oil burners began to change this picture early in the war. It became important for the great maritime powers to consider oil fields and naval-oil storage.

Even the *Leviathan* was a coal burner when transporting our troops, although she had been one of the latest of the luxury liners to be built before the war, and for some time after the 1921-1922 Washington Arms Conference the United States still had a few coal-burning battleships.

It was not until 1916 that this government began to take an interest in *industrial* preparation. Both the army and the navy in that year undertook surveys. The problem was simplified by the fact that every industrial concern in the country that could figure out a way to do so was converting to war production. The profits made by the big steel corporations in producing munitions for the Allies were enormous, and most manufacturers were eager to get some of this business. There was little competition, the Allies wanted *all* they could buy and did not seem to care *what* they paid!

With young Franklin Roosevelt taking a keen interest, the naval committee, appointed by the Naval Consulting Board, really did a big job. It listed no less than 18,000 industrial plants, cataloguing them as to type of production, quantities that seemed conservative, and possible expansions.

The army went into a somewhat similar inquiry. A body that became known as the Kernan Board was appointed by the Secretary of War. The army effort, however, seemed to be directed more at reform than at preparedness. The chief idea was to determine whether the government should set up its own plants and thus help "take the profit out of war." That phrase, however, was not to be used until long afterward.

Such a motive was absolutely in line with the spirit of Congress and with what seemed to be the spirit of the Wilson administration. As we have seen, Congress had appropriated $50,000,000 for the Alaska railroad, chiefly to prevent the big interests from exploiting our resources. But Congress had also very strong feelings about the profits made by munitions makers. It was particularly bitter about the price of armor plate, and there was much talk about the Steel Trust. Congress had appropriated the money for a government armor plant in West Virginia, which was rushed to completion but never operated until the Second World War loomed.

Neither of these inquiries seemed directed at the vital war problem of getting an adequate supply of raw materials. This may appear strange, in retrospect, but even what was attempted was a long step forward, to meet a situation brought forcibly to our attention by the mad scramble of the Allies to arm themselves.

The action that was to bring Baruch into this picture was the inclusion, in the Army Appropriation bill enacted toward the end of August in 1916, of a provision providing for a Council of National Defense.

"That a Council of National Defense is hereby established," reads this act of Congress, "for the coordination of industries and resources for the national security and welfare, to consist of the Secretary of War, the Secretary of the Navy, the Secretary of the Interior, the Secretary of Agriculture, the Secretary of Commerce, and the Secretary of Labor.

"That the Council shall nominate to the President, and the President shall appoint, an advisory commission, consisting of not more than seven persons, each of whom shall have special knowledge of some industry, public utility, or the development of some natural resource, or be otherwise specially qualified, in the opinion of the council, for the performance of the duties hereinafter provided."

The council, the act continued, should "supervise and direct investigations and make recommendations to the President and the heads of executive departments as to the location of railroads with reference to the frontier of the United States, so as to render possible expeditious concentration of troops and supplies to points of defense; the coordination of military, industrial and commercial purposes in the location of extensive highways and branch lines of railroad; the utilization of waterways; the mobilization of military and naval resources for defense; the increase of domestic production of articles and materials essential to the support of armies and of the people during the interruption of foreign commerce; the development of seagoing transportation; data as to amounts, location, method, and means of production, and availability of military supplies; the giving of information to producers and manufacturers as to the class of supplies needed by the military and other services of the government, the requirements relating thereto, and the creation of relations which will render possible in time of need the immediate concentration and utilization of the resources of the Nation."

Actually, of course, part of this language was inserted for purely political purposes and part of it to disguise the true significance of the move. There was no serious thought at the time of any need for new railroad lines leading to the "frontier." There was plenty of political sentiment for waterways. Both were appeals to sections of the country that had been very strongly opposed to any increase in military and naval appropriations.

The cluttering language, also, was aimed at preventing any fear throughout the country that the Administration was getting ready for war, for there was a presidential campaign on. But the machinery thus provided was actually a much more important step toward effective preparation than the small increases in the army and navy that the Administration had approved.

The Advisory Commission consisted of Daniel Willard, president of the Baltimore and Ohio Railroad, Hollis Godfrey, president of the Drexel Institute, Howard E. Coffin, a leading figure in the automobile industry, Dr. Franklin H. Martin, secretary general of the American College of Surgeons, Julius Rosenwald, of Sears, Roebuck & Co., Samuel Gompers, president of the American Federation of Labor, and Baruch.

After a number of preliminary conferences, this advisory council began to get very busy, rapidly organizing committees to deal with the various problems. It is interesting to note that in addition to itself developing into the War Industries Board, committees of this council actually sprouted into the Railroad Administration, the Fuel Administration, the Food Administration, the Shipping Board, and the War Trade Board.

On February 28, 1917, the Munitions Standards Board was created, with Frank A. Scott, president of the Warner-Swasey Co., manufacturers of machine tools in Cleveland, as chairman. Within a month came the General Munitions Board. This meant another important step on the road the War Industries Board was to take to prevent competition in buying between various governmental units. The General Munitions Board, with Mr. Scott as chairman, included members of the original Munitions Standards Board, with representatives of the army and navy.

It must be realized here that the new bodies faced a very tough problem in obtaining fair prices for the government, because the Allies had been bidding against each other to get the needed war supplies and were still heavily in the market. Also, in the General Munitions Board's appointment of many committees to deal with different industries, irritation developed among concerns that were not represented on these committees. They felt that they were being discriminated against in favor of competitors who had friends at court.

A new setup was needed to meet these objections, with a new name, and one important change in character. No one with any authority in the new organization should have any financial interest, no matter how remote, in any of the concerns from which purchases were to be made.

On July 28, 1917, the War Industries Board was created. Mr. Scott was the first chairman, with Baruch as commissioner of raw materials, Robert S. Brookings, commissioner of finished products, Robert S. Lovett, priorities commissioner, Colonel Palmer E. Pierce for the army, and Rear Admiral F. F. Fletcher for the navy.

During the first few months of its existence the Board worked along as the creature of the Council of National Defense, a group of terribly busy Cabinet members. To make matters worse, the two Cabinet members obviously most interested in what the Board did were the War and Navy Secretaries, who really had very little time to attend meetings of any sort.

Handicapped as it was in dealing with this entirely new problem of providing unified direction of production and unified buying, the Board invoked two methods of control: price fixing, a time-honored governmental function, and priorities, which seemed to the board members something new under the sun.

A considerable reshuffling of powers was necessary to provide for smooth execution of the functions that Baruch and the President realized were essential, so Mr. Wilson had a bill drafted that gave him wide authority to transfer functions and powers from one governmental agency to another. This proposed bill was first sent to Senator Thomas Martin, of Virginia, then chairman of the Appropriations Committee. Martin was aghast at this grasping for power from the White House. He refused to have anything to do with it, so the bill was put in charge of Senator Lee S. Overman, whose name it bore when it became law.

Thereupon, on May 28, 1918, the President issued an executive order, taking the War Industries Board from under the Council of National Defense, making it an independent body, and outlining its functions. All of these powers were actually set forth in a letter that President Wilson wrote Baruch dated March 4, 1918, the discrepancy of the dates being due to the delay in surmounting the opposition to the Overman bill. Of course, there was no delay in actual operation.

Originally pecked out on Wilson's own typewriter, this letter is such a clear exposition of the precise thought in the minds of both Wilson and Baruch that it warrants careful reading. The text is as follows:

"My dear Mr. Baruch:

"I am writing to ask if you will not accept appointment as Chairman of the War Industries Board, and I am going to take the liberty at the same time of outlining the functions, the constitution and action of the Board as I think they should now be established.

"The functions of the Board should be:

"(1) The creation of new facilities and the disclosing, if necessary, the opening up of new or additional sources of supply;

"(2) The conversion of existing facilities, where necessary, to new uses;

"(3) The studious conservation of resources and facilities by scientific, commercial, and industrial economies;

"(4) Advice to the several purchasing agencies of the Government with regard to the prices to be paid;

"(5) The determination, wherever necessary, of priorities of production and of delivery and of the proportions of any given article to be made immediately accessible to the several purchasing agencies when the supply of that article is insufficient, either temporarily or permanently;

"(6) The making of purchases for the Allies.

"The Board should be constituted as at present and should retain, so far as necessary and so far as consistent with the character and purposes of the reorganization, its present advisory agencies; but the ultimate decision of all questions, except the determination of prices, should rest always with the Chairman, the other members acting in a cooperative and advisory capacity. The further organization of advice I will indicate below.

"In the determination of priorities of production, when it is not possible to have the full supply of any article that is needed produced at once, the Chairman should be assisted, and so far as practicable, guided by the present priorities organization or its equivalent.

"In the determination of priorities of delivery, when they must be determined, he should be assisted when necessary, in addition to the present advisory priorities organization, by the advice and cooperation of a committee constituted for the purpose and consisting of official representatives of the Food Administration, the Fuel Administration, the Railway Administration, the Shipping Board, and the War Trade Board, in order that when a priority of delivery has been determined there may be common, consistent, and concerted action to carry it into effect.

"In the determination of prices the Chairman should be governed by the advice of a committee consisting, besides himself, of the members of the Board immediately charged with the study of raw materials and of manufactured products, of the labor member of the Board, of the Chairman of the Federal Trade Commission, the Chairman of the Tariff Commission, and the Fuel Administrator.

"The Chairman should be constantly and systematically informed of all contracts, purchases, and deliveries, in order that he may have always before him a schematized analysis of the progress of business in the several supply divisions of the Government in all departments.

"The duties of the Chairman are:

"(1) To act for the joint and several benefit of all the supply departments of the Government.

"(2) To let alone what is being successfully done and interfere as little as possible with the present normal processes of purchase and delivery in the several departments.

"(3) To guide and assist wherever the need for guidance or assistance may be revealed; for example, in the allocation of contracts, in obtaining access to materials in any way preempted, or in the disclosure of sources of supply.

"(4) To determine what is to be done when there is any competitive or other conflict of interests between departments in the matter of supplies; for example, when there is not a sufficient immediate supply for all and there must be a decision as to priority of need or delivery, or when there is competition for the same source of manufacture or supply, or when contracts have not been placed in such a way as to get advantage of the full productive capacity of the country.

"(5) To see that contracts and deliveries are followed up

where such assistance as is indicated under (3) and (4) above has proved to be necessary.

"(6) To anticipate the prospective needs of the several supply departments of the Government and their feasible adjustment to the industry of the country as far in advance as possible, in order that as definite an outlook and opportunity for planning as possible may be afforded the businessmen of the country.

"In brief, he should act as the general eye of all supply departments in the field of industry.

"Cordially and sincerely yours,

"WOODROW WILSON."

The Board now consisted, besides Chairman Baruch, of Alexander Legge, vice-chairman (Legge had been vice-president of International Harvester; he later became its president and then attempted to improve the agricultural situation under President Hoover), Rear Admiral F. F. Fletcher, Robert S. Brookings, chairman of the price-fixing committee, Major General George W. Goethals (builder of the Panama Canal and later a member of the Shipping Board), Edwin B. Parker, priorities commissioner (an outstanding lawyer of Houston, Texas), George N. Peek, commissioner of finished products (Peek, who was with Deere & Company, manufacturer of agricultural implements, Moline, Illinois, was brought into the setup on the advice of Alexander Legge), Hugh Frayne, labor representative, J. Leonard Replogle, steel administrator (president of the American Vanadium Co.), L. L. Summers, technical adviser (a New York consulting engineer who had been acting as adviser on Allied purchases), Albert C. Ritchie, general counsel (later Governor of Maryland for three terms), H. P. Ingels, secretary (vice-president and consulting engineer of the Milton Manufacturing Co., with experience in producing explosives for the Allies).

In addition Herbert Bayard Swope, later executive editor of

the *New York World,* was an associate member of the Board and assistant to the chairman. Harrison Williams and Clarence Dillon were also assistants to the chairman.

General Goethals was soon replaced by the War Department with Brigadier General Palmer Pierce, who served until May, 1918, when Brigadier General Hugh S. Johnson took his place.

Peek and Johnson, who were later to be Baruch's close lieutenants in his campaign to keep this country prepared for war emergencies and in many of his other activities, were both thrown into a close connection with him in the War Industries Board, Peek on the recommendation of Legge, and Johnson by appointment of the War Department. Swope, as a very important figure on the *New York World,* had known Baruch intimately for years and has been perhaps his closest friend and adviser ever since.

The final setup of the War Industries Board, which functioned so smoothly and successfully that there was very little criticism either during the war or in the brief attempts at muckraking after the Republicans came into power, approached astonishingly close to the final setup of the War Production Board in the Second World War.

There was this interesting difference in the history of the two organizations. The War Industries Board functioned so smoothly, among other reasons, largely because the chairman was given almost complete authority. In fact he had the final decision on everything save price fixing, and actually he had considerable to say about that. Most of the changes in setups that occurred in the War Production Board of the Second World War resulted from futile attempts to conduct such an organization without giving one man anything approaching complete power.

Donald B. Nelson finally gained one-man control in the Second World War board after the two-headed Knudsen-Hillman organization and various others had failed. Even at the height of his power Nelson did not have anything approaching the authority that Baruch was granted by Wilson during the First World War.

In fact, Baruch was granted so much power that his first actions after the new board got to functioning was to delegate as much of it as possible, making each of his colleagues a czar in his own field and granting him as much responsibility, along with the power, as practical.

The Board organized speedily, setting up a huge number of committees to deal with specific problems or materials. On each such committee was a representative of each government agency interested, who would bring to all discussions the point of view of the agency involved.

On Capitol Hill there were grave wonderings about all this. Never had the senators and representatives seen so much power exercised without their having made the grants of authority, approved the appropriations to exercise them, and had something to say about the personnel. There was criticism in the cloakrooms, not of the actual deeds of the War Industries Board, but of this method of governmental functioning. Critics insisted that Congress had signed its life away when it passed the Overman bill.

Bills were repeatedly introduced legalizing this exercise of power by the Board. Sometimes they reached the stage of being discussed in committees, but none was ever brought out on the floor of either the House or Senate. The general impression on the Hill, despite the questioning of constitutional lawyers and champions of the prestige of the lawmaking branch of the government, was that the Board was doing a good job, and any attempted legislation would be more likely to do harm than good.

Nobody, not even in the Republican minority, ever made any important attempt to change the setup. This attitude may have been due, in part, to the many close friends Baruch had acquired in the years just preceding. It was found that he had a champion or an enthusiastic admirer in every corner of the Capitol, including all the committees that discussed the various proposals to give legal sanction to his activities.

If this unwillingness of Congress to rock the boat, despite the obvious encroachment on its prerogatives, was astonishing, there is no fitting adjective to describe the fact that in the years following the war no single figure in the War Industries Board, in memoirs, interviews, or in any way that has ever reached the public has ever indulged in any criticism. When it is remembered that there were more than a hundred men who occupied what were termed "key positions," that there were sixty important commodity sections, that there were tens of thousands of businessmen whose very economic lives had been in the hands of this Board, it seems almost a miracle that no one ever felt the urge to tell the world of the wrongs he had known!

One explanation of this loyalty Baruch inspired is that he had a system. Years later he revealed a part of it. He was discussing, rather disappointedly, the repudiation of a prominent official by his chief. It had been front-page news for two or three days, and the results were highly embarrassing to the chief, to the subordinate, and to the Administration.

"I would never have done it that way," he said, musingly. "If I give one of my lieutenants, or any employee for that matter, directions on how to proceed on a piece of business, and he violates my instructions and gets in trouble, I stand by him. I take the blame.

"If he does it two or three times, of course, I transfer him to some job where he cannot make trouble, or get rid of him. But I would never admit to outsiders that he had exceeded his authority or violated my orders. I would manage to placate the outsiders involved in some other way. To make my aide the scapegoat destroys the morale of whatever organization I may be heading. My loss as a result of that demoralization would be much greater, in the long run, than anything I could possibly gain by putting the blame on the chap who really deserved it."

His eyes twinkled as he looked across Winyah Bay.

"Besides," he added, "the other fellows might not believe the repudiation anyhow."

The best chapters of many biographies have been fattened by disclosures made by repudiated lieutenants. This author has lacked such assistance. Like "neutrality" and "controlled inflation" in Baruch's dictionary, there "ain't no such animal."

CHAPTER . . . EIGHTEEN

WHAT convinced Woodrow Wilson that Baruch was the right man to head the War Industries Board?

That question was frequently asked at the time and has been asked many times since. Even some who thought that Baruch turned out to be a very fortunate choice for the job have been inclined to term the selection of Baruch a bit of luck on Wilson's part.

The argument has even been advanced that Wilson knew Baruch had been lucky on the stock market and figured that he would like to have a lucky man handle problems so vital to the war effort. They cite the fact that Wilson believed that the number 13—thirteen letters in his name, etc.—was good luck for him. The words Bernard Baruch contain thirteen letters.

It is of course true that if Baruch had not become one of the close circle about Wilson, he would probably never have been considered for the place, but it is just as true that this friendship, warm as it had become, would not have moved Wilson to make the appointment.

Wilson simply did not make that sort of appointment. He appointed Baruch for two reasons. Baruch was one of the barest handful of men available who could, without tearing up his roots, divorce himself utterly from any private interest, so that he would not be embarrassed in dealing with business interests of every possible variety throughout the country. Wilson had been enormously impressed, moreover, in the immediately preceding years, with the accurate knowledge that Baruch displayed about so many lines of business.

Naturally Wilson, getting to know and like Baruch, had been interested in his success story. Perhaps when he first met Baruch he was curious, as so many people have been, about how Baruch had done it—how one managed to beat the stock market! He may even have suspected that Baruch had the Midas touch. Certainly there were many conversations between the two, during the 1913-1917 period, when the President drew his friend out to see just what made him tick.

Now it happens that Baruch resented the popular supposition that he has been just a lucky gambler. With no provocation at all he would tell his friends stories of particular operations to illustrate his theories about how one should operate in the market. He freely admitted that he had been at times very lucky but insisted that very hard work, plus intelligence in judging situations, was of the essence.

Wilson soon learned how very deep and comprehensive a knowledge of the different industries of this country Baruch had. The President learned also that Baruch was in a very small minority so far as stock-market operators were concerned. Some of the most spectacular, for instance, were generally far more concerned with winning the control of specific properties, whether industrial or railroad, than in the profit or loss involved. Some were floor traders primarily, men who bought and sold huge blocks of stocks for others, with the commissions their chief objective. Some were speculators who thought they could make money by operations but who did not think a painstaking research job a primary requisite for a plunge.

Most successful businessmen were so wound up in their own operations that it would have been practically impossible for them to sever completely all ties. If they took on a wartime job it would be with the idea of getting out of the government service at as early a date as possible after the coming of peace and returning to their regular work. Such men, the President believed, could easily be of great service, but only in working under the direction of someone else, who would pass on actions that might hurt or help their own company or competitors.

Being a market operator and not permanently identified with any particular line of business, Baruch could eliminate personal financial interest by the simple expedient of selling all securities he held in any corporations that might possibly be affected by government action.

When the President decided to appoint Baruch, they talked this situation over and agreed at once that Baruch should do precisely this. Such odds and ends as could not be immediately sold he directed his office to hold as a sort of trust fund, applying all dividends that might be received to the Red Cross and similar charities.

Baruch approached his duties with no hard and fast blueprint of the precise type of organization needed. In the first place, he was not sure just how the new body should be organized and, in the second, he was a firm believer that *any* organization would work well if it had the right men doing the job and that *no* organization, no matter how technically perfect, would function well if the men in key positions were inept.

His first job was to pick a staff for the important positions. The selections were made largely from the host of men from all types of industry, mining, and business who had been in contact with, or connected with, the Advisory Commission of the Council of National Defense or the Munitions Board during the months preceding.

Politics did not enter into the selections. As usual, Wilson, having decided to give the job to Baruch, did not embarrass him by demanding that any particular men should be appointed. Few of the positions were salaried, so senators and representatives did not covet them for their political lieutenants. Baruch himself was not interested in the politics of any particular man he wanted.

Almost his first objective was to eliminate competition between the buying agencies of the government and for the Allied governments. Actually by far the most difficult of all the problems with which the Board had to deal was to control the buying agencies of the army. The army officers resented the authority of the War Industries Board, tried their best to circumvent it, and made trouble from first to last. As soon as the war was over the army got back to its own time-honored and uneconomical purchasing methods as rapidly as possible.

It is characteristic of Baruch that nowhere in his writings, his testimony before congressional committees, and his printed interviews does this criticism of the army appear. It is characteristic also of General Hugh S. Johnson that, although he represented the army on the War Industries Board, he made the most scathing criticism of the army supply departments of anyone who has ever discussed them. Years afterward, in *The Blue Eagle from Egg to Earth,* Johnson disclosed that he had not mellowed about this army attitude, though some seventeen years had elapsed.

It was soon realized that it was virtually impossible to draw up a hard and fast schedule of requirements. The "fluidity of war," as it came to be called, prevented this. What the various war agencies wanted from American industry changed not only from month to month and week to week, but almost from day to day. At that time this was almost a brand-new idea. It seemed almost scandalous to the old-timers of 1918 that the army should not be able to say in January what it would want in October.

This trouble with the army was simplified, a few months after this country entered the war, by what turned out to be a marvelous break of luck. General John J. Pershing, in command in France, knowing that he had the complete confidence and backing of both President Wilson and Secretary of War Baker, grew very impatient with the way the army supply departments were functioning. So he sent General Peyton C. March back to Washington to be chief of staff.

Technically, March thereupon became Pershing's superior. Actually he was Pershing's agent in Washington. He threw the weight of his four stars around the War Department, with the complete approval of Secretary Baker and to the dismay of the old bureaucrats, cut red tape, and ignored tradition in getting whatever Pershing wanted done.

From that time on, when supplying the army, Baruch had to satisfy one man—a man who knew just what he wanted because he had almost hourly cables from Pershing.

There was another army difficulty that Baruch was never able to remedy. This was the desire, particularly of the ordnance department, though it naturally applied also to airplanes, to improve items before starting production of them. The public understands fairly well, today, the difficulties that constant change impose upon mass production. In 1917 and 1918 this was not a matter of common knowledge. There was considerable outcry about the lack of production of certain things, notably airplanes, artillery, and rifles.

Even at the time this criticism hit the bull's-eye. There was virtually a revolt in the Senate, led by Chairman George E. Chamberlain of the Military Affairs Committee, a Democrat from Oregon. Chamberlain made himself very unpopular at the White House. In fact it was generally believed that his defeat at the next election resulted from President Wilson's supporters in Oregon voting against him. However, he accomplished part of his purpose. The quartermaster general and the chief of ordnance were "promoted" to a very important commission that Wilson created and were replaced by men who, in the congressional view at least, were much more efficient.

There has been much criticism because, with all the productive capacity of this country, our armies in France right up to the end of the war were supplied with artillery and airplanes by France and Britain. One illustration explains a great deal.

In 1917 it was general military opinion that the best gun of the 3-inch size was the French 75. This being so, the French, at our own request, shipped several of these guns to the United States, so that our manufacturers could produce them. Naturally they went to the Ordnance Department. At once our experts began to figure out how this gun could be improved.

It is not of record whether any of the "improvements" were really good, but when the Armistice came not a single one of the guns had been produced! They were still in the study stage.

This is cited because there has been a tendency in some quarters to belittle the job the War Industries Board did and to cite in proof such facts as the nondelivery of artillery and airplanes and the slowness in production of rifles.

At that time I was Washington correspondent of the *New York Tribune* (this was before its merger into the *Herald Tribune*). The editor who gave me the most orders was Garet Garrett, an old friend of Baruch from his stock-market days. Every time Garrett came to Washington he would spend some time with the Chairman of the War Industries Board, and every time he would emerge with a brand-new idea about some phase of war production that ought to be investigated.

Sometimes it was the price of some article being bought by the government that seemed to Garrett, after a conference with Baruch, to be too high. More often it was the amazing delays due to "improvements." Garrett hired experts to investigate ships, rifles, artillery, and airplanes. On two occasions I was supplied with proofs of the muckraking articles and directed to get the reaction to them of a group of the most critical senators. These were Chairman Chamberlain, of the Military Committee, and

Senators Gilbert M. Hitchcock, of Nebraska, James W. Wadsworth, of New York, and John W. Weeks, of Massachusetts. In each case the senators were unanimous in thinking that no useful purpose would be served by printing the articles and that harm would almost surely result.

The expert who investigated ship construction praised the job being done, so there was no question about printing his articles.

All this shows that Baruch sometimes resorted to channels outside his official sphere in order to bring pressure on agencies over which he had no control, in the hope of expediting the war effort. I remember distinctly the impression of the senators that the investigation by possible muckrakers had a very salutary effect on the government agencies involved.

One of the practices of the government procurement agencies that the War Industries Board encountered not only tended to boost prices but also to produce confusion. This was making inquiries as to whether so much steel, for example, might be supplied and the taking of options on materials that *might* be needed. No one in any given industry, by adding up his firm orders, his options, and his inquiries, could possibly tell if a few months later he would be giving the government what it needed, whether he would be falling far short, or whether he would be embarrassed by a surplus that he could not dispose of at a profit.

The Board set out at once to solve this difficulty by a system of clearances. Soon a clearance list was set up. Government agencies were requested not to make any orders, take any options, or make any inquiries about articles on this clearance list without consultation with the Clearance Committee of the War Industries Board. On this committee were representatives of the various army divisions, including the General Staff, the Navy, Marine Corps, and eventually the Allied Purchasing Commission.

It was the job of the Clearance Committee to thrash out the

conflicts between the conflicting claimant agencies, avoiding bloodshed if not high blood pressure and doing its best to distribute available or obtainable supplies where they would do the most good, without the competitive bidding and inquiries that had been boosting prices.

Naturally this became an enormous job, which had to be broken down into various groups handling individual commodities. On the whole the plan worked extremely well.

In his official report Baruch admitted that this clearance system never resulted in a program of what was to be required, which would have permitted long-range planning. By the spring of 1918, however, a Requirements Division was set up, with Alexander Legge at its head and the usual representation of all government purchasing agencies.

It has been said that this was the first time in the history of government that a plan was adopted by which all the government agencies sat round a table and mapped out what could be done without one interfering with another. It seemed to promise great improvement during the brief period in which it was in operation. The end of the war came so quickly after it was set up that the system did not have a thorough test.

In his final report to the President, Baruch observed that much of the confusion in providing war supplies could have been avoided had there been accurate estimates of requirements by the various government agencies, but he sugar-coated even this criticism by hastening to add that this would have been exceedingly difficult.

He went this far in criticism only in order to make a strong point in favor of the creation of a permanent body consisting of army officers whose function would be, in time of peace, to keep in close touch with the industries, resources, and possibilities of the country so that they could always have an up-to-the-minute plan for their utilization in the event of war.

The industry of the country was already turned very heavily to war production when the War Industries Board came into being. Du Pont was making powder, the year this country entered the war, at the rate of 30,000,000 pounds a month, a jump from 500,000 pounds a month before 1914.

As it was the desire of the government to create a war production for our own forces without curtailing the supply the Allies were getting, the immediate problem was to obtain conversion, in addition to that already effected.

The Board had the navy list, which included 18,000 plants. It was necessary, however, not only to expand this list, but to revamp it so as to provide additional information. For example, the navy list showed what a plant made, and in what quantity, according to the 1914 census. It did not show the processes, the type of machinery used, and therefore the possibility of any given plant's being converted to some other purpose.

By May, 1918, the new list compiled for the Board by its Industrial Inventory Section, with all the information required, had reached 28,000 plants.

In its decisions on clearances and priorities, particularly with regard to new construction of war facilities, the Board early ran into the transportation problem involved in the concentration of so many war industries in the northeastern section of the country. That there is little new in the difficulties that government complicated by human nature tends to create is shown by the fact that the Board was confronted by a storm of complaints by manufacturers of war supplies over the number of questionnaires that they were obliged by various government agencies to fill out.

In an optimistic effort to correct this abuse a Questionnaire Section was set up and an order issued to all government agencies (just 3 months before the Armistice) that all questionnaires sent out by any branch of the Board must be approved in advance by this section. To curtail these questionnaires at the source an Editorial Section attempted to provide, through frequent bulletins, all the information already in hand for every branch of the board that might conceivably find it useful.

So real was this problem, and so satisfactory seemed the solution, that Hugh Johnson wrote into the original National Industrial Recovery Act, in which NRA was created, a provision for a separate agency known as the Central Statistical Board. This survived the Blue Eagle, and its functions were transferred to the White House offices.

Questionnaires persist and complaints about them continue. Maybe Baruch hoped that the reforms he forced, both on questionnaires and on army bureaucracy, would live. But he had read a good deal of history, and he knew a good deal about human nature. Hugh Johnson scolded later about reversal to type. Baruch, highly pleased with Johnson's words though not liking to say them himself, turned to things that might have some hope of accomplishment.

While there was, of course, nothing like so all-inclusive a control by the government over business in the First World War as in the Second, long steps in that direction were taken in 1917 and 1918. The War Industries Board exercised its power under various laws, but it could deny nonessential enterprises not only fuel but railroad transportation. It prevented the construction of a huge soldier memorial in Chicago. It forbade the building of a tabernacle for Billy Sunday, the evangelist, an act which that popular figure applauded when the reasons for it were explained to him. It banned an $8,000,000 public school in New York City.

Actually a special committee was appointed by President Wilson to study the question of eliminating all nonessential industries during the war. This committee consisted of: Vance McCormick, chairman of the War Trade Board; Baruch, chairman of the War Industries Board; Herbert C. Hoover, Food Administrator; and Harry A. Garfield, Fuel Administrator. A subcommittee was appointed, consisting of Clarence M. Woolley, of the War Trade Board, chairman; Edwin B. Parker, priorities commissioner, T. F. Whitmarsh, of the Food Administration; Edward Chambers, of the Railroad Administration; Edwin F. Gay, of the Shipping Board; P. B. Noyes, of the Fuel Administration; Felix Frankfurter, chairman of the War Labor Policies Board; and George May, of the Treasury.

It was decided not to shut down any industry completely but to work out a program for curtailment so as to provide the maximum of men and materials for the war effort and at the same time maintain the nonessential industry in such position that, on the coming of peace, it could expand promptly and help in providing employment.

That idea of cushioning as much as possible the economic consequences of sudden peace was ever present in Baruch's mind.

CHAPTER . . . NINETEEN

BARUCH did not browbeat the British in his conduct of the War Industries Board. He did not beat them down to the last penny in any of the deals. There were loud screams, of course, but actually it would appear that he applied the same formula for fixing prices to them that he did to American producers—a fair profit on top of an allowance for the advance in prices already in effect when the Board was set up. But this was not easy. It took a shrewd stock-market Yankee-type trader—if Baruch will forgive the word "Yankee"—to do it. For instance, he forced the British to cut the price of jute when they had claimed they could not control prices in India. This was a triumph, since everyone knows that the most sensitive spot in the British pocketbook is that concerning profits on their overseas investments.

He cajoled the neutrals, getting Spain to sell us mules, when she did not even want gold, by finding something she *had* to have, ammonium sulphate, to trade her. The ramifications of War Industries Board dealings, intrigues, and manipulations were on a global basis. Negotiations for a needed Chinese product were followed by more dealings for Japanese ships to bring that product to America.

Most of the really exciting stories of Baruch and the Board will never be told, unfortunately, unless, some years hence, Herbert Bayard Swope should take pen in hand and tell all. The answer is that Swope and Baruch are the only two men living as this is written who know enough, and Baruch simply will not do it. It would be out of character.

There is a very full record of what the Board did in Baruch's book, *American Industry in the War*, published in 1941, but the excitement is carefully omitted. It is all sweetness and light, in the best Baruch manner. To tell what really happened in some of the negotiations and deals would be to criticize, very sharply, certain individuals, here and abroad.

There was a proposal, for instance, for a new plant, the operation of which would save hauling millions of tons of coal each year nearly a thousand miles. Certain gentlemen in whom President Wilson had confidence were so persuasive about this that the President sent for Baruch. The President was willing to allot some $40,000,000 for the construction of this plant, he told Baruch, provided Baruch could be satisfied by proper tests that the project was sound.

The strain on the railroads was approaching the breaking point, and the need for coal had already resulted in heatless days. The new process would help in both problems. The President was enthusiastic.

Baruch directed tests to be made at the Bureau of Standards. These were begun. Before their completion, however, Baruch learned, from one of the young men at the Bureau, whom he was questioning about the tests, that the new process was far from being as economical as the promoters claimed. This young man told Baruch that the promoters had secretly installed a gas pipe around the meter, with the result that the amount of gas required for the process was made to appear far less than was actually the case.

Employees of the Bureau, noting the extra gas pipe, calmly put a meter on it. They were not supposed to know about the extra pipe; the promoters did not know about the extra meter!

Brown Brothers

LONDON, 1919

Bernard Baruch with Loucheur, Churchill, Lloyd George.

"Baruch certainly gave me a grilling," said the Bureau man later. "He wanted to know everything about it, and to hear the evidence of all my boys. He soon saw that we were right."

This was far from being the end of the episode. The promoters stopped the experiment at the Bureau of Standards, insisting that the test was unfair. Very important political figures interested themselves. They put pressure on the Bureau and on Baruch and even tried it on the White House.

Baruch was firm. He made no public accusations, contenting himself with telling the President he would not approve the appropriation for the new plant unless he could obtain better demonstrations of the efficiency of the process. The promoters squawked, but Wilson followed his usual rule of relying on the man he had assigned to the job.

The government was saved some $40,000,000, and President Wilson was spared considerable embarrassment.

Hugh Johnson could have written a hundred such interesting stories about Baruch's experiences in the War Industries Board, but for years afterward he worked for Baruch and then got so busy with NRA and his newspaper-column writing that he never had time, even if Baruch would have let him.

The best proof that Baruch was not unfair to the British is that, despite his harsh trimming of war profits, he cemented friendships with leading figures in Britain that lasted for years. Winston Churchill and he found they were kindred souls. Britain's great Minister of Munitions in the First World War paid high tribute to Baruch soon after that war ended. "No British Minister had, I believe, a greater volume of intricate daily business to conduct with United States representatives than I had during 1918," said Mr. Churchill. "It is my duty to record that no Ally could have been given more resolute, understanding, and broadminded cooperation than the Ministry of Munitions received from the War Industries Board of the United States."

Further on in the same statement he said:

"It was not until after the war that I had the pleasure of meeting Mr. Baruch, the Chairman, but almost daily telegrams soon put us on excellent terms. I could feel at the other end of the cable a strong clear mind making quick decisions and standing by them."

It was the squabbles on the home front that would really make good stories should Baruch choose to tell them. For example, it was only from a boasting remark, long afterward, by Elbert H. Gary, of the United States Steel Corporation, that it was revealed that Baruch had threatened to "take over" that company.

Gary's long-delayed comment was that he had kept the United States Steel Corporation from being nationalized. Baruch admitted, after Gary had unsealed this chapter, that the War Industries Board had only obtained what it wanted in the way of prices, production, and compliance with its regulations generally by threatening to commandeer the plants of various steel companies.

The Board had a great deal of trouble with many other industries beside steel. It merely happens that steel is the one that was eventually dragged out into the light of day and then only because Baruch considered that the seal of secrecy had been removed by Judge Gary's remark.

It was never widely publicized, even then. This particular statement was blanketed by other stories the same day that newspaper editors considered of greater news value. The fact remains that future historians, or economists trying to figure out the best way to take the profit out of war, will have to do a great deal of shrewd guessing about the difficulties the Board had with industry and may even jump to erroneous conclusions as to the willingness of selfish human beings to give up profits.

Let's make no mistake about this. The Board used a big stick ruthlessly. It used powers that might be called farfetched, chiefly the power to commandeer and the power to cut off fuel and railroad facilities from anyone who dared to resist. It wasn't the excess-profits tax that made the industrialists so amenable to patriotic pressure to fight inflation by keeping prices down, it was the mailed fist quietly revealed across a conference table in a temporary shack down near the Potomac, *never* brandished in the newspapers.

Nor was this ruthless campaign done without the approval, in advance, of the Administration. The President had said, "Let the manufacturer see the club behind your door." (This also did not become public until many years later.)

In the heat of a discussion afterward, in which Baruch differed sharply from proposals supported by Newton D. Baker, Secretary of War under Wilson, Baruch said: "Agreement there was in the sense of acceptance of a Federal price determination by a few leaders in each industry, and in many of our conferences the government had the enthusiastic support of some producers and in some conferences the unanimous support of all, but, as a practical matter, *there was no alternative to such acceptance and there was a distinct threat of effective reprisal in case of refusal.*

"I bore the heat and burden of nearly every one of the principal price determinations except food, and I am speaking from intense experience when I say that in most cases those prices, while eventually accepted wholeheartedly, were not unconstrained free-will offerings of all by any manner of means. We used a good many euphemisms during the war for the sake of national morale, and this one of 'price fixing by agreement' is a good deal like calling conscription 'Selective Service' and referring to registrants for the draft as 'mass volunteers.' Let us make no mistake about it; we fixed prices with the aid of potential Federal compulsion, and we could not have obtained unanimous compliance otherwise."

Steel, of course, was one of the war-baby products that simply had to be handled. Its average weighted price reached 370 per cent of normal by July, 1917. Connellsville coke had been $1.67 a ton in September, 1915. It was $12.25 in July, 1917. Basic pig iron was $12.59 a ton in June, 1915. By July of 1917 it was $52.50 a ton. Bessemer steel billets were $19.50 a ton in May, 1915. By July, 1917, they were $95 a ton. Structural steel shapes were $1.20 a hundredweight in December, 1914. By July, 1917, they were $6.20. Steel tank plates rose from $1.22 a hundredweight in July, 1915, to $22 in September, 1917.

J. Leonard Replogle was appointed director of steel supply for the War Industries Board, and the negotiations with the industry began. The steel people were willing to cut prices, but they insisted that the price to the public should continue to be determined by a free market and that the price to the Allies should continue subject to such contracts as had been or should be made.

Baruch, with the approval of the President, insisted that the public should receive the advantage of the lowered price and that the new prices should apply to sales to the Allies. There was little delay. The first formal meeting, following much consultation, was held on September 21, 1917, and on September 24 the President proclaimed the new prices. They were: iron ore, $5.05 a gross ton at lower lake ports; coke, Connellsville, $6 a net ton; pig iron, $33 a gross ton; steel bars, Pittsburgh-Chicago, $2.90 a hundred pounds; shapes, $3 a hundred pounds; plates, $3.25 a hundred pounds.

This fixing of prices as of Pittsburgh and Chicago, which applied to the last three items, is believed to have been the first time this was done. The steel industry liked the old Pittsburgh-plus-freight-rate-from-Pittsburgh system of fixing prices, resumed it after the war, and continued it for several more years.

It has been estimated that this regulation of steel prices alone saved a total of more than a billion dollars.

The winter of 1917-1918 was a particularly bitter one and played havoc with the already badly strained railroads. To help out in this situation the War Industries Board worked out many hundred eliminations of cross hauling. In his report Baruch cited the case of a Buffalo steel manufacturer who was shipping a tremendous tonnage of projectile steel in bar forms to a forge plant in Cincinnati, which turned the bars into projectile forgings. Then these were shipped back to Buffalo for machining! There were complications, chiefly in that the price contracts were very different, but arrangements were made so that the steel bars made in Buffalo were forged near by, while other work was found for the Cincinnati plant.

Then as now copper was second to steel on the munitions list. The price had risen from 16 cents before 1914 to 35.74 cents in March, 1917. The copper men were in a better position to trade than the steel people had been. For one thing, there are few commodities in which so large a percentage of the production cost is wages. Since 1915, they pointed out, the average wage in their industry had advanced 50 per cent. Moreover, some of the contracts with the miners fixed the rate of pay directly on the price of copper, and the workers would strike if the price were reduced too sharply. After much dickering the price of copper was fixed at 23½ cents on September 21, 1917, but was raised to 26 cents on July 2, 1918, remaining there for the duration.

The aluminum negotiations fell into a different pattern from those of steel and copper. Then, as for many years thereafter, aluminum was virtually a monopoly. The Aluminum Company of America proposed to Baruch that it would sell the government all it could produce at any price the government might fix. Before the outbreak of war in Europe the price had been 20 cents a pound. It had soared to 60 cents, with contracts in the neighborhood of 38 cents. This wide discrepancy was due to the fact that the trade practice was to make annual contracts, so that, in a rapidly advancing market, the contract price would be considerably lower than the open-market price.

The government accepted this offer of the company and bought 2,000,000 pounds at 27½ cents, agreeing that the final price should be whatever the government should fix. The Federal Trade Commission, at the instigation of the War Industries Board, made a study of costs. A price of 32 cents was recommended and approved by the President. However, the company came forward with the argument that it had been urged to increase its facilities, that the Allies were paying a much higher price, and that an extra 3 cents a pound should be allowed. Eventually this was compromised to be 33 cents, which continued until after the end of the war.

Aluminum, of course, was a fairly new industry, having grown from a production of 23 pounds in 1885 to 1,000,000 pounds in 1896 and 130,000,000 pounds in 1918. It must be remembered that the United States did not get into real production of airplanes until the end of the First World War. Use of aluminum for planes was not recited in the report of the War Industries Board, though many other uses, both for war and peace, were mentioned.

Actually aluminum was used for planes in this country only where no great strains were involved. There were some aluminum castings—for instance, one for the Hispano-Suiza engine. The alloys that were to make aluminum strong enough for wings had not been developed in this country, though the Germans actually made a few all-aluminum planes toward the end of the war. Even these, however, were too late to get into the fighting.

Steel, copper, and aluminum are mentioned here as samples, steel and copper because they were the two more important metals, and aluminum because of the ease of the negotiations.

Actually, of course, the Board dealt with hundreds of metals, materials, chemicals, and other articles. A mere list would fill many pages. An attempt to trace their history in the War Industries Board record would fill many volumes the size of this.

In a report by Baruch to President Wilson dated December 24, 1918, in which he paid high tribute to his associates on the War Industries Board and praised both industry and labor, he said:

"It is not within the province of the writer to render judgment upon the success achieved by the organization of which he was the head, but it is not amiss for him to say not one default was recorded on any demand made by the military establishments. They were given all they asked in measure so full and so quick as to be noteworthy, especially when it is remembered that most of the years of our existence had been given over to life and thought of peace with small inclination or opportunity to familiarize ourselves with the arts and needs of war. If the love of country shows itself in the readiness of men to fight it is equally proven in the willingness of capital and labor—of the men and women workers—to serve."

Another section of that letter is worth repeating here, because it is the first chapter, so to speak, of the volumes Baruch poured out in his efforts to get this country in such shape that no international danger should ever again catch us off balance, so that we would be prepared for any emergency, so that we would be ready, when some international bully should swagger down the international street, to hit, and hit effectively.

"It would be impossible in any statement of the activities of the War Industries Board," wrote Baruch in the same letter to President Wilson of December 24, 1918, "or any story of the mobilization of the industries of the country, not to conclude with definite recommendations based upon the lessons learned. A similar emergency may arise in the future and it can more easily be coped with if the experiences of the last two years are profited by. The writer believes:

"First. There should be created a peace-time skeleton organization based on the experience of the war-making agencies. It should be headed by a chairman, who, when the emergency arises, should be granted the powers necessary to coordinate and synchronize the economic resources of the country. With him should be associated the representatives of the Army and the Navy or any other department vitally interested, as the Shipping Board, who should have centralized under them the various purchasing branches of their departments. There also should be in the skeletonized organization a vice chairman, a secretary, a counsel, and members in charge of raw materials, finished products, facilities, prices, labor, planning and statistics (during peace under the Department of Commerce), priority and conservation. Under these there should be also the various section or commodity heads. The peace-time organization would meet at least once a year to discuss and outline plans and to keep in touch with the general world situation and with one another. Each sectional head would name committees in each industry in order that, in the event of an impending crisis, it would be possible within a few days to create an organization which immediately would mobilize all of the industries of the nation and quickly make available for the government all of its resources. These men, with the exception of the Secretary, who would keep the records, would serve without compensation and the actual expense of maintaining such an organization would be small. I would recommend that all priorities, including those of shipping, should be centralized in the chairman.

"Second. Through a system of stimulation by a protective tariff, a bonus, an exemption from taxation for a limited period, licensing, or any other effective means, every possible effort should be made to develop production of manganese, chrome, tungsten, dyestuff, by-products of coal, and all such raw materials usually imported but which can be produced in quantity in this country. Above all, immediate and persistent effort must be made to develop production of nitrogen and its substitutes, not alone for war but for agricultural purposes.

"Third. Under the supervision of the proper departments of the Government some industries must be given encouragement to maintain a skeleton organization through which can be developed the rapid manufacture of guns, munitions, airplanes, etc. Some facilities already developed might be kept alive through outright purchase or by small orders for munitions and airplanes while at all times there must be kept on hand the necessary dies, jigs, fixtures, etc., needed for the manufacture of munitions. The expert personnel of the War and Navy Departments in addition to keeping abreast of the times in new war-making agencies should keep the industries of the Nation attuned in a skeleton form to meet immediately that enlarged demand. which would come through war."

A lot of grief might have been saved had that advice been taken!

The best evidence of what Woodrow Wilson thought about Baruch's conduct of the War Industries Board lies not in any particular thing he said, but in the fact that he wanted to keep the financier not only at his right hand, but in an official position if possible. The situation was very different from what it had been shortly after Wilson's first inaugural, when he tried to discharge the obligation he felt toward Baruch on account of the latter's heavy contributions to his campaign fund.

This time he wanted him in the Cabinet. He offered him the post of Secretary of the Treasury. Baruch had always said he did not want to hold any office, but many men have said that and then accepted important diplomatic posts, and the list of men who have refused seats in the Cabinet is not very long. Baruch's name is now on it.

Wilson may have been surprised, but he was probably glad of it later. Soon he wanted Baruch very badly for the Versailles Peace Conference in which Wilson's heart was much more concerned.

CHAPTER . . . TWENTY

On October 7, 1918, President Wilson received official word from Berlin, via the Swiss, that Germany wanted to end the war on the basis of his famous Fourteen Points. The war effort had to go on, for no chances could be taken, but Baruch was advised of the situation and told to govern the activities of the War Industries Board accordingly. The President also told him that he was being drafted for service at the Peace Conference, whenever it should be held, because Wilson considered no one so well qualified to work on the economic sections of the treaty.

After this first request for an armistice and before the President and Baruch sailed for Europe, however, occurred something which was to "break the heart of the world." This was the congressional election on November 5, just 2 days before the false armistice and 6 days before the real one.

Somebody—the blame has never been clearly fixed, though most Democratic politicians blamed Postmaster General Albert S. Burleson—persuaded President Wilson to issue an appeal for the election of a Democratic Congress. This was done on October 24. The Democratic leaders were worried about the House of Representatives. In the election of 1916 the House results had been so close that only by some shrewd maneuvers and several lucky breaks were the Democrats able to organize the House and elect a Speaker.

The general public, of course, did not realize that the end of the war was in sight. Wilson's political advisers thought that if the President, as war leader, appealed for a Democratic Congress as necessary to the war effort, the people would vote the Democratic ticket.

The appeal backfired. It made the Republicans furious, naturally, and it resulted in driving the Republicans who had been supporting the President back to their own party. As a result not only was a strong Republican majority in the House elected, but control of the Senate passed to the GOP also. No one, not even the most optimistic Republicans, had expected this.

The number of Democrats in the Senate dropped from fifty-one to forty-seven, the Republicans gaining five seats and losing only one. Had the Democrats held just one of those five seats they lost, the whole story would have been different. Forty-eight votes instead of forty-seven would have resulted in a tie, and the Democrats had Vice President Marshall to settle any tie in their favor.

In Delaware, Senator Willard Saulsbury, a strong Wilson man, was defeated for reelection by L. H. Ball by only 1,406 votes! In Colorado, Senator John F. (Honest John) Shafroth, who always voted precisely as the White House asked, was defeated by Lawrence C. Phipps, with a vote of 107,726 to 104,347. Normally heavily Democratic Missouri elected Seldon P. Spencer, Republican, to the Senate over Joseph W. Folk by a plurality of 35,283.

Had the war continued, this loss of control of the Senate might not have had such repercussions. The Republicans were cooperating on all war measures. Besides, the new Congress would not take office until March 4, 1919, this being before the Constitution was changed by the Norris "lame duck" amendment.

But with peace arrived, and not overlooking the Republican trend, which seemed to promise a presidential victory for the

GOP in 1920, the new senators did not wait for March 4 to act. A round robin was arranged, signed by more than one-third of all the senators who would be in office after March 4, and dispatched to Paris. This round robin stated that the senators signing it objected to the League of Nations covenant being included in the peace treaty.

As it so happened, the British and French underestimated the importance of this, but Colonel E. M. House did not.

Under the skillful direction of Senator Henry Cabot Lodge, of Massachusetts, the Foreign Relations Committee was packed against the League, against the treaty, against everything that Wilson wanted. With control of the Senate passing to the Republicans, they not only obtained the chairmanship of this committee, but a majority as well, in conformity with the time-honored tradition that the membership of important committees is divided roughly on the proportion that the parties have in the Senate. Senator Lodge, with the approval of the Committee on Committees, added four Republicans, Hiram Johnson, George H. Moses, Warren G. Harding, and Harry S. New, to the committee. Johnson and Moses became "irreconcilables"—treaty killers—while Harding and New became Lodge reservationists.

Saulsbury's defeat at the polls eliminated him from the committee. Two other Democratic senators were dropped from it, one of whom, Joe Robinson, was a thick-and-thin Wilson supporter.

Wilson and Baruch worked in Paris as though nothing untoward was happening back home. The task Baruch faced was the nearest to impossible of any in his career. Revenge, greed, and politics conspired against him. Even when the delegates from other countries wanted to be reasonable, they could not. Their peoples would overthrow them if they did not insist upon the very demands that the Americans thought unreasonable.

Nor was there much incentive for Baruch and other Americans

to encourage heroism on the part of many of the foreign delegates. It was obvious, from the temper of the peoples of the Allied countries, that if the British or French or Italian delegations should suddenly yield to reason, their governments would be overthrown, there would be new delegates, and the new delegates would be even tougher in their unreasonable demands.

There was no doubt about the temper of the peoples back home. Lloyd George had just gone through an election on the slogan of "Hang the Kaiser" and, on the reparations issue, of "Shilling for shilling and ton for ton."

One of the first big rows was over the division among the Allies of whatever reparations Germany should pay. Britain insisted on the inclusion of war costs. Baruch opposed this. At the head of the American group he worked out a percentage of payments to the Allies as follows: France, 43 per cent; British Empire, 19 per cent; Belgium (under a special formula), 24 per cent; Italy, 6 per cent; Serbia, 4 per cent; Rumania, 3 per cent; and 1 per cent scattering.

The British plan of including war costs, Baruch pointed out to the other delegations, would result roughly as follows: France, 24 per cent; British Empire, 40 per cent; Belgium, 1.7 per cent; Italy, 6 per cent; Serbia, 1.3 per cent; United States, 25 per cent; and 2 per cent scattering.

It will be observed that the French share of the reparations would be barely more than one-half under the British plan what it would have been under the American and that the United States would get nothing under the plan of its own delegation, but 25 per cent under the British plan. Naturally the Americans figured that the French would give the American plan some support. They did not. Neither did the other nations that would get less under the British plan.

It may be argued that the French, Serbians, and others thought they would eventually get more under a plan that called for the payment of war costs than under one that did not, even if their own percentages were less. Whether that is true or not, it was not the *real* difficulty. This was simply that these delegates would not have dared face their countries with a reparations plan that did not include repayment of war costs.

How much Germany could be paying 3, 5, or 20 years later was on the academic side. Nobody had the slightest idea anyhow. Estimates of experts ranged all the way from $8,000,000,000 to $120,000,000,000, with no two agreeing on any particular figure.

Furthermore, the delegations would not present a bill of particulars for the war damage they wanted to collect. The British eventually went through the motions, but the French refused even to start.

Confronting this confusion of ideas and motives, Baruch finally came to approve the idea of a Reparations Commission. When he came home he said he hoped such a commission would be able to solve the problems as they arose, with less boiling blood and more cold-blooded analysis of what could be done. He had done the best he could to work out the economic and reparations sections so that there was a minimum of intrinsic harm in them.

Baruch's tour of duty at the Peace Conference was not all hopeless problems and frustration. There were bright moments. For one thing, the financier reveled in his meetings with the economists of Europe at the council table. It was like the satisfaction of a great chess player at finding an opponent worthy of his best efforts.

For another thing, Mrs. Baruch accompanied him, and they did a great deal of entertaining. Always a delightful hostess, she was very popular. Her remark to an American that he was "lucky to meet the two most beautiful and witty duchesses of Britain at one dinner party" was quoted for years afterward; the duchesses appeared to like it.

Nearly every afternoon Baruch had a pleasant session at the Crillon with three or four of his old cronies from the War Industries Board. The only difficulty was that Alec Legge could not find any of his favorite chewing tobacco, Piper Heidsick.

"You'd think with a name like that the Paris tobacconists would carry it," he grumbled.

Sidney Kirkpatrick, then a young lieutenant serving as aide to one of the group, informed Legge that his brand could be obtained at a certain commissary in one of the suburbs.

"Would you mind taking my car and running out there for some?" inquired Baruch.

A few moments later a very proud lieutenant was lolling in the tonneau of Baruch's Rolls-Royce, a startling black and white, wicker-bodied affair that somehow conveyed to those who saw him that this young lieutenant must be one of the most important personages in Paris.

"After that it was a regular assignment," said Kirkpatrick, afterward. "The proudest I had been in Paris before that was when I would go out to the same commissary in an army Cadillac to get a pound of butter for my landlady."

Back in America after the signing of the treaty, Wilson plunged into the fight to obtain its ratification by the Senate. It was apparent that there had been a drift in sentiment away from the League. Opposition senators proved adept in producing interesting attacks on this or that phase of the treaty. Wilson made his well-remembered swing around the country, trying to work up a popular enthusiasm so great that individual senators would not dare oppose his dream of world peace. He collapsed physically. Opposition senators fought on. It was, Baruch thought, a time for compromise.

Canvassing the situation with his friends among the Democratic senators, he soon discovered the political difficulties. All the racial groups, virtually without exception, were against the treaty for one reason or another, especially the Irish, the Germans, and the Italians. He studied the reasons and saw that there was no hope that education would change them in time to do any good.

The Irish, normally Democratic in most states, were off the reservation because of the six votes to one for the British Empire. In the League Covenant it was provided that Britain and the Dominions would have a total of six votes in the League Assembly; the United States would have only one vote. The Irish were also indignant because Ireland had not been given its independence. The Germans thought Wilson had betrayed Germany after she had laid down her arms on the basis of the Fourteen Points and were bitter against Wilson for having entered the war in the first place. The Italians would never forgive him for not giving Fiume to Italy.

On top of this were the pacifists and isolationists, who did not want to see American boys killed in Europe's quarrels and who had the backing of William Jennings Bryan. Baruch found that Bryan's following could be placated if Wilson would accept one of the Lodge reservations, that on Article X. Most advocates of world cooperation to preserve peace insist today, as President Wilson vainly did in 1919, that something in the nature of Article X is the only possibility for preventing aggressive wars. Its text as written in the Covenant of the League of Nations approved at Versailles follows:

"The high contracting parties undertake to respect and preserve as against external aggression the territorial integrity and existing political independence of all States members of the League.

"In case of any such aggression, or in case of any threat or danger of such aggression, the executive council shall advise upon the means by which the obligation shall be fulfilled."

Many normally stanch supporters of President Wilson among the Democratic senators wanted a reservation to this section. The President eventually wrote a letter to Senator Hitchcock, which was read to the Senate.

"There is no escaping," said President Wilson, "the moral obligations which are expressed in positive terms in this Article of the Covenant. . . .

"Any reservation which seeks to deprive the League of Nations of the force of Article X cuts at the very heart and life of the Covenant itself."

He added that Article X "is the bulwark, and the only bulwark of the rising democracy of the world against the forces of imperialism and reaction."

Many diplomats today believe Wilson was right about that and that the British and French were wrong in thinking it unimportant whether America accepted Article X. Of course, there enters into this controversy the question of whether America would have agreed with other members of the League in ignoring Article X when the Japanese and Italian aggressions occurred. Wilson was acting on the premise that treaty pledges would be kept. Baruch's position was that while this country might not bind itself by approval of the treaty with Article X intact, at least, if the U. S. joined the League, our representative would sit in on any conference called to consider an act of aggression and probably would agree to any concerted action to prevent aggression and therefore war.

Senator Lodge eagerly accepted the President's comments on Article X.

"Article X," he said, "is not diplomatic; it is an appeal to naked force. That is why we so much object to it; that is why the country so much objects to it. It is naked force for which each nation is made individually responsible. It is well that he has said it; the issue can be veiled no longer; it justifies the position that we on this side [the Republican side of the aisle in the Senate], all alike, have taken, that there must be no obligation imposed on the United States to carry out the provisions of Article X."

In his canvass Baruch found that other groups could be placated by accepting other Lodge reservations. He soon found, indeed, that the Lodge reservations composed a masterly job of appealing to all the groups and minorities of the country and that it took a very brave politician indeed to oppose all of them.

A close student of history, Baruch knew that several states, including Rhode Island, had joined the union in the first place with reservations but that the reservations had not made any difference later. In fact they had been forgotten. He talked to some of his British friends and discovered that, while they could not say so openly, actually they were not perturbed by the reservations.

Wilson was brooking no opposition. He was discarding advisers right and left. Everyone who had dared oppose him was dropped overboard. Baruch did not want to be dropped overboard. He did not want to end a friendship that meant so terribly much to him. He did not want to be excluded from the stage of world affairs on which Wilson had placed him. But this time he *knew* his idol was wrong—that it was impossible, no matter how right Wilson might be as to principles, for him to get a whole loaf. He wanted Wilson to take half a loaf, believing that if he did it would turn out eventually to be pretty nearly the lion's share.

He had seen the strength of political tides at Paris outlaw sound reasoning. He knew that the political tide in this country was running so strongly that Wilson could not possibly obtain ratification without reservations for the Versailles Treaty and the League of Nations; that the Republicans were bound to win the presidential election on an isolationist platform if Wilson kept on fighting. He knew finally that Wilson could put the United States in the League, and make that instrumentality a force for world peace, if he would only compromise.

With a clear conscience, therefore, but a sad heart he urged the President to accept ratification with reservations. The President stuck to his guns. Baruch, hating to see a total loss when he knew it might be so easy to salvage such an important fraction of the whole, appealed to Mrs. Wilson. We have evidence that she, for the time being, was very sympathetic. She also was afraid of the effects of this long-drawn-out fight on her husband. She added her appeal to the argument Baruch had made. The President was determined to go down with his flag flying.

After the Senate had adopted the Lodge reservations, the President sent word to his followers in the Senate that they were to vote to reject the whole business, rather than accept it thus compromised. So the United States stayed out of the League.

Baruch knew at the time that the French did not care very much about the details of the League. He knew, for instance, that Clemenceau would not have given a sou to have obtained elimination of the Lodge reservation to Article X, for the simple reason that Clemenceau did not have any confidence that the member nations would ever, as required by Article X, send men and ships to prevent any act of aggression by one nation against another.

The Tiger had taken quite a fancy to Baruch during the Peace Conference and the journeys that the two happened to make together. He always called Baruch Prince, having personally dubbed him Prince d'Israël. Knowing that both Wilson and the British were enthusiastic about the League, Clemenceau had calmly exacted a price for his final support. This was a treaty under which Britain guaranteed France against aggression and another by which the United States did the same thing.

Certainly Lord Robert Cecil, one of the best friends the League ever had, thought Wilson made a grave mistake in not taking Baruch's advice. There are those who believe he would have compromised, as he did in the case of the Federal Reserve Act, if he had not been a sick man at the time.

There was another reason why Baruch did not share Wilson's determination to have the treaty approved without changing the dotting of an *i* or the crossing of a *t*. He knew there would have to be revisions of the sections of the treaty on which he had worked in Paris. He knew that the Reparations Commission that had been set up as a solution for presently irreconcilable views would make drastic revision of the reparations program from time to time. He was just as anxious as Wilson for the United States to become a member of the League and to have a voice in this international effort to maintain peace, but he was naturally more keenly concerned than even Wilson about the functioning of the economic sections, and these were not importantly affected by the Lodge reservations.

Baruch had realized, during the reparations negotiations in Paris, the possibility of reparations payments becoming more harmful to the nation receiving them than to the nation paying them.

Baruch pointed out to his fellow members of the economic section of the Peace Conference that reparations payments would have to be made in goods. All removable property presumably would be taken at once, so that only work could produce reparations payments. Hence Germany, in order to make reparations payments, would have to export goods. This would mean that the markets of the world would have to be kept open to Germany, and this in turn would mean that, by the time Germany had finished paying the reparations, she would dominate these markets. Meanwhile, presumably, there would be no unemployment in Germany, but there would be serious unemployment among Allied nations taking the reparations!

Once this had been stated by Baruch, most of the delegates realized that the situation promised plenty of trouble. It was brand-new. Most tributes and ransoms in the past had been exacted in immediate payment. The huge tribute levied on France in 1870 by Bismarck might have developed this new idea had it not been that the French paid it off so rapidly.

But the politicians at the Versailles conference realized instantly that, sound as this principle might be, it was not one that would readily be understood by their peoples. So here was another reason for postponing decisions—handing them over for future settlement by the Reparations Commission.

Baruch wanted the United States to be in a position to act as moderator when these decisions were made, to be in a position to inject sanity into the bitter arguments he foresaw. But Wilson saw himself as a soldier carrying the flag; death was preferable to surrender.

There is an anticlimax to this story, a chapter that was a tightly held secret until several years after Wilson's death.

In March, 1920, months after the first vote in the Senate on the treaty with the Lodge reservations, President Wilson asked Baruch and a number of other friends to hold a meeting at the Chevy Chase Club, just outside Washington. Among those present were Chairman Homer S. Cummings of the Democratic National Committee, Senator Gilbert M. Hitchcock, who was leading the treaty fight for the President in the Senate, Secretary of State Bainbridge Colby, Joseph P. Tumulty, the President's secretary, Secretary of the Treasury David F. Houston, Secretary of Labor William B. Wilson, Postmaster General Albert S. Burleson, Chairman Edward N. Hurley of the Shipping Board, and Senator Carter Glass of Virginia.

Homer Cummings produced a bit of paper on which, in Wilson's handwriting, were the words: "What shall I do politically this year?" That, apparently, was the purpose of Wilson in asking this group to confer.

The conversation revealed that most of those present believed that the President wanted to be a candidate for a third term. Only Burleson, however, expressed a desire for Wilson to be a candidate. His health, most of them thought, made such a strain as the candidacy would involve unthinkable.

The meeting then passed to consideration of the political aspects of the treaty fight. Burleson agreed with the others that to go to the country on the issue of ratifying the Treaty without reservations would be political suicide for the Democratic Party.

The President, meanwhile, had been insisting that the action of the Senate, in failing to approve the Treaty, had not been a rejection, but merely a failure to act. The Treaty, he insisted, was still before the Senate. In fact, it seemed to be his position that the Treaty would remain before the Senate until it should be approved.

Senator Hitchcock and other followers of the President on this issue obeyed orders. There was nothing the other senators could do about it. They could not muster a majority to kill the Treaty outright, by indefinite postponement. Too many Republican senators would vote against such a motion, as they actually wanted the Treaty ratified, provided that they could get satisfactory reservations.

When the meeting at Chevy Chase was held the Treaty was still an issue in the Senate. Everyone knew that there would have to be another vote and that it would be a mere repetition of the previous vote unless Wilson permitted his loyal followers to vote for ratification with the Lodge reservations. Hitchcock made this very clear to the others at the meeting.

It was agreed by those present that if Wilson did not change his position the League of Nations would become a tremendous issue in the campaign. They agreed that this was what Wilson wanted, that he wanted to be the candidate on that issue and believed the people would sustain him.

Not one man present thought this was wise. Even Burleson, who wanted the President renominated, wanted the treaty issue disposed of by ratification with reservations. A letter was read to the gathering from Frank I. Cobb, editor of the *New York World*. This adoring friend of Wilson urged that the Lodge reservations be accepted, so as to get the treaty ratified.

At this point Senator Glass said that it was obviously the opinion of all present that President Wilson should accept the reservations and that he should be advised that all present were in agreement about it.

"But," added the Virginia Senator, "in the present condition of the President's mind and his state of health, who among us will be willing to go to him and tell him that he should accept the reservations?"

Baruch sat there uncomfortably. He had already tried telling the President precisely that and knew how useless it would be. But keeping what presidents said to him in confidence had already become a personal law. He could not tell his friends. He wondered what his duty was, as the seconds clicked by, and one man looked at another. Soon it appeared that no warning from him was necessary. No one volunteered to carry the unwelcome news to the White House!

CHAPTER . . . TWENTY-ONE

BARUCH found himself helpless as a result of Wilson's sick-bed decision. Senator Henry Cabot Lodge had won his objective. He had carefully compromised with the so-called "mild reservationist" Republican senators until he had worked out reservations *every one* of them would support. This was quite an achievement, because actually some of them were far more enthusiastic for the Treaty than many of the Democratic senators.

Porter J. McCumber, of North Dakota, was probably more favorable to ratification of the treaty and getting the United States into the League, regardless of reservations, than anyone else in the Senate. Senator Colt, of Rhode Island, told a group of newspapermen who were in favor of killing the treaty that he did not see how they could sleep at night. Senator Kellogg, of Minnesota, was bedubbed Nervous Nellie, which was to haunt him after he became Secretary of State, because he kept wavering as to whether he could agree to this or that one of the Lodge reservations. Public sentiment was for strong reservations. Senator Charles L. McNary, of Oregon, was one of the few mild reservationists to be reelected.

Having worked out reservations as strong as he could and yet have every one of the forty-nine Republican senators vote for them, Lodge prayed that Wilson would refuse to accept them. Had Wilson accepted, Lodge knew that only about twenty to twenty-two senators at most would vote to reject and the United States would be in the League.

Lodge's motives have often been misstated. Many have chosen to believe that personal hatred of Woodrow Wilson was the one that dominated. Certainly Lodge did not like Wilson, but the mere fact that he worked so hard to get a solid Republican front gives a clear insight into his mental processes and reveals his chief motive. This was to capitalize, for the Republican Party, an issue that every political sign, particularly the vote in every primary and special election, indicated was overwhelmingly popular.

There was another perfectly natural political motive. Lodge was ambitious to play a more important role in the Republican Party. At the 1916 Republican national convention Theodore Roosevelt, in withdrawing his own name, had suggested to the convention that it nominate Senator Lodge. It is seldom that anyone who has been mentioned for the presidency ever entirely gives up hope. He may be sane on every other subject, but logic departs from him on that one question. Perhaps with T.R. off the scene, Lodge thought seriously of the White House.

Be that as it may, there is no doubt whatever that Lodge resented the leadership in his party of certain gentlemen who were championing the League of Nations, notably his former colleague from Massachusetts, ex-Senator Murray Crane, former President William Howard Taft, who had stumped the country for the League, George Wharton Pepper, and others.

At the Republican convention the Lodge issues triumphed, but the man who had so successfully united his party in the Senate behind them was passed by. Warren G. Harding, who was nominated, had been a so-called "strong reservationist," in other words, a Lodge reservationist.

Baruch played his usual role of generous contributor in the 1920 election, but, knowing from his political friends that it was a hopeless fight, he was not greatly surprised at the result. He had no urge to return to active operations on the stock market. He had sold his seat on the New York Stock Exchange in 1917 and never considered buying another.

He settled down to what he regarded as his job—to keep the country prepared industrially for any emergency that might come—and to enjoyment of life at his South Carolina plantation.

Following the 1920 election Baruch saw that there was not going to be any assurance that the world could avoid another war or that the United States could avoid being dragged into it. He did not say a word to discourage his chief, President Wilson, or his daughter, Belle Baruch, who not only largely financed but worked tirelessly for an organization called the Non-Partisan League (no connection with the agrarian movement of the same name in the Northwest), which was fighting for eventual entry of the United States into the League of Nations. But he knew from his political friends that the trend against joining the League throughout this country was too strong to be reversed in the near future, and, knowing the skepticism of Clemenceau and certain other European friends, he thought it wise for this country to be on guard against war.

Hence he embarked, shortly after the inauguration of President Harding, on what he confidently expected to be an even greater service to his country than he had performed in the War Industries Board. He started a one-man crusade to have the United States always ready for war. He wanted an adequate armed force, well trained and equipped. He wanted a never-ceasing study of new developments and inventions, so that our army, navy, and air force would always be abreast, if not ahead, of possible enemy powers.

Most important of all, he wanted a skeleton directing body always working on industrial preparedness, backed by powers lodged in the President that could instantly, in emergency, be brought into play. He wanted to assure not only military strength, but also government control of prices. Thus he would prevent inflation, hold down the cost of war, avoid civilian hardship, and avert the hitherto inevitable postwar depression following demobilization of fighters and war workers.

Baruch's optimism at the time was based, in a way, on previous successes. In the stock market and business he had dealt with keen minds concentrated usually on one objective, the making of money; men, in short, who did not have to have a brick house fall on them to know that a wind was blowing; men who, once the pattern was made clear to them, followed it instantly; men who did not have constituents to worry about; men whose pride of opinion never prevented their doing a quick about-face if so doing would save them a dollar. As head of the War Industries Board he dealt also with businessmen, while, as we have seen, Congress, though grumbling about his powers, never got to the point of interfering. He learned something about bureaucracy in dealing with the army, but he was to learn much more.

Early successes obscured the difficulties. Congress in 1920, with the unpreparedness situation of 1917 still recent, passed amendments to the National Defense Act of 1916. These authorized the Assistant Secretary of War to set up a Planning Branch for "M day" to provide for the mobilization of industry in the event of war, and, through the Army and Navy Joint Munitions Board, to coordinate the demands of the two services and thus avoid the competition for supplies that had been such a headache before Baruch took charge in the First World War.

There was set up also the Army Industrial College, where Baruch, Hugh Johnson, and other Baruch lieutenants in the War Industries Board gave frequent lectures. Everybody was fairly happy about the situation. Baruch enjoyed his own lectures and those of his fellow War Industries Board veterans thoroughly. The army was getting a first-class education in war supply planning. The army bureaus were covertly recovering their old powers. The public thought of the war as having accomplished, if not the making of the world safe for democracy, at least the ending of all wars that might conceivably involve the United States.

Starvation of the navy started with the Arms Conference, which met through the winter of 1921 and 1922. This not only stopped new naval construction, save for small vessels, but scrapped several battleships nearing completion. It also drew up a number of treaties that seemed to promise peace and good will in the Far East. Japan not only gave Shantung back to China, but joined eight other powers in what Sir Auckland Geddes called a "nursing ring" around China, in the protection of which the Chinese people were expected to prosper.

To nearly everybody but Baruch, and the army and navy officers outraged by the armament limitation agreements, the prospect of another war and the necessity of being ready for it seemed a distorted dream—nothing like as important as whether Germany would be able to pay the reparations, and that seemed not as important as whether the Allies paid us the interest on the war debts promptly.

Even war debts were just a little on the academic side. Secretary of the Treasury Mellon was encouraging Congress to reduce taxes and was actually paying off our national debt at an increasing tempo. It seemed a golden age. The isolationists gave thanks that elimination of the armament race had made this possible. The prohibitionists were convinced that outlawing rum had done it. Peace and prosperity forever, in ever-increasing volume, was the prospect.

Coolidge, with his "They hired the money, didn't they?" became President. The country was delighted with him, liked the idea of Yankee thrift in Washington.

Baruch knew perfectly well that the Allies had "hired the money," but he knew two other things. One was that they probably *could not* pay, the world trade situation being what it was. He also knew that it would be very difficult for us to take the money.

It was the same problem that Baruch had discovered at Versailles with respect to reparations. It was new because it had been created, virtually, by the industrial system, with its attendant unemployment factor.

If John Smith owes you a hundred dollars, and pays, that is all right. But if one government owes another government a debt that involves paying a hundred million dollars a year, *that* payment must be made in goods. The nation taking the goods gets them without using work to produce them. That sounds as if the receiving nation was getting something for nothing, until unemployment raises its head. Political pressure at once develops for economic barriers to protect the receiving nation's employment. This produces interference with world trade and starving of the have-not nations and fertilizes the soil in which the seeds of war can and will sprout. This principle is generally recognized now, but it was brand-new at Versailles, and it had not percolated generally enough to be politically important when Coolidge succeeded Harding as President.

Actually it was politically important in reverse, as Baruch soon found out. He had talked to Harding about the economic effect on this country of taking vast amounts of goods as payments of war-debt principal and interest. Harding was grateful for Baruch's interest, expansively pleasant as he would naturally be to a man who was such a close friend of so many of Harding's old Senate friends. He said nothing that showed he really understood what it was all about, which is not surprising, for many men with far greater intelligence than Harding regarded the whole theory as a smart talking point by people who wanted to get out of paying their just debts.

Coolidge said very little, though he too expressed gratitude for Baruch's advice. The problem continued to worry the financier. He came to realize that no administration could afford, politically, to cancel the war debts, that it would seem to too many voters a wicked wasting of this country's hard-earned substance. He knew, from his talks with Coolidge, that the intention was to cut the debts down to somewhere as near as possible what was believed to be the capacity of the Allies to pay.

Thinking this over, as he sat on the wharf at Hobcaw, looking over Winyah Bay, a plan occurred to him that would not only sugar-coat the reduction in war-debt payments so far as the American public was concerned, but would tend to create a friendlier attitude toward the United States on the part of the peoples, if not the governments, of the Allied countries.

Proceeding on his normal get-all-the-facts routine, he made a quick survey of just how much was lent to each country, just when the loans were made, and whether any of the money went for anything but armaments and if so what.

Armed with these data he called on President Coolidge with the suggestion that, instead of the scaling down in proportion to ability to pay, a different formula should be applied. This was simply that *every dollar* lent *before* the Armistice should be forgiven, leaving only the sums advanced by the United States to the various Allied nations *after* the Armistice to be paid.

Baruch's argument favoring this was that the amount of scaling down that he expected would be done would amount to just about the same ratio of reduction, but that to accomplish this by forgiving loans made during the war, for the purpose of defeating the common foe, would deprive Europeans forever of the cry they were already making that their countries had lost lives, but we were getting our dollars back. He further pointed out that it would forestall the European reaction that America came into the war too late.

His advice was thankfully received and pigeonholed. On this

occasion, incidentally, he did not even get the publicity that such an argument before a congressional committee would have given him. The country as a whole never knew that the proposal had been made. He was still advising presidents, not Congress or the people, and talks with presidents, he considered, were confidential.

After the announcements of the debt settlements were made, Baruch had all the factors recalculated. He discovered that his suggested plan would have reached almost identically the same figures! But of course the settlements as made did not stop European critics from branding Uncle Sam as Shylock demanding his pound of flesh.

While Baruch was plotting constant preparedness for war and how to win good will through debt settlements, in the late fall of 1923, his former chief, in retirement at his house on S Street, was still hoping for American entry into the League of Nations. Thrilled over a "wonderful plan" they had conceived to help this cause, Belle Baruch, B.M.'s elder daughter, and Evangeline Johnson, her coworker, had dinner with the former President and Mrs. Wilson one October night, accompanying them later to Keith's vaudeville playhouse, Wilson's favorite theater.

Mr. Wilson promised the girls that he would do as they wished, make a radio address on the night of November 10 on "The Significance of Armistice Day." It was to be his first radio address. He had talked by radio to a plane in the air during the war but had never made a speech over the air.

The invalid grew more and more enthusiastic, especially when told that the girls were trying to arrange a debate over the radio and that, while lots of prominent figures were willing to argue *for* the League, they could get no one, not even Senator Lodge, to take the opposition side. He made that speech, with great physical difficulty, and was terribly discouraged when he had concluded, Mrs. Wilson tells us.

Wide World

"ALUMNI OF THE PEACE CONFERENCE"

With Mrs. Woodrow Wilson and Frank L. Polk, 1929.

The next day, though visibly tired, he was enormously pleased at the reception his speech had been given by the country. That night a huge delegation, headed by Senator Carter Glass, of Virginia, appeared on S Street in front of his house. The former President had insisted on dressing meticulously and appeared on the front steps of his house. After a speech by Senator Glass and a reply by Wilson, there was a band selection, following which Wilson insisted on speaking again.

"Just one word more," he said. "I cannot refrain from saying it. I am not one of those that have the least anxiety about the triumph of the principles I have stood for. I have seen fools resist Providence before, and I have seen their destruction, as will come upon these again, utter destruction and contempt. That we shall prevail is as sure as that God reigns."

It was Wilson's last public utterance. He died February 3, 1924.

Within hours of Wilson's funeral the former President's friends and lieutenants who had come to Washington to pay him a last tribute were jolted by a political explosion on Capitol Hill. The Teapot Dome committee, investigating the leases of naval reserve oil lands, had been smearing various Republican leaders for months. Few Republicans, much less Democrats, realized the hold that Coolidge had taken on the American people. Most Democrats, and many Republicans, thought 1924 was going to be a Democratic year.

Democratic sentiment had been swinging to McAdoo. As Wilson was lowered into his grave it seemed very likely that the former President's son-in-law would be elected President the following November. Three Republican Cabinet members had been smeared. Republican senators had been caught red-handed trying to hush up the whole thing.

Suddenly it developed that Edward L. Doheny, the oil magnate who had sent the little black satchel to Albert B. Fall, that satchel which contained $100,000 in currency, which the committee insisted was the payoff for Fall's putting through an oil lease to Doheny's company, was also paying a princely salary to William G. McAdoo.

It was not charged that McAdoo had anything to do with the oil leases. In fact, it was known that one reason why Franklin K. Lane had resigned as Secretary of the Interior was that Wilson had refused to approve oil leases. McAdoo's service to Doheny had been a trip to Mexico in an effort to induce the Mexican government to grant Doheny some concessions.

The reaction to this disclosure next day was terrific. The country seemed to think anything about Mexico and oil was bad, per se. Also McAdoo had undertaken this mission while his father-in-law was still in the White House. The President's good will was very valuable to the Mexican government. Wilson had landed marines at Vera Cruz and had sent Pershing into that country on a punitive mission after Villa.

There was a gathering of the McAdoo leaders at the old Shoreham Hotel, in Washington, to discuss what should be done. Baruch was there. So was Daniel C. Roper, who had been Collector of Internal Revenue under Wilson, Thomas B. Love, of Texas, and many others.

It was one of the unhappiest nights of Baruch's life. He loved McAdoo. It was McAdoo who had really brought him close inside the Wilson picture back in 1913. They had been intimate ever since, talking over problems as they arose during the 8 years Wilson was President, shooting together and talking in front of the fire nights down at Hobcaw. He was fond of McAdoo's wife, his idol's daughter. He had hoped to see McAdoo President. Perhaps he had envisaged 8 more years of usefulness to his country at the right hand of the President.

Yet here were men in whose political judgment he had confidence, one after another saying that McAdoo was ruined, politically, regardless of how innocent he might be personally. They believed that it would be folly to try to nominate him at the Democratic convention scheduled for New York in June. One man there insisted it did not make any difference, he was sure that McAdoo could be nominated and elected. This was David Ladd Rockwell, of Ohio. Baruch's friends did not seem to have much confidence in his judgment.

Facts are elusive things, in politics, where it is not what is true that is important, but what people *believe* to be true; and even this is often not so important as what politicians calculate the people will believe on the following election day. Baruch could not gather facts for the sort of study he wanted to make. He had to take people's opinions—the opinions of people in whose political judgment he had confidence.

Working out this unsatisfactory sort of jigsaw puzzle, Baruch finally made up his mind. He advised McAdoo to declare that he was not a candidate but to defend his actions vigorously. Baruch believed that this would result, in plenty of time before the convention, in a revulsion of sentiment against McAdoo's critics and a swing to McAdoo that would make his nomination inevitable.

Rockwell's view prevailed. McAdoo did not withdraw, and Rockwell became his campaign manager. It did not turn out very well. Rockwell had been a delegate to the previous Democratic convention but was not elected to the one at Madison Square Garden. Furthermore, he was not able, in that long-drawn-out battle between Alfred E. Smith and McAdoo, in which more than one hundred ballots were taken, to obtain a single vote for McAdoo on any one of them from the delegation of his own state of Ohio, although the forty-eight delegates were not bound by any unit rule and split all over the field at various times.

When that convention, which split the Democratic Party so badly that the election of Coolidge was assured, ended, Baruch made himself a solemn promise. Never again would he help *any* presidential candidate in advance of the convention. No more preconvention contributions!

CHAPTER . . . TWENTY-TWO

BARUCH found little silver lining in the black cloud that hung over Madison Square Garden in those hot days when the Democrats fought each other with all the bitterness of a civil war, with brother against brother, fellow teammates clouting each other, altogether making a spectacle so menacing with its threat of religious and racial intolerance that even the Republicans deplored it.

He heard orator after orator attack his candidate, McAdoo, as the beneficiary of this intolerance.

Not anticipating the bitterness, Baruch with other McAdoo leaders had become rather hopeful for McAdoo's nomination, and even his election, just prior to the convention. Word had come from Senator La Follette (the Elder) that the Progressives, scheduled to meet in Cleveland right after the Democratic convention, would endorse McAdoo if he were nominated. The South was almost a unit for McAdoo. California, his adopted state, was rampant for him. This optimism may seem to have had little foundation, viewed in retrospect, but Ed Moore, of Ohio, leader of the anti-McAdoo forces and one of the smartest and most practical politicians of his time (he had led the fight to nominate James M. Cox at San Francisco 4 years before), told a group of newspapermen he was afraid McAdoo would win.

This was not all that discouraged Baruch. In the fight over the platform Newton D. Baker, Wilson's Secretary of War, poured out a passionate, idealistic appeal for the convention to endorse United States entry into the League of Nations. Unused to microphones (broadcasting of convention proceedings was new that year), Baker hoisted himself on his elbows, which rested on the speaker's reading desk, so that his feet were inches off the floor, in an effort to talk over the unfamiliar obstructing instruments and reach the hearts of the delegates.

Baruch heard another good friend, Senator Key Pittman, of Nevada, scorn this "hysterical" plea for a plank that Pittman said would certainly defeat the party's candidate if adopted. The delegates booed Pittman's slur at Baker, but they voted, in a close roll call, as Pittman wanted. In short, the convention refused to endorse the League and thus repudiated Baruch's idol, Woodrow Wilson.

Baruch and his friends did not believe the country was so violently against the Woodrow Wilson plan for the maintenance of world peace as the 1924 election figures seemed to indicate. There is no way to prove that they were wrong, despite the accepted conviction that Coolidge was amazingly popular. The election returns, though overwhelming, are subject to various discounts.

For instance there was the "Coolidge or chaos" issue. Many in the East never appreciated the power of this slogan. What happened was that certain Democratic leaders sent word to the Democratic organizations in western states, where Robert M. La Follette was reported to be very strong, to throw their states to La Follette if possible. This meant taking votes away from John W. Davis and having them cast for La Follette.

The hope was to give La Follette enough electoral votes to prevent any candidate having a majority and thus throw the election into the House of Representatives, where there would have been a tie. Hence the Senate, proceeding under the constitution to elect a Vice President, would have elected Charles

Bryan, brother of the Great Commoner, and he would have become President!

Democrat after Democrat in Washington, Oregon, and other Western states told me about that plan, when I visited the West in early October. Most of them said it scared them to death and that, while I could not mention their names, they proposed to vote for Coolidge!

In San Francisco, William H. Crocker, old friend and occasional business associate of Baruch, said to me earnestly:

"I don't have to tell you what I think about La Follette, but I would rather have La Follette elected in November than have this election thrown in the House of Representatives. I shudder to think of what would happen. There would be terrific temptations to individual members of the House. If any Representative yielded, many people would suspect bribery. Our very form of government might fall into disrepute. There might be chaos. I remember the 1876 Hayes and Tilden situation, and I would rather have La Follette as President than see this country go through anything like that again."

Of course Mr. Crocker was merely illustrating the strength of his feelings when he said he would rather have La Follette. A vote for La Follette, everyone knew, was the very thing that might bring about throwing the election into the House.

Some may have forgotten the full import of what Mr. Crocker meant by speaking of a member of the House switching his vote. Under the Constitution the House votes for President—in the event no candidate has a clear majority in the Electoral College—not by individual roll call, as it votes on a bill or resolution, but by state delegations. Each state has one vote. Delaware counts as much as New York. As a number of states had House delegations evenly divided between the Democrats and Republicans, there were many opportunities for such switches.

At the Gridiron Dinner following this election two singers,

representing the Bryan Brothers, William Jennings and Charles, sang a parody on "It Ain't Gonna Rain No More." It started off:

> We are the Bryan Brothers,
> We've been in every race.
> We ran three times for President,
> And once for second place.
> But we ain't gonna run no more, no more,
> We ain't gonna run no more.
> There's no use trying to elect a Bryan,
> So we ain't gonna run no more.

But there were a couple of lines in one of the verses that were extremely accurate. They went, with Brother William singing:

> So I lost all the eastern states,
> And Charley lost the West.

Calvin Coolidge, sitting across the well from the singers, did not smile so broadly as some of the guests. He knew too well how much truth there was in the humor and that the 1924 election had not been half so much a Coolidge landslide as a Democratic debacle.

Coolidge's election did not hamper Baruch's progress toward industrial mobilization planning. He had obtained a public endorsement of this proposal from President Harding, and, in October, 1925, President Coolidge urged it in his speech before the American Legion Convention at Omaha.

Baruch was now well fitted into the extraordinary role he played for 12 years, under three Republican presidents. He was constantly doing his utmost to make the administration of each Republican president better. His advice on knotty problems was to be had for the asking and sometimes without its being asked. But he was constantly aiding his own party and hoping that his party would be strong enough at the next election to throw the President he had been advising out of office.

There have been court favorites and counselors all through history who hoped to oust their kings. What was unique about this Baruch performance was that each of the three Republican presidents he advised and helped knew all the time that Baruch was hoping for a Democratic victory at the next election, that he would give his money and his ideas freely to movements that if successful would hurl them back into private life.

Perhaps all three felt so strong that they could smile indulgently at any effort to help the opposition. As a Republican senator of the period put it: "We need a strong Democratic Party, but not *too* strong!"

Whatever their mental processes, they all used Baruch's advice. Not only did it seem sound to them, but it came with all the prestige of success and achievement that *was* Baruch. They had seen their own party, coming into power immediately after the conclusion of Baruch's handling of billions, go through his record with a fine-tooth comb and fail to find anything the criticizing of which would provide political nutriment. They knew what the leading figures abroad, who had good reason to be familiar with what Baruch had done, thought about that record.

Hindenburg wrote in his Memoirs, speaking of the United States:

"Her brilliant, if pitiless, war industry had entered the service of patriotism and had not failed it. Under the compulsion of military necessity a ruthless autocracy was at work and rightly, even in this land at the portals of which the Statue of Liberty flashes its blinding light across the seas. They understood war."

Clemenceau, the Tiger, said in 1922:

"The United States declared war in April, 1917. It was only in March, 1918 [the month Baruch was put at the head of the War Industries Board], that their industrial mobilization found its final form. Even in the land of quick decisions, the routine of peace days struggled hard to live. But the High Command of Industry was created. It was a splendid company of men who at the call of their country had come from all parts of the United States. It had no congressional birth certificate; a mere decision of the President, and in a few weeks resources were perfectly adapted to needs, the whole coordinated by the War Industries Board, which was supreme in all matters of production, priority and distribution."

Further on in the same statement he added:

"The steel they sent us represented the raw material for a hundred and sixty million '75' shells. The foodstuffs they sent us fed twelve million Frenchmen for a year and a half. If this help had not been forthcoming, our army could not have held, the army of the United States could not have fought."

To Harding and Hoover, who had both started from nothing and made fortunes, the fact that Baruch had done so more spectacularly carried great weight. To Coolidge's Yankee thrift the fact that Baruch, unlike so many who had made money in Wall Street, still had plenty of money despite his lavish expenditures, made a peculiar appeal.

In the writing of his Omaha speech President Coolidge had been greatly impressed not only by Baruch's personal arguments to him, but by an exchange of letters between Baruch and Owen D. Young. Young was interested in the Walter Hines Page School of International Relations at Johns Hopkins University, and after this exchange of letters Baruch financed a course of lectures before this school on industrial mobilization, taking the profit out of war, and the necessity of planning for war in time of peace.

One of the earliest of Baruch's magazine articles seeking to arouse public interest in the necessity for this advance planning was published in the *Atlantic Monthly* shortly after President Coolidge's Omaha speech. He never gave up fighting for the idea, both in this country and on his trips to Europe, where he conferred frequently with world leaders. He believed that there might be much less danger of war if adequate precautions were taken in advance, and were well advertised, to prevent any individual making any money out of it and any nation gaining anything by it.

But there were plenty of domestic problems in this period. Since he had been a small boy in South Carolina, Baruch had been deeply sympathetic with the farmers in their constant battle against not only natural hazards but artificial trade practices. He had heard his mother complain that it took too much of Dr. Baruch's professional fees to keep his farm in operation. He learned what happened when the neighboring farmers sold their crop, mostly cotton in that section. Having worked all year to "make" the crop, the farmer at harvest time would be deeply in debt to the storekeeper and pretty nearly everybody else.

These creditors would press him to sell at once, so that they could be paid. They might know that the price was too low and that by waiting the farmer would get enough more to make the difference between profit and loss on his year's work. But the storekeepers and other creditors would be in debt themselves, to the wholesalers and who not, and they could not wait.

That was only part of the trouble, young Baruch had observed. The cotton—and, he learned later, other crops—might not grade so high as it should. The men who did the grading could not lose if they fixed a grade poorer than the cotton really merited. They would be in trouble later if they happened to grade it too high. So they seldom gave the farmer the benefit of any doubt. In his Wall Street career he ran into the same problem.

During the period when Baruch was unofficial adviser to Republican presidents there arose what amounted to a real farm revolt. There had been a simply appalling situation in the

Middle West as a result of the inflation of farm-land prices following high grain prices during the First World War. Tens of thousands of farmers, from the Dakotas down to Kansas, sold their farms at these high prices to land-hungry neighbors and retired to the pleasanter clime of Southern California.

Tens of thousands of others mortgaged their farms in order to buy worthless oil stocks. The fake-stock salesmen cleaned up.

"One group alone," said an investigator in 1922, "took in $100,000,000 in the one state of Nebraska, and they took Iowa like Grant took Richmond."

With the deflated prices following the war, the farmers could not possibly pay the interest on the money they had borrowed from the insurance companies and from their local bankers.

In Iowa the local bankers were called "bird-dog bankers" because they "pointed" farmers who had good credit for the fake-stock salesmen. There was no allegation of fraud on the part of the bankers. Gardner Cowles, who published the *Des Moines Register* at the time, commented that most of the bankers were just as much suckers as the farmers, that the bankers took their commissions for "pointing" in the same fake stocks the farmers were buying.

This extraordinary situation came on top of the natural and always-with-us problem of the farmer. This time it was so widespread, and hence of such political significance, that it stirred up things on Capitol Hill. Congress wanted to do something about it. It was as popular with the legislators, this desire to remedy the farm situation by some sort of law, as was the desire to curry favor with the four million veterans by voting them a bonus.

This sentiment in Congress gradually crystallized in what was called the McNary-Haugen bill, named after Senator Charles L. McNary, of Oregon, and Representative Gilbert N. Haugen, of Iowa. The chief feature of this bill was the so-called "equalization fee." It was to work like this: The government would buy all wheat offered for sale at what the government considered a fair price. Then the government would sell all domestic users of the wheat at the same price. Whatever surplus should be left over would be sold abroad at a loss. This loss would then be prorated among all the farmers who had sold their wheat to the government in the first place. Thus the farmers would receive the benefit of a high price for wheat consumed inside the country and would have to take a lower price only on that percentage of their crop which was exported. It was contended that the desire to hold down this percentage on which a loss must be taken would restrain farmers from overplanting.

In a way it was the same idea as applying tariff protection to industrial products. Actually many big corporations, including the steel industry, had been taking advantage of the same idea, selling their products domestically at a price held up by the tariff wall, while selling more cheaply abroad.

Nearly every conservative in the land, including Presidents Coolidge and Hoover, fought this proposal during the long battle that ensued. Baruch flabbergasted the Republican presidents, his old friends in Wall Street, bankers, advocates of sound economics generally by endorsing the McNary-Haugen bill.

He not only endorsed it. He worked for it, telling the large group of senators who had come to be his close friends that it was absolutely sound and workable. It was particularly annoying to the safe-and-sane economists who were advising first Coolidge and then Hoover and screaming in the newspapers against this proposed subsidy, to encounter Congressmen influenced by Baruch every time they visited the Capitol. They found senator after senator and representative after representative merely amused when it was insisted that this bill was economically unsound.

"Bernie Baruch is for it," the legislators said. "I guess he knows something about business and finance, doesn't he?"

It was pretty hard to answer that.

Twice both houses of Congress approved the McNary-Haugen bill, and sent it to the White House. Vetoes by Coolidge and Hoover killed it, but the farm problem marched on.

Hoover wanted to solve the problem another way. He set up the Farm Board and appointed Alexander C. Legge, of the International Harvester, who had been Baruch's right arm on the War Industries Board, as chairman.

"Do you think," a friend asked Baruch, "that the new Farm Board can help the farm situation without something like the McNary-Haugen bill's equalization fee feature?"

"I don't know," said Baruch slowly. The shade of a big live oak had reached his chair on a path back of the Hobcaw mansion. He moved his chair back into the sun. His face brightened up as though with a pleasant memory. "But if *anybody* in the world can do it, Alec Legge can," he said. "Hoover could not have picked a better man."

Much later, when the Hoover administration was frantically trying to hold up the sagging price of wheat, Secretary of Agriculture Arthur M. Hyde charged in a speech that the Soviet government was selling wheat short and that this was wrecking the government's efforts to keep the price up. There was considerable excitement about the charge. Some believed that Russia was deliberately trying to force revolution in this country.

Baruch was puzzled. He had not been consulted, or the speech would not have been made. He knew that *if* anybody were selling wheat short, that somebody would have to buy it back, sooner or later, so *if* the Russians *had* sold wheat short, there should now be a bullish factor in the picture.

Pretty soon he had the answer. Admiral Frederic R. Harris,

who had just been superintending some navy-yard and dock construction for the Soviet government, sent him word that these Russian sales had been *advance* sales, not *short* sales. The Russians had unloaded a huge wheat crop while Uncle Sam unwittingly held the price up for them!

CHAPTER . . . TWENTY-THREE

As THE battle for the Democratic presidential nomination in 1928 developed, Baruch kept the promise he had made himself in 1924, that he would never again help any candidate *before* the convention. But had events shaped just a little differently he might have been forced to break it. This was because one of the candidates was Senator James A. Reed, of Missouri. Reed had been one of the bitterest critics in the entire country of President Wilson, and Baruch felt very strongly against him. Curiously enough one of Baruch's warm friends, Sam W. Fordyce, of St. Louis, then a law partner of Bennett Champ Clark, was Reed's manager.

The fight was really settled in the California primary, in which all three leading candidates, Alfred E. Smith, Senator Thomas J. Walsh, of Montana, and Reed were entered. Smith won so handsomely, despite heavy newspaper support for Reed by the strong anti-League of Nations newspapers, that the other two did not figure seriously after that.

William G. McAdoo took little part in the campaign that followed Smith's nomination, though he did yield sufficiently to Baruch's advice to make a sizable contribution to the Smith campaign fund. Most of Baruch's old friends in the Democratic Party stuck by Smith. He had never been close to Senator Furnifold M. Simmons, of North Carolina, or Senator Tom Heflin, of Alabama, who bolted. (Both were beaten in their primaries the

Press Association, Inc.

SENATE HEARING, 1935

With Senators Nye (l.) and Barbour (c.).

next time their voters got a chance at them.) He helped hold his own state of South Carolina in line for the New York governor and did what he could elsewhere. He knew the fight was hopeless but was inexpressibly shocked, as were many of his friends, at the vote against Smith in New York, where as a candidate for governor Smith had made such magnificent runs.

Early in the Hoover administration, Baruch toyed, for at least the second time, with the idea of becoming a newspaper publisher. He had often thought of what he might be able to do, in advocacy of the plans he thought so vital to the nation's interest, if he owned a New York morning paper, which would be read by the political figures in Washington and perhaps quoted throughout the country.

His first move in this direction was in 1920. The old *New York Herald* was for sale by the executors of the Bennett estate. Baruch was wondering what to do with himself now that Wilson was about to leave the White House. He placed a bid with the Guaranty Trust Co., which was handling the estate.

It soon developed that he was up against pretty keen competition. Among those who seemed interested were William Randolph Hearst, Governor James M. Cox of Ohio, General Cornelius Vanderbilt, Herbert Hoover, and Clarence H. Mackay.

The Guaranty officials had figured the property worth $2,250,000. Frank A. Munsey, who had already combined the *New York Press* with *The Sun,* calmly offered $4,000,000 for the property as it stood, without current assets. It would have gone against Baruch's instinct as a trader to have bid higher. His own investigation had shown the property to be worth much less than Munsey's offer.

Nine years later *The World* was sold, and this time there was even more wonder why Baruch did not figure, especially as it was the general opinion that the paper could have been bought at a very low price considering its standing. Besides, Baruch had been rather close to *The World*. His good friend Herbert Bayard Swope was executive editor. Baruch and Frank Cobb, who had been the chief editorial writer during the Wilson regime, had seen eye to eye on all the Wilson issues.

"I realized," Baruch said afterward, "that if I had bought *The World* I would have been so interested in its problems, editorial and otherwise, that it would have taken all my time. I would not have been able to devote sufficient attention to other problems which I considered it my duty to study. So, much as I would have liked to own *The World*, I did not buy it."

In the months following the election of Hoover, in 1928, there was a wild stock-market boom. Most speculators, most businessmen, most people thought the country was moving on to a new high plateau of prosperity. Hoover was the miracle man. He *knew* about business and would help it prosper. Stocks were already high the day Hoover was elected; for example, American Telephone, which had sold around 150 in the spring of 1927 and was around 200 on election day, 1928, soared to a high above 310.

Baruch saw the storm coming. His sulfur interests in Texas had proved very profitable in the years following the war, and he was still hopeful about Alaska Juneau, which had not begun paying dividends. As always, he had a lot of cash—just in case. Except for Alaska Juneau he began withdrawing from everything speculative, putting his money into tax-exempt state and local bonds.

As a matter of fact, some of the most profitable investments he made at that time were, in a way, wished on him. The town of Georgetown, for instance, needed very badly to raise some cash and offered bonds to Baruch at a sharp discount. Senator Robinson persuaded him to help out the state of Arkansas by buying a big block of her bonds. They were selling at a fraction of their real value, but nobody wanted to buy bonds in that get-rich-quick era. People with some money to invest wanted to buy something that would double or triple in price in a few weeks.

Lots of people made fortunes, on paper, after Baruch started turning his fortune into bonds and cash. Baruch, with one eye cocked on the income tax and the other at the cloud he so clearly saw rising over the stock market, passed up these "opportunities." As a result, he was able to save a lot of his friends in the period beginning in October, 1929, and dragging on until the early thirties. He saved them with his strongbox cash, never selling any of his tax-exempts. Actually he kept on accumulating sound state and municipal bonds all through the early years of the depression.

It has been estimated that he at least doubled the money he so invested, in addition to receiving the tax-free interest and to avoiding stock-market pitfalls during those terrible years.

Two questions present themselves here. (1) How was Baruch able to foresee the crash? (2) Why did he not sound a note of warning to the country?

The answer to the second is the simpler. The great figures of politics and finance, economics and business were joining in a chorus of optimism. To listen to them, the country had crossed a new frontier into a new era of prosperity. It was not just a few stock-market operators and promotors who talked in dreamy-eyed fashion. Professor Irving J. Fisher was *proving* it with careful statistics.

Besides, most of the optimistic talk was just conversation anyhow. Each individual buying stocks, in 999 cases out of 1,000, was not thinking about general conditions. He read Fisher's statements, if he read them at all, merely with a nod of general approval. He glanced through interviews with big bankers and businessmen with the mental comment "of course." What he really was doing, each time he bought, was figuring that the particular stock he was acquiring was bound to go up and that he would make a profit on *that* individual transaction. Having sold it, at a profit, he bought some other, that had already had a rise, because he had a tip or a hunch that this one was going up enough to give him a good profit.

Baruch did do a little private warning. So did Ogden L. Mills, who said rather ruefully afterward that he had certainly made a lot of enemies by talking people out of purchases that would have made them good profits and destroyed his reputation for economic intelligence with a great many more who had ignored his advice.

In short, the country was in no mood to pay any attention to sober advice. The few who tried to give it were regarded as reactionary stick-in-the-muds.

But what made Baruch sell stocks and buy tax-exempts at such a favorable time?

Baruch was not sure *when* the market was going to break. Just when the high or the low of any given moment of a stock would occur was something he never had tried to figure except as a mental exercise. He never attempted to buy at the bottom and sell at the top—the amateur speculator's dream. He knew that it simply was not done save by miracle, and even that could not be achieved if one were dealing in large blocks. To sell a large amount of stock one requires considerable buying demand, and that has disappeared when the peak is reached.

Always studying the *value* of securities he held, or thought of buying, Baruch reached the conclusion long before the crazy peaks of 1929 were attained that most stocks were selling for more than they were worth. He *knew* he was not getting what was going to be the top price, but, according to the theory on which he had operated so successfully for so many years, it is always a good idea to let the other fellow make a little.

Besides, another of his maxims was always, in case of doubt, to sell. "Sell to the sleeping point," he said once, meaning until one would not be kept awake at night worrying. And he has said hundreds of times that one should never be regretful because someone else tells of how much better he has done. "That fellow," said Baruch positively, "always goes broke."

On top of the fact that Baruch, months before the crash, believed the individual stocks in which he was interested at the time were selling at higher prices than their real values justified, the whole market, he thought, was bucking the law of supply and demand. The law of supply and demand is fundamental with Baruch. He says it is suspended in time of war by government intervention, but otherwise it is like the laws of the Medes and Persians, which change not.

It so happens that Baruch is the only person I have ever heard mention the law of supply and demand in connection with the amount of securities available for purchase at any given time. Occasionally, Baruch points out, such vast quantities of new securities are floated, or come upon the market, that there are actually more securities than there is investment money to buy them. Whereupon the situation is precisely like an overproduction of anything else, be it wheat, or little pigs, or cotton. The law of supply and demand will start to operate on this the moment artificial restrictions are removed. Its operation may be postponed; it cannot be prevented.

When there is overproduction of wheat, the law of supply and demand forces down the price. At some stage people who want more wheat are able to buy it, and the surplus gradually disappears. But when the same conditions operate to drive stock prices down, the very elements that had been pushing the prices up too high disappear. There is no longer what looks like a certain profit if one buys stocks.

Baruch saw the vast quantities of new security issues being

brought out, and knew that not only were individual stock prices too high, but that Old Man Supply and Demand was waiting with a club for that market.

"Last-chance betting," he has often said, "leads over the hill to the Poor House." Lots of people made fat profits in the market in the first three quarters of 1929, but Baruch regarded it as last-chance betting.

Incidentally, he was just a little skeptical about all the "new-era" interviews with leading bankers and corporation officers and directors. He thought that the market was long overdue for a jolt, but, as he has often pointed out, no one can tell either when the jolt will come or what sort of fuse will touch off the explosion.

As spring turned into summer in 1929, production began to slacken in some quarters. Automobile companies were curtailing orders to makers of parts. The automobile men knew that the farmers would not be able to buy so many cars. Buying power was shriveling. Few people noticed that Birmingham had some 18,000 less workers in its steel plants than 1 year earlier, because Birmingham, owing to improved machinery, was making just as much steel. The same thing was happening in other steel centers and in other industries.

Baruch had helped prevent legislation, back in the Wilson days, that he feared would include a prohibition of short selling. He always thought short selling was a useful function and that bears were often public benefactors. In fact he has said that a market without speculators and without bears is comparable to a country without a free press—there is no one whose function it is to criticize absurdities.

This country, being optimistic, he pointed out, dislikes bears. The bear, therefore, performs a very unpopular service, but one which is vitally necessary if crazy booms are to be kept in some limits. When the GOP leaders, after the crash, tried to make the few bears on Wall Street the goats—to make them responsible for the crash in the eyes of the public—Baruch pulled a few of his wires leading to the Capitol and managed to quiet the hysteria a little.

The most notorious bear of that particular period was Ben Smith, of whom Baruch was very fond and of whose intelligence he thought highly. Smith finally was brought before a congressional committee, but not until some of the heat had cooled. Baruch thought Smith had done the nation a better service than had certain corporation officers and directors who, in the months preceding the crash, had issued statements inducing more "suckers" to put their money in overpriced stocks.

Long before there was any public agitation on the subject Baruch, during his stock-market days, had developed a pronounced feeling against directors and officers of corporations speculating in the securities of those companies or of companies with which their corporations did business. He not only objected to the evil itself—of an insider taking advantage of information withheld from other traders—but to the appearance of evil.

Some of his friends have always thought that it was the appearance of evil more than the evil that caused Baruch to have such strong views, for it was obvious from his occasional comments that he utterly distrusted inside information.

There is a story he was fond of telling about an operation in Soo Line stock. A friend told Baruch the line proposed to build an extension that would result in its getting a lot of business. He looked into the stock, which was paying $4 and selling at from 60 to 65. Friends in the company admitted that they proposed to build the line, but added that this would not be done for some time, so that it was too early to start buying the stock. Baruch bought.

Continuing his investigation he discovered that, although a bumper wheat crop was boosting the earnings, it was certain that later on most of the crops of the new region being opened up would move to the head of the Lakes and then east by water. He therefore began selling, getting as much as 135.

The point of the story is that he bought largely from insiders in the first place and sold to insiders in the second.

Baruch not only disapproved of directors speculating in their own or allied corporation stocks, but was also unfavorably impressed by the motives that influenced some of the big figures in selecting men for their boards and even more by the motives that induced men to accept such appointments. He objected to flattering the vanity of men appointed in order to gain some ulterior objective and to putting men on a board in order to dazzle, and thus frequently mislead, the public. He commented that this practice was an abuse even for charity bazaars but certainly should not be followed by business corporations.

As a result of this conviction he declined many directorships. Anthony N. Brady, one of the giants of finance of his day, wanted him on the executive committee of the Central Trust Co. He was also offered a directorship of the Phoenix Life Insurance Co. He declined, gratefully but firmly.

Some time after his return from Paris, however, regarding himself as having concluded his career as an active speculator, he yielded to two old friends and broke the practice of a lifetime. At the urging of Daniel Willard, president of the Baltimore & Ohio, of whom he had grown very fond in their War Industries Board relationship, he became a director of that railroad, and, at the request of Simon Guggenheim, his friend for many years, he became a director of the American Smelting & Refining Company.

As he came to be more and more consulted in Washington, however, and particularly as he had agreed to a request of insurance and savings-bank officials to serve on a committee looking into the railroad situation, he concluded that his old rule about directorships was best. He desired to continue as the unofficial adviser to presidents and wanted to keep himself free from any entangling relationships that, even if he were able to render cold and unselfish judgment, might seem to critics not to be disinterested. Eventually, therefore, he resigned these two directorships.

CHAPTER...TWENTY-FOUR

IN THE second week of February, 1930, occurred perhaps the most striking episode of the 12 years in which Baruch served Republican presidents. On this occasion he saved from an extreme humiliation two men, whose election as President he had fought with all his power. Incidentally he saved his own Democratic friends from an egregious blunder.

On February 3 President Hoover nominated Charles Evans Hughes to be Chief Justice of the Supreme Court of the United States, to succeed William Howard Taft, who had resigned because of ill health. At once a storm rose both among the Democratic senators and the progressive Republicans, who between them had enough votes to defeat Hughes for confirmation.

Baruch heard that his beloved friend, Joe Robinson, Democratic leader of the Senate, intended to vote against Hughes. He hurried to Washington, anxious to prevent Robinson from doing a thing he was sure Robinson would regret bitterly later on. By the time he reached Washington the lines in the Senate had been drawn. Newspapermen covering the upper house were confident Hughes would be beaten when the roll call should be reached.

Actually, as the situation stood when Baruch walked into Robinson's office, a poll had shown a majority against Hughes without counting a single doubtful vote, so that it was just a question of how much the doubtful senators would increase the unfavorable ballot.

Baruch was one of the very few men in the country to whom Robinson would listen. He not only loved the financier but had long since learned that Baruch had no selfish motives, that his only thought when he gave advice was for the good of the country, first, and the Democratic Party, second.

Baruch now stressed the party angle. He pointed to Hughes's fine record as governor of New York, as a justice of the Supreme Court up to his nomination for President by the Republicans in 1916, as Secretary of State, as an advocate of world peace.

Baruch said he feared independents all over the country would feel that the Democratic senators had played cheap, partisan politics if they rejected a man of such outstanding ability. He said that they would not even have the defense that the Democrats were entitled to this vacancy on the Supreme Court, because Hughes was appointed to succeed a Republican.

Robinson saw the force of the arguments. He finally agreed that it might hurt the Democratic Party to take the responsibility for Hughes's defeat. When Baruch walked out of the Democratic leader's office he had Robinson's promise to vote for the confirmation of Hughes. Baruch did not stop there. He went on to visit other friends among the Democratic senators. He turned more than enough votes in the next few days to change the result. Hughes was confirmed by the Senate on February 14. Had Baruch remained at Hobcaw, Hughes would have been defeated.

There was an interesting aftermath to this. Hughes had been opposed by some of the Western Republican senators because they regarded him as a reactionary. In the few years following his appointment the liberality of his opinions from the high bench so impressed them, as well as some of the Democrats Baruch had induced to change their votes, that several of them admitted that he had been right about Hughes and they had been wrong —which in politics is just a little bit unusual.

A few months later (September 16, 1930) came the Eugene Meyer, Jr., appointment as governor of the Federal Reserve Board. Baruch had long admired Meyer's intellect. Also, he said, Meyer had character. To illustrate this he told of Meyer's firm policy of refusing to enter any arrangement for the sale of securities unless he was convinced that the proposition was so sound that the purchasers would have nothing to regret.

When Baruch urged President Hoover to appoint Meyer to the Reserve Board, it developed that the board was already top-heavy in two respects—with Republicans and with New Yorkers. Meyer was both. Baruch looked the situation over. In a few days a Republican member of the board, Edmund Platt, a former New York Congressman, received such an attractive offer in private business that he resigned, and the way was cleared for Meyer's appointment not only to the board, but as governor. Baruch just grinned when asked if he had done it, but his trail was rather obvious.

Meyer himself, in the hearings on his confirmation, disarmed his former chief critic, Senator Smith W. Brookhart, of Iowa, but Baruch did not spare the horses in rounding up a good majority for him.

In the preceding June (1930) Baruch had been delighted by the passage by Congress of the act setting up the War Policies Commission. He had been working for the objective at which this Commission was aimed since his report to President Wilson on the War Industries Board. Patrick J. Hurley had become Secretary of War in December, 1929. As Assistant Secretary he had come to favor Baruch's ideas about constant industrial preparedness, and he favored strongly the War Policies Commission Act.

Hearings by the new Commission, with Hurley as chairman,

opened on March 5, 1931. Other members were Secretary of the Navy Charles Francis Adams, Secretary of Agriculture Arthur M. Hyde, Secretary of Commerce Robert P. Lamont, Secretary of Labor William N. Doak, Attorney General William D. Mitchell, Senators David A. Reed, of Pennsylvania, Arthur H. Vandenberg, of Michigan, Robinson, of Arkansas, and Claude A. Swanson, of Virginia, Representatives Lindley H. Hadley, of Washington, William P. Holaday, of Illinois, Ross A. Collins, of Mississippi, and John J. McSwain, of South Carolina.

In his statement before this commission, on March 6, 1931, Baruch urged the adoption of practically the same permanent setup as he had recommended to President Wilson in his report on the War Industries Board. He laid great stress, in an exhaustive discussion that contained all the pros and cons of every debatable point, on the necessity of fixing ceilings for *all* prices at figures which prevailed on some date to be selected by the President, prior to the beginning of the war, preferably some date on which supply and demand fixing of prices was as nearly normal as possible. With these ceilings fixed, governmental authorities could determine whether any injustices had been done, whether ceilings of particular articles should be raised or lowered.

Again and again Baruch insisted that this was not freezing prices, that it was merely fixing *ceilings,* which could be changed on proper study.

His chief trouble, before this Commission, came from persons who extravagantly admired the work he had done in the War Industries Board. Wilson's Secretary of War, Newton D. Baker, Commander John M. Hancock, who had represented the Navy on the War Industries Board, General Douglas MacArthur (Chief of Staff at the time of the hearing), and Leonard P. Ayres, the Cleveland economist.

All of them approved the Baruch ideas in general and price

fixing in particular, but they wanted it done the way Baruch had done it during the First World War! In short, they wanted fixing of particular prices, instead of fixing *all* prices at the figures prevailing on a day selected by the President before the war emergency had thrown economic relationships askew.

Mr. Baker had been counsel, in the summer of 1930, for the Bethlehem Steel Corporation in the famous litigation at Youngstown that arose out of its attempt to absorb The Youngstown Sheet & Tube Co., and dwelt at some length on the amiability with which the steel industry had complied with government requirements in 1918. It was as a result of this testimony by Baker that Baruch revealed for the first time that he had threatened to take over various steel plants if the industry did not fall in line with the government's price ideas.

Baruch explained patiently, in his rebuttal, that the War Industries Board was not brought into the situation in the First World War until prices had already soared enormously and irregularly. The best thing to do then was to lop off the peaks. This had been extraordinarily difficult because no price stands alone but is the component of scores or hundreds of other prices, including the cost of living, which affects wages. He pointed out that despite the best efforts of the War Industries Board it had *not* been able to prevent a considerable degree of inflation.

"If what you have naturally at the beginning is the very thing you are striving to recreate artificially at the end," he told the Commission, "why not preserve the initial relationship? This thing you are trying to recapture, in an irregularly rising market, by arbitrary piecemeal stabilization—no matter how comprehensively—is, by its very terms, arithmetically impossible. . . .

"It is like a dog trying to catch himself by running rapidly around a tree. Or (because the free components of the fixed price continue to increase) it is like a command to a moving regiment—'Regiment, halt!' But all the soldiers shall keep on marching!

"When we reflect that the price of anything is simply the resultant of the price of everything, it must be clear that, in war, we cannot justly or practically halt the rise in the price of anything unless we halt the rise in the price of everything, and this is true—in different degree—whether we start with a balanced schedule or a distorted schedule.

"For this reason even in a repetition of 1917, I can see no logical argument against general stabilization first to stop the rising trend everywhere—followed by an immediate attack on each exaggerated price. . . .

"One method *stops a runaway* and keeps the whole team in line. The other submits to a runaway and then tries to keep some of the horses from running faster than the rest."

In the same hearing Baruch set forth his often-expressed view that labor must not be drafted to work for the private profit of employers. He advocated high taxes and excess-profits taxes but insisted that these without price-ceiling fixing would not prevent inflation. On the contrary, they would be a temptation to increase prices so that the net profits resulting would not be cut.

"I am confidently of the belief," Baruch said in concluding his prepared statement to the Commission, "that, on the policies here briefly outlined, this country would achieve the following benefits:

"(1) It would pass from a peace to a war status with a minimum of confusion, waste and loss.

"(2) It would mobilize war supplies almost as quickly as it could mobilize men.

"(3) It would reduce the cost of war by 50 per cent and I believe by an even greater figure.

"(4) It would eliminate war profits and inflation.

"(5) It would preserve its credit and its economic prestige throughout the world.

"(6) Its war effort would be conducted with less interference with normal economic processes and the lives of the civil population than has ever been the experience of any nation in the history of the world.

"(7) It would conserve its resources and preserve the morale of its people to such an extent that it would be able to outlive any antagonist in a long-drawn-out struggle.

"(8) It could pass from a war status back to a peace status with a minimum of the prostrating economic aftermath that has hitherto been the invariable experience of every ex-belligerent in a great war.

"(9) The efficiency of the combined military and economic machine that could be derived from these policies would constitute this nation an instrument for war effective beyond the imagination of any military expert even of this advanced date—powerful beyond the possibilities of any antagonist and perhaps of any combination of antagonists.

"(10) Considering the obvious fact that the military aspirations of this nation will never disturb the peace of the world, the mere acceptance of (and deliberate provision for) the kind of organization here suggested would go very far toward keeping the peace of the world.

"And the last result, I take it, is the hope and aim of all of us."

What happened after all this? Three volumes of the lengthy proceedings of the Commission were carefully filed away in the archives!

For some time before this hearing Baruch had been concerned about the "draft dollars as well as men" slogan of some of the Progressive senators. They had prepared "war plans" that called for capital levies and seemed to Baruch to be much more likely

Press Association, Inc.

SENATE HEARING, 1939

Surrounded by microphones, flash-cameras, and an audience.

to disrupt our economic structure and lead to socialism than to render any aid to a war effort.

Patiently he expounded to the Commission his convictions on this subject, in language so clear and convincing that the idea of confiscating capital to finance a war has not been seriously proposed on Capitol Hill since.

"The total of our expenditure for the World War," he told the Commission, "was 39½ billion dollars. The nearest antecedent census estimate of total national wealth was 186 billions in 1912, of which only 1.4 billions was in gold and silver bullion. Real estate, plant and equipment (including railroads) was 141 billions. Transportation systems (except railroads) was 10 billions and all other forms of wealth (agricultural, manufactured and mining products, clothing, furniture, carriages, etc.) was 34 billions.

"It is interesting to inquire how the war could have been financed by confiscating any or all of these items. The billion and a half in hard money would not have been a drop in the bucket if all had been taken. As to the seizure of physical properties their use for finance would require resale. But who, under the patent threat of reconfiscation, would buy such properties? And since such capital levies would of course first reach the more liquable forms of wealth, who would have anything to buy them with?

"There may be an idea that seizure would nevertheless finance war because we would simply take war material without paying for it. The error in this is that there is no considerable amount of material available for war under peace conditions. It has to be manufactured from raw resources. The bulk of all fabricated costs are labor costs. We cannot conscript labor, therefore we would have to pay labor and that requires finance. There being no available war material for seizure no one would expend his money to produce war material merely to have it seized as fast as he made it and without reimbursement. The whole idea is absurd.

"There has been a good deal of talk of drafting dollars. Even if there were ample Constitutional authority there is a very cogent reason why that could not be done. Every man with fair warning that his dollars were about to be taken away from him and never given back would cause them to disappear with amazing rapidity on the first rumor of war. The experience of France and Germany in attempting to draw existing distributed supplies of gold into their treasuries for war purposes clears this point. [This was long before anyone dreamed of the government's commandeering all privately held gold.]

"I think I was the very first advocate of the plan to take the profit out of war and to make every man, dollar and thing bear an even proportion of the burdens of war. I hold no brief for especial protection of wealth in war, but my experience tells me that the draft of dollars is quite as absurd and impossible as the draft of labor. Such wholesale impressment is both impossible and unnecessary, but in the considerations under this heading it is crazy. The fiscal strength of a nation lies not in what government owns but in what its people own. The sinews of war are not dollars—they are efforts. In order to produce things, money is necessary but it is not necessary that government *own* the money by taking it away from the people who do. Monetary wealth is potential productive capacity just exactly as a factory is and, exactly as the factory capacity of the country must be administered, rationed and controlled for war purposes in order that the vastly increased demands of war may be met and, at the same time, that the normal requirements of the civil population be not denied, so must wealth be similarly administered, rationed and controlled."

Baruch told the commission about an episode in the First World War, when it was proposed for the government to take over a certain plant. The proposal split, he said, on the rock of this argument:

"Who will run it? Do you know another manufacturer fit to take over its administration? Would you replace a proved expert manager by a problematical mediocrity? After you had taken it over and installed your government employee as manager, what greater control would you have then than now? *Now* you can choke it to death, deprive it of transportation, fuel and power, divert its business, strengthen its rivals. Could any disciplinary means be more effective? If you take it over, you can only give orders to an employee backed by threat of dismissal and with far less effort than you can give them now. Let the management run the plant and you run the management."

What happened after all this? Three volumes of the lengthy proceedings of the Commission were carefully filed away in the archives!

CHAPTER... TWENTY-FIVE

BARUCH will give us all the money we want *now*, when he knows Franklin is going to be President. He wouldn't give us a nickel before the Chicago convention, when we really needed it."

The speaker was Louis McHenry Howe, gnomelike secretary to, political manager for, and worshiper of Franklin D. Roosevelt. The time was October, 1932, when the Democratic National Committee, though always needing money, was beginning to weigh each financial contribution tendered against the potential obligation it might impose on Roosevelt *after* inauguration.

It was not a mere casual statement made in conversation. Again and again during the campaign Louis, brooding over the before-Chicago struggle, would march into the office of anyone he knew liked Baruch and shoot this statement provocatively.

"Well, Baruch doesn't want anything in return for the money he is now offering," Senator Key Pittman said rather sharply to Howe on one of these occasions.

"And he isn't going to get anything," said Louis angrily as he walked away.

Howe and Pittman were not talking the same language. Pittman knew that Baruch had refused the secretaryship of the Treasury under Wilson and that he did not want any office or any special favors for any private interests, so he resented what he thought Louis meant. But Howe didn't mean anything of the kind. He was in no doubt about what Baruch wanted—to become Roosevelt's Number One Adviser.

Howe had watched Baruch for 8 years while Wilson was President, when Howe was Roosevelt's secretary in the Navy Department. He had seen the effects of Baruch's personal charm and wisdom at work on Wilson, Mrs. Wilson, and Admiral Grayson. He did not want anything of that sort to happen while Franklin was in the White House. He wanted the Number One Adviser to be Louis McHenry Howe.

Actually both Roosevelt and Howe were convinced that Baruch had helped Albert C. Ritchie, the "more or less permanent governor of Maryland" as he was once called, in his campaign for the 1932 nomination. There were certain indications that Louis was reflecting his beloved chief when he said Baruch "isn't going to get anything." Louis did not have to bother with being tactful. He could say things that would be impolitic for Roosevelt to mention, just as for years Hugh S. Johnson would say things that could not be dragged from Baruch by wild horses but that most of his friends thought reflected his views.

The truth is that Baruch did not lift a hand to help Ritchie, did not give a penny or an idea to his campaign, did not assign any of his personal "brain trust" to help the Maryland governor, and did not tell anybody he wanted Ritchie nominated. Many who knew about his warm friendship for Ritchie, who was an extraordinarily lovable person, suspected that down in his heart he hoped Ritchie would be nominated, but they could never check this. To borrow a phrase from Baruch's political idol, Woodrow Wilson, Baruch tried to be "neutral in thought." Whether he succeeded or not is unimportant. It never got beyond thinking.

Actually, if Baruch *had* gone the limit for Ritchie, it is not half as wild as it may sound to wonder if the course of history might not have been changed and Ritchie nominated and elected President of the United States instead of Roosevelt.

Most political observers at the time believed that if the Ritchie campaign had been properly financed it would have been possible for him to have captured most of the Pennsylvania delegation, whereas actually Joe Guffey delivered a majority of that big unit to F.D.R. Despite this Pennsylvania strength it was well known at the convention that, right after the next to the last ballot, four state delegations that had been voting for Roosevelt were going to break.

One of these, the Mississippi delegation, led by Senator Pat Harrison, planned to switch to Newton D. Baker. This news, plus various other reports, were relayed to William Randolph Hearst, who hated Baker violently. The deal with Garner resulted, and Roosevelt was nominated on the following ballot.

Hearst was utterly wrong in being afraid that Baker might be nominated. No delegation from any heavily German state, which includes all of the Middle West, would have dared vote for Baker. Yet this was a very general belief. Raymond Moley in his book *Seven Years After* expressed the view that if Roosevelt had failed to win the nomination Baker would have won.

Baker's unpopularity with the Germans, plus his championing of the cause of some of the big interests, notably Bethlehem Steel, made him utterly unavailable. He would have had a brief ride in the convention and then been abandoned.

Now suppose that when the Mississippi delegation caucused, Ritchie had been a strong candidate. Remember that Pat Harrison, one of Baruch's best friends, was head of the Mississippi delegation! Word that Mississippi was switching to Ritchie from Roosevelt would not have infuriated Hearst. He might even have been pleased. But whether he liked it or not he would not have thrown Garner overboard in a panic. Many thought Hearst had backed Garner to head off Roosevelt.

There was no hostility to Ritchie anywhere in the convention. He had admirers in almost every delegation. As one old political reporter put it, "Ritchie has more friends and less votes among the delegates than any candidate at any convention I ever covered."

Whether Baruch ever regretted not helping Ritchie probably will never be known. He has written a great many things that have never found their way to any printing press, some of which I have seen and some of which I have heard about. Something may be found in his papers on this subject, although it is unlikely.

Long afterward, when told one day that Roosevelt suspected he had helped Ritchie, he merely said, "I made up my mind after McAdoo that I would never again interest myself in any candidate for President until after he had been nominated."

Certainly he lost no time in making his aid available to Roosevelt once the New York governor had the nomination. Ray Moley, worried over the Roosevelt acceptance speech, tells of his annoyance at seeing Baruch and Hugh Johnson taken into Howe's private office at Chicago. Moley was in despair. He admitted frankly that he suspected the worst. He had never met Baruch, and he feared a Wall Street and Big Business slant might now be forced on Roosevelt for the sake of expediency.

While still worrying about this, Moley was approached by Jesse Straus and asked to show to Baruch the draft he had of the acceptance speech. Straus explained that it was desirable to be nice to Baruch, who might contribute a good deal to the campaign.

Moley apparently thought merely of a *money* contribution. At any rate he made a rather sarcastic answer to Straus, in giving him a copy of the draft for Baruch, making no bones of his opinion that this represented a long step toward the surrender of Roosevelt's ideals to the practical exigencies of the campaign.

So Roosevelt's Number One Brain Truster, as he was known for some time after that, was amazed when Baruch, less than an hour later, appeared, told Moley he had read both drafts (Howe and Moley) and infinitely preferred what he called the "Albany version."

"It's magnificent," said Baruch.

Moley would have been even more flattered if he had known then how seldom Baruch used superlatives. Baruch persuaded Moley to take the speech to Herbert Bayard Swope, whom he found with Hugh Johnson and Joseph P. Kennedy. He read it to the three of them, and, after Swope expressed regret that it did not mention the glorious work of some of the party wheel horses (Moley thought he meant Al Smith), all approved the draft.

What followed is history, how Roosevelt read the first page of Louis's draft and the remainder of the text Moley had helped write and was championing. Baruch, with two of his important experts, Johnson and Swope, had made an auspicious entry into Roosevelt's Brain Trust. But it was not an entry calculated to enthuse Louis Howe nor to deter him from reminding Franklin from time to time that Baruch had been for Ritchie, and "wouldn't give us a nickel when we needed it."

Louis had another needle to apply to Roosevelt whenever the subject of Baruch came up. It will be remembered that F.D.R. had had a good deal to do with the Navy Board that had made an industrial study of the United States as a step toward preparing this country for war. Actually this board had done a good job in a new field. It had not been a complete job, as the War Industries Board later considered, but after all it had catalogued some 18,000 plants. As stated earlier, the chief weakness of this report seems to have been that it did not show the sort of detail that would reveal whether any particular plant could be converted to some other purpose. Be that as it may, the job had been almost revolutionary when done, and the Navy never got any particular credit for it.

In vivid contrast, F.D.R. personally got tremendous credit in 1917 for his daring in having ordered, prior to the declaration of war, supplies for the Navy, far and away in excess of the authority granted the Navy Department by Congress. These supplies turned out to be very useful indeed after the United States got into the war.

Louis, who had been Roosevelt's secretary then, always blamed the War Industries Board in general and Baruch, its chairman, in particular, for thus smothering the industrial-survey feature of Franklin's work.

After the acceptance-speech episode, when Howe had made such an effort to get Baruch and Hugh Johnson to approve *his* draft, only to have both favor the Albany draft, Louis just *had* to blow off steam to somebody, as he secretly whetted his ax for both Moley and Baruch.

In the frequent conferences between Baruch and the Brain Trusters during the campaign, Ray Moley long afterward revealed not only that Baruch had been in complete sympathy with their viewpoint and ideals, but that his intellectual contributions had been regarded with admiration. Eventually, wrote Moley in his book, *After Seven Years,* Baruch became just a Brain Truster—"and one of the best at that."

It is no wonder that Moley appreciated what Baruch was doing. The financier played the Moley game by writing a memorandum to Roosevelt advising that the policy group, of which Moley was the recognized head, should be kept distinct from political headquarters. He was not only a valued adviser in personal contact with the Moley group, but he donated the services of the experts on his pay roll, notably Hugh Johnson, whose pungent and forceful speech-writing proved of enormous value.

Moley wrote, in *After Seven Years:* "Johnson had, by now,

become a fixture of our little group. Baruch had dropped him into our midst casually enough, but, once there, he exploded, like an elaborate fireworks display, into a series of enchanting patterns. We had a preview of all the color, spirit, and versatility that were later to fix the eyes of the country on him, and it captivated us."

There is not the slightest evidence that Baruch was aware of the jealousy that Louis Howe felt toward Moley or of Howe's resentment against Baruch himself. On the contrary, he and Hugh Johnson cheerfully worked with Howe from time to time, notably when Moley was with Roosevelt on the campaign trips.

In fact, Baruch and Johnson worked out a speech on the budget and Federal finances, showed it to Howe, and aroused him to such enthusiasm that he pestered the life out of both Roosevelt and Moley trying to get Roosevelt to use it on the trip back from California. One of Howe's telegrams, including the text of this speech, was 8,000 words long. Having worked for a New York newspaper in the old days, it never occurred to Louis to spare the horses when it came to telegraph tolls!

It must be stated in fairness to Howe that his loyalty to F.D.R. came first, his resentments and personal aversions second. He might beware of Greeks bearing gifts, but he didn't spurn the gifts if he thought Franklin could use them. He only used the needle to arouse F.D.R.'s animosity when he was convinced that the gift might not be worth much.

One of the Republican attacks that worried all the Roosevelt group during that campaign was the change that F.D.R. might take the country off the gold standard. Roosevelt did not want to answer this himself, and Senator Carter Glass, of Virginia, who had been Wilson's Secretary of the Treasury for a short time, was induced to make a speech denying this. Glass seldom minced words when he talked, and the resulting oration was a philippic. It left no doubt in business circles that Roosevelt would be for sound money.

When Baruch learned that Glass had refused the offer to be F.D.R.'s Secretary of the Treasury he was greatly disturbed. Baruch was always a strong gold man. He knew that gold had stood the test for thousands of years, whereas every attempt to fix some other base for money had failed and failed usually with disastrous consequences to everyone concerned.

It may have been intuition, it may have been actual suspicion of F.D.R.'s intentions, it may have been fear that some form of inflation might make an irresistible appeal to Roosevelt after inauguration as a temporary escape from the financial troubles the world was undergoing, but he went to work on Glass in an effort to get him to change his mind. Baruch was sure that there would be no inflation if Glass was Secretary of the Treasury. The assurances as to F.D.R.'s soundness on the money question did not seem to satisfy Glass, however, and he persisted in his declination.

Roosevelt promptly put Baruch on the spot by offering him the post of Secretary of the Treasury. This was not known at the time—in fact, it was not revealed for many years—but any of Baruch's friends could have told F.D.R. that the place would not appeal to Baruch. He had declined precisely the same portfolio under Woodrow Wilson, under whom he literally adored to work.

It was never a particular job that Baruch wanted, no matter how glamorous the job might be. What he wanted was to be trouble shooter for the President of the United States, minister without portfolio.

This particular offer was opportune—he thought it of the essence that a sound-money man be Secretary of the Treasury. But definitely he wanted the job assigned to somebody else, so that he would be free to function in the way he knew he could be of greater service.

There was perhaps an additional reason why he declined. He was just a little dubious of Roosevelt's currency views. He knew that if Roosevelt should follow an unorthodox course on money while he was Secretary of the Treasury, he would have to resign. That would make it impossible for him to play the role he wanted to play. His resignation would prove a barrier to continuance of his role as adviser.

Louis Howe had his revenge on Moley when the latter went to London, to the floundering Economic Conference, in a role that was regarded by some as that of Supersecretary of State and direct personal representative of the President, and by a minority as that of a glorified messenger boy. Baruch was involved in two ways. In the first place, at the suggestion of Moley and with the approval of the President, Baruch was "sitting in" on Moley's job in Moley's absence. In the second, Herbert Bayard Swope, Baruch's right bower, went with Moley. This last lent a peculiar relish to the mission as newspapermen interpreted it. It happened that two former subordinates of Swope, Charles Michelson and Elliott Thurston, were respectively director and assistant director of publicity for the American delegation to the London Conference. Michelson and Thurston had worked under Swope when Swope was executive editor of the *New York World*.

Thus not only was Moley apparently taking over the reins by direct mandate of F.D.R., but he was bringing along a publicity man who ranked those already on the job. The whole thing was spotlighted by a flight by plane and a rush trip by destroyer for Moley to consult Roosevelt just before going abroad and by wide publicity for the hiring of a special plane to take the two from Ireland to London.

Meanwhile, back in Washington, a cautious visit by Baruch to Moley's office resulted in a fanfare of publicity, in which the title of Assistant President was given to the financier in many headlines and editorials. The fact that with scarcely a discordant note these were all approving did not relieve Baruch of concern about this untoward publicity. He suspected that Roosevelt might not like it!

He paid no further visits to the office, but he did keep in touch, only to become involved, though this time without immediate publicity, in the episode that proved the final death blow to the conference.

At that time France and some of the smaller countries were still clinging to gold, but with a precarious hold that the slightest jar might loosen. What they earnestly wanted was some forceful statement from the United States that would allay the paniclike fear which was still engulfing the world and from which the United States gave promise of emerging. Britain earnestly wanted an agreement that would fix the relative value of the pound and the dollar. Roosevelt wanted to retain his freedom to do anything about the value of money and exchange he wished in order to boost domestic prices, particularly farm prices. Secretary of State Hull, head of the United States delegation, was more concerned about cutting tariff barriers than monetary questions.

Wall Street, bankers, and businessmen generally were all strong for stabilization; that is, fixing the price of dollars in pounds. As the British had an agreement with the French concerning the relative value of the pound and the franc, this would really have meant that the value of the dollar would be fixed, indirectly but positively, in gold. This was precisely what F.D.R. did *not* want to do at that time.

Virtually all the newspapers, bankers, speculators, and businessmen generally, however, were certain that stabilization was about to be announced. The "inside dope" on Wall Street was that the agreement had already been reached. Importers and exporters were making their plans on this basis. Business generally ignored one or two Washington correspondents who insisted that Roosevelt would not—could not—permit stabilization because it would make the carrying out of his economic objectives impossible.

So little did Secretary Hull appreciate this that, on the eve of his departure for London, he said, among other things, "There should be an agreement as to the fundamentals of the situation in a few weeks, that should equally apply to currency stabilization as well as to trade barriers."

Roosevelt not only repudiated the idea of any immediate stabilization, but scolded the entire London Conference for not going ahead with other objectives in a statement that has been often called the "bombshell." That statement sealed the fate of the conference and ended the mild boom that the stock market was enjoying. Many critics have said that it delayed the return of prosperity for years.

What was not generally known for a long time afterward was that there was a desperate effort on the part of the gold-bloc countries (France, Italy, Switzerland, Holland, and others) to soften the blow. Their delegates in London prepared a statement that they insisted did not really commit the President to anything, but which they thought would save the situation.

Oliver M. W. Sprague sent this statement to the President, to Secretary of the Treasury William H. Woodin, and to Baruch. Moley arranged by transatlantic telephone for Baruch and Dean Acheson, Undersecretary of the Treasury, to meet at Woodin's bedside (he was seriously ill) in New York for a telephonic conference. All agreed that the statement would do no harm and might do a great deal of good. George L. Harrison, governor of the Federal Reserve Bank of New York, was also present at the Woodin home and agreed with the others. They wirelessed the President to that effect.

Nothing happened. Moley sent frantic messages to the President direct. F.D.R. was on the Atlantic, aboard the cruiser *Indianapolis*. With him were Henry Morgenthau, Jr., and Louis Howe. Finally F.D.R. sent a message to London. It was a flat rejection. It was interpreted as a repudiation of Moley. It would have been interpreted as a repudiation of the Assistant President, the Secretary and Undersecretary of the Treasury, and Mr. Harrison if the public had known at the time about the telephonic conversations.

All that came to light *then* was that a transatlantic call made by Moley cost $400. Howe was not the *only* person gunning for the Number One Brain Truster!

"Don't leave your nice warm bed," Baruch had said to Moley before Moley set out for London. "Somebody will be in it when you get back!"

CHAPTER . . . TWENTY-SIX

When Moley returned from London he found Thomas Corcoran and Benjamin Cohen snugly bundled in the "warm bed" he had left, while Rexford Tugwell had donned his pajamas and dressing gown. It wasn't long before he began to see newspaper photographs of Baruch and Tommy Corcoran walking through the park, each obviously exuding the charm for which both are so justly famous.

Baruch was overlooking no opportunity for steering the ship of state so as to avoid the economic reefs so clear to him in the waters ahead and apparently, as he listened to the bright young men around Roosevelt, so enticing to the New Deal. He had lost his fight to keep the country on the gold standard. He hoped by his persuasiveness and sound logic to protect the country from running on the shoals of other nostrums that seemed so millennium-like to the starry-eyed professors.

Apparently he had plenty of friends at court. His lieutenant Hugh S. Johnson had just been made head of the newly established NRA. Another of his boys, George Peek, was Administrator of the AAA. Between them they directed the entire effort at business and agricultural recovery.

But there were dangers outside the scope of these two trusted friends. For instance, there was the obvious fact that President Roosevelt was impressed with the theory of Professor George F. Warren that changes in the price of gold would result in pro-

Press Association, Inc.

BETWEEN THE ACTS

At a performance of *I'd Rather Be Right* with Admiral Cary T. Grayson.

portionate changes in the prices of commodities, which seemed to Baruch to have been the motivation of Roosevelt's action in spurning the plea of the gold-bloc countries at the London Conference.

He found it more and more difficult to present his views adequately to the President. Roosevelt was just a little impatient, remarked frequently to others and at least once to Baruch himself that Bernie was "very stubborn." On that occasion Baruch smiled broadly and just waited. Finally the President broke out laughing, probably because it occurred to him, watching Baruch smile, that maybe he was a bit on the stubborn side, too.

Socially, the President was always at his delightful best when Baruch came around, whether at Washington or Hyde Park, but it was very apparent that he was avoiding opportunities for arguments over his plans. He did not manifest any great desire for serious discussions. On one occasion, at Hyde Park, when Mrs. James Roosevelt said she had invited Baruch to come by, F.D.R. said that that was all right—by all means have him to lunch. But the President added that he would have to go into a conference with some other visitor right after lunchtime, and so he would not have to argue with Baruch.

"Why are you so stubborn when you see the President?" a friend asked Baruch shortly after this episode.

"My dear fellow," said Baruch, somehow conveying the notion of a patient teacher with a very stupid pupil. "How can I be otherwise? I say that two and two make four. I am *very* stubborn about that. Am I supposed to yield, for the sake of being pleasant, and say that maybe they could make six, if the government insisted upon it?"

Baruch had thought of giving up his annual vacation in Europe that first summer of the New Deal. He felt he was badly needed. But a few newspaper articles and editorials played with the idea that he was really running the NRA, with "his boy" Johnson as the figurehead. This distressed Baruch. Even as head of the War Industries Board, when he had had the power and responsibility, he had never interfered with his lieutenants once he saw them well started on a good job, but he feared the publicity would have a bad effect. It would not be fair to Johnson. It might prejudice certain left-wingers against Johnson and cause trouble for him at the White House.

After doing his best with such White House advisers as he could, therefore, he sailed for Europe.

For a brief time it seemed as though both Baruch and Moley had dropped out of the cloistered group of advisers to the President. Actually Moley was slipping in and out, quietly, and continued to do so until after the 1936 convention. Baruch was never entirely "out." Indeed, early the following summer it appeared to the public that he was in high favor, for when the President went to the baseball park, to throw out the first ball for the opening game, the trip was made in an open car, with the top down, and there was Baruch, beside him for all the populace to see, basking in the two kinds of sunshine he so dearly loved—that from Old Sol and that of the favor of the President of the United States.

Curiously enough, it was none other than Louis Howe who had suggested that Baruch be brought to Washington on this occasion. Louis was worried about the political situation, and he knew that Baruch could help in certain important quarters. Never did Louis Howe let his personal fears and jealousies stand in the way when it seemed to him that Franklin might be hurt by them.

Indeed, it seemed to many of his friends that he was perfectly willing at all times to sacrifice himself for his chief. One wondered whether he worried more about the possibility of someone else becoming the Number One Adviser or about his fear that, should he loosen the reins a moment, someone else would persuade the President to do something that might result in an unfavorable reaction.

This was the time for the first congressional election since Roosevelt entered the White House. There were certain spots that looked dangerous, both for the primary and for the election campaigns. Howe wanted something done about it. Apparently it was largely due to Baruch that things were done in those particular states and districts. At any rate the election returns carried virtually a vote of confidence in the New Deal.

It was far more characteristic of the kind of contribution that Baruch had been making to his country since the Wilson days, however, that this same year, 1934, Baruch began to urge stockpiling of strategic materials. This particular warning was adroitly calculated to meet the then political situation. The country was rather bitter about war debts. All the debtor countries except Finland had stopped paying. The depression was still pretty bad. To have urged public spending *outside* the United States when there was such an orgy of government spending inside the country to provide employment would not have had the slightest possibility of a sympathetic hearing.

Baruch did not like what he had learned on his previous two trips to Europe, when he had been seeing a great deal of the friends he had come to know as a result of his war and peace-conference activities. He listened more gravely to Winston Churchill than anyone else, the two having become like Damon and Pythias.

Churchill was afraid of another war, which he envisioned not only in Europe but in the Pacific. Baruch knew what that would mean to the United States on strategic materials, particularly tin and rubber. He knew that in any modern war shipping is of the essence and that ships could not be spared for the long haul to bring tin and rubber from the Far East to the United States once a world war had broken out, whether the United States was in it or not.

Baruch proposed to the House Foreign Affairs Committee that the United States stockpile tin, taking the tin as payment on account of the war debt. He thought that that would be an entering wedge and that this country could pile up stocks of tin, rubber, and other strategic materials so that, by the time some spark should touch off the next world war, this nation would be guarded, to that extent at least, against the economic dislocations that an acute shortage of tin and rubber would produce to our domestic, not to mention our war, economy.

There was scarcely a month, in the more than seven years between this 1934 testimony and Pearl Harbor, that Baruch did not try to persuade individual senators, representatives, writers, and officials of the wisdom of stockpiling. No matter what problem was brought to him for advice, no matter how high or low the statesman, politician, or writer who brought it, Baruch always managed to lead the subject around, at some stage, to the vital importance of stockpiling.

No action by the White House in that 7 years indicated that F.D.R. had actually been convinced by Baruch's arguments in favor of stockpiling or of proper planning for industrial mobilization and prevention of inflation.

Yet the President appointed Baruch and Hugh Johnson to a commission to study the idea of planning for industrial mobilization. Hugh Johnson said, long afterward, that Baruch had been directed to recheck his findings! However, the appointment looked important at the time. The newspapers played it up, just as they had played up his idea for obtaining stockpile materials as part payments of the war debts.

Congress and the public were inclined to yawn, both being very pacifist-minded at the moment and only reconciled to Roosevelt's bigger navy plans because they would provide employment. The Baruch ideas, however, and this indication that the President might go along with them, did not pass unnoticed by the shrewd gentry who were playing the German game.

Pretty soon many who were consciously or unwittingly helping the Nazi operations in this country were pouring abuse on Baruch, attacking his record in the War Industries Board, intimating that he and his friends had made millions through war profits resulting from the Board's actions. Those preaching anti-Semitism took it up.

Father Coughlin, in a radio address, went back into ancient Jewish history, changing Baruch's middle name to make a biblical reference fit better, and tore the financier to shreds over the air waves. The drive seemed very timely. Senator Gerald Nye, chairman of the committee that was to look into the munitions industry, had some very positive views. He was violently against the munitions industry and regarded its desire for profit as the chief instigating motive for most wars. He deplored that this country had gone into the First World War and questioned the motives of those who, as he saw it, led us into it. Further, he was vigorously opposed to everything connected with Wall Street.

It looked as though Baruch was being led to the slaughter. All sorts of whispers were circulating, just as they had in 1916, about Baruch profits. Care was taken to have them reach Senator Nye. The committee promptly subpoenaed Baruch's records, income-tax returns from 1916 to 1919, inclusive, etc., and called on him to appear.

Baruch wrote Senator Nye a letter, under date of March 22, 1935, which Baruch read into the record when he appeared before the committee on March 27. The letter was an answer to all attacks. As a result of sending the letter in advance, the way was cleared for Baruch to devote all his testimony to advocating (1) his own ideas for taking the profit out of war, and (2) the plan he had urged many times before for having the country ready not only for war itself but for its economic and financial impact.

The letter follows:

"In response to your letters of March 8 and of March 18 and your telegrams of March 20, copies of which and of my replies thereto are attached, I am turning over to your messenger the material relating to my income and my taxes during the years 1916 to 1919 inclusive, for which you asked.

"Immediately upon learning that the Committee was interested in my personal finances during the period in question I had a search made of all my records which might supply the data you seek. I supplemented this effort with a request made to the Bureau of Internal Revenue that copies of my tax returns in their possession be forwarded to me. Copies of my letters of March 14 and 18 to the Internal Revenue Bureau and of the reply thereto are attached. In that reply you will notice that the Bureau supplied photostatic copies of my income tax returns for the years 1916 and 1917, which I enclose, although an impression was somehow created that your committee was unable to get any copies of my returns. Further, the Bureau informed me that, while the original returns for 1918 and 1919 had been destroyed and my copies had not been sent back, they were supplying to me full copies of the reports made by the field agents of the Internal Revenue Commission based upon my returns for those years. My examination of them indicates that they are comprehensive and supply the basic facts as contained in the returns themselves.

"You ask me for 'a statement of the stocks and other securities held from 1916 to 1919.' In a memorandum attached I am making an effort to comply with this request, although it is not easy to do so, for it deals with accounts from 16 to 20 years old. However, I think the list is fairly complete. It shows all those securities which I held then and hold still, mostly bonds, and it is as complete as I can make it with respect to other securities. It is based upon an old list which my secretary unearthed. I am unable to set down the precise date on which it was drawn, but to the best of my belief and that of my secretary, who has been with me for thirty-odd years, it was compiled about 1919. It shows my total worth at that time. The amount in bonds was about $8,500,000 exclusive of the three investments which I mention later and which were worth perhaps $1,300,000 additionally. Further, I probably had some cash balances, the size of which I cannot recall. If there were any changes in this list, they were due to shifting from some of my Liberty Bond holdings into state, municipal and other types.

"In an effort to aid your committee, I am summarizing the facts contained in the returns or reports covering the four years in question. They show the following:

"1916 Income	$2,301,028.03
1916 Tax	261,169.91
1917 Income	617,061.67
1917 Tax	263,762.53
1918 Loss	
1919 Loss	

"During the four years in question I paid taxes, apart from the Government, to Washington, to New York City, to New York State, and to South Carolina.

"You will observe that my income steadily decreased after 1916. I was called into the Government service in 1917. I thereupon arranged to dispose, even at a loss when necessity arose, of all those securities affected by the War. I also sold my seat on the New York Stock Exchange, severing myself from all active business. That is why my income in 1917 shows a decline of almost seventy-five per cent from the previous year. In 1918 and 1919 I reported no taxable income, as I had sold large portions of my holdings, showing actual losses each year, and reinvested the money in Liberty Bonds. My income from them was somewhere around $200,000. My holdings in Liberty Bonds may have been as high as seventy-five per cent of my total wealth.

"Never from the moment I was called to the Government service did I have a dollar's worth of interest in any concern manufacturing munitions of war. Immediately upon my coming to Washington, although I was at first merely in an advisory capacity and not charged with procurement or executive responsibility, I divested myself of all holdings that even remotely touched upon my official activities. I took this step freely and at a heavy cost to my fortune. I made absolutely no purchases of securities except bonds, mostly governments. In buying these bonds I was, of course, under the necessity of selling some of the other securities I had in my box, which, as the records show, were sold at a loss. From the time I entered the service until I left in July, 1919, I was not a participant either directly or indirectly in any market transactions.

"I carried through the war three major investments in which I am still interested. They were, first, Alaska Juneau Gold Mining Company, in which I invested before the war and which for many years had no value; second, Texas Gulf Sulphur Company, in which I originally invested about twenty-five years ago and which never produced an ounce of sulphur during the entire war; and third, the Atolia Mining Company, a producer of tungsten to which you have made previous and public reference.

"I originally invested in this mine in the year 1905 or 1906. Its potential value lay in the fact that it was the most promising tungsten development in the United States. It took several years to bring it up to profitable productivity. It went on a dividend basis several years before the war. Tungsten was used for electric lamps, contact points, steel tools, etc. It became important as an alloy before and during the war because of the absence of other alloys in American mines.

"America never fixed a price on tungsten or similar materials during the war. The Government itself never bought an ounce of tungsten. It was sold to innumerable private buyers and was never allocated by quota. It was not a direct munition of war, but its use in steel caused its price to be affected in common with almost all other commodities.

"At this point let me emphasize the fact that the U. S. War Industries Board did not fix prices, nor did its Chairman. They were made by a special committee, distinct and separate from the War Industries Board, reporting directly to the President. Neither did the Chairman of the War Industries Board make contracts. Those were made by the various departments interested.

"More than a year before America entered the war the price of tungsten had risen to as high as $100 a unit. Before the demand was stimulated it had been around $10 a unit. An endeavor was made in the early part of 1917 to bring about agreements with producers of raw materials to grant lower prices to the Government, but neither then nor later was there a department of the Government interested in tungsten. The greater part of the sale of tungsten was directly to the Allies, and the price at which it was sold was set in the London markets by the Allies. In 1917 the price of tungsten dropped below $25 a unit, induced by fear of the establishment of an international executive and due to overstimulation of world production.

"As nearly as I can recall, my income from tungsten in 1916 was around $600,000. When in 1917 I set myself the program of getting rid of all holdings even remotely affected by the war, I tried to dispose of this investment. I offered it to my associates at a price which was to be one-half the dividend it would pay during the calendar year, and they refused to buy. Their refusal was based on the fear that there was no ore reserve; that there was a sharp limitation on the life of the mine; and that the foreign governments, which were the chief consumers, might limit the price. There was no market whatsoever for the shares of the mine in spite of the dividends it had paid. Accordingly I was compelled to retain my holdings. I did not resort to the subterfuge of a fake transfer.

"I informed certain officials in Washington, including the President of the United States, the Secretary of War, the Attorney General, the Secretary of the Interior, and my fellow board members of this interest and also of a plan that I had devised. Because tungsten had become increasingly important as an alloy, although its use was largest by civilian industrial enterprises, I ordered the segregation of every dollar that the mine paid me and directed that all the dividends should be paid to various charities. After this decision from the end of 1917 to the close of the war, I made contributions approximately of $400,000 to the Red Cross, the Knights of Columbus, the Y.M.C.A., the Y.M.H.A., the Salvation Army, and other relief agencies and also for other war purposes. In this period I had received Atolia dividends of approximately $300,000. Incidentally, the mine became practically worthless due to exhaustion of visible ore reserves, with an occasional trifling dividend since then. I still have the stock.

"I hope I have answered fully as to my personal affairs. I shall be present at the time you set—Wednesday—to answer as to any further details you may wish to go into, and, at the same time, to further the work of the Committee, which I had understood to be an investigation of the munitions industry.

"I have no request to make as to the course to be followed with reference to publicising this communication except to ask that you be good enough to inform me of your intention in advance of action.

"With assurances to you and your fellow Senators of my esteem, I am

"Respectfully,

"(Signed) BERNARD M. BARUCH."

CHAPTER...TWENTY-SEVEN

THE unique spectacle of a snooping, smearing, senatorial committee apologizing to the witness it had seemed all set to tear to pieces occurred on the second day of Baruch's appearance before the Nye group. All the barbed arrows of the previous few days, hinted to the newspapers by individual committee members and officials—income-tax returns destroyed, millions of profit, favoritism to friends, etc.—proved boomerangs. Committee members were embarrassed after publication of Baruch's letter. They were still more embarrassed, that morning of the second day, by a surprise appearance of Senator James F. Byrnes, of South Carolina.

"Mr. Chairman," said Senator Byrnes, "I want only a few minutes, and I appreciate your giving me the opportunity to make a short statement, so that I can go to my own committee meeting.

"This morning I read the newspaper report of this hearing yesterday, in which references were made by the witness, Mr. Baruch, to some criticism made heretofore with reference to his financial transactions during the period that he was chairman of the War Industries Board. It caused me to make this request to be heard at this time.

"During the war I was a member of the Deficiency Committee of the Appropriations Committee [of the House of Representatives]. That committee handled nearly all of the appropriations for the conduct of the war. After the Armistice there came before a subcommittee one day Mr. Ritchie, then Attorney General of the State of Maryland, who said he desired to call our attention to certain actions of Mr. Baruch.

"He told us that it was necessary for a mission to be sent to Great Britain by our Government for several purposes. First, to see that the material that the United States was shipping to Great Britain and our allied nations was really being used for military purposes and not commercial purposes to advance their export trade; and, secondly, inasmuch as we had fixed prices upon commodities in this country, and our Allies were receiving the benefit resulting from the fixing of prices, that as to certain commodities, such as tin and jute, that there should be a price fixed by Great Britain, so that this Government would not be paying an excessive price for such commodities.

"There were other purposes that I do not now recall. About the time that the mission was scheduled to leave, it was discovered that there were no funds to pay the expenses of this mission representing the Government of the United States. Mr. Baruch paid the expenses of that mission out of his pocket, and, according to the statement of Mr. Ritchie and his associates in the War Industries Board, it amounted to something like $85,000.

"By reason of the mission going to Great Britain for the purposes mentioned, millions of dollars were saved to the Government of the United States. After the matter was presented to the subcommittee of the Appropriations Committee, on which was Mr. Mondell of Wyoming, among others, and myself, we agreed that we would put into the appropriation bill an item reimbursing Mr. Baruch for this expenditure, and about two or three days later Mr. Ritchie again came to the committee to say that he had mentioned the matter to Mr. Baruch, who stated that under no circumstances would he accept the money, and, because of that fact, it was not included in the bill.

"Because it was an unusual occurrence, it caused me to discuss the matter with an official of the War Industries Board, a man who was familiar with all the activities of that organization; and he told me that that was not the only occasion that Mr. Baruch had spent his money for the Government of the United States during the war; that the expenses of the Council of National Defense, when the offices were first opened in Washington in the Munsey Building, and before the appropriations were made available, were paid out of the pocket of Mr. B. M. Baruch; and that at the conclusion of the War when our committee, in an endeavor to bring to an end the activities of these war boards, introduced a bill repealing the appropriations made for such boards in order to hasten the winding up of their activities, a very serious situation confronted us here in Washington.

"The boys had gone to War. Many of them had been drafted out of the Departments. Their places were taken by young girls from all over the country, who desired to serve their country in the only way that they could. And when it became necessary to abandon this activity of the War Industries Board, and hundreds of girls were to be dismissed, with no chance on earth of securing employment in Washington, at that time, this official of the War Industries Board told me that Mr. B. M. Baruch had employed a matron, and directed her to call upon every girl in the organization and try to persuade her to return to her home, instead of walking the streets of Washington securing employment.

"He said that she succeeded in persuading them, and the inducement offered was the cost of transportation of every girl in the War Industries Board from Washington to her home, including Pullman berth and all expenses.

"I thought they were two fine things. I have never heard of Mr. Baruch mentioning them. I have never seen them printed in any newspaper, and this morning when I read that he was under criticism about his financial transactions during the War, I felt it was only fair and right that somebody should put into the record this statement, showing that while other men may have used the power given them to accumulate wealth, that this man was using his wealth to serve his Government and to help young women return to their homes."

"Senator Byrnes," said Senator Nye, chairman of the committee, "I hope you have not been under the impression that the committee was the party that was critical of Mr. Baruch's wartime record. The committee's purpose in having Mr. Baruch here has been to ascertain from him the background, the information which he can so readily afford, concerning wartime activities, a background which we need in determining the issues which are going to be presented, when any war comes. I am making this statement only in the hope that the record may be clear as respects the attitude of the committee."

"I am very glad to know that," said Senator Byrnes. "As a matter of fact, my desire to do this was based upon the impression that I got from newspaper statements that he was under some criticism because the Secretary of the Treasury, or the Treasury Department, had destroyed his income tax return during the War."

"This seems an appropriate time," said Senator Bennett Champ Clark, of Missouri, another member of the Nye Committee, "to say, that as far as Mr. Baruch's personal income tax return is concerned, that that matter arose last December by reason of the inclusion of Mr. Baruch's name in a list of other gentlemen, put in by a committee investigator, whose income tax returns were found for certain years and not found for other years.

"Now the next morning after that exhibit was put in, I took the trouble to go to the Bureau of Internal Revenue and found out that that was entirely an ordinary course, and was done under an Act of Congress, and found that it was the practice of the Bureau of Internal Revenue to destroy income tax returns from time to time, simply as a matter of reducing the number of records necessary to be kept, but that it was not their practice to destroy any records on which there was a possibility of a claim for refund on the part of the taxpayer or for additional tax on the part of the Government. That would explain the fact that the income tax returns of any taxpayer might be destroyed for certain years and not for others.

"I also think it appropriate to say at this time, that Mr. Baruch furnished the committee with his income tax returns and income tax data from which the returns were made up, for the purpose of careful examination by the committee, and also with a list of his holdings of securities during the years of the War, and that there is not only nothing in those returns or those papers which could in any way be considered a reflection on Mr. Baruch, but they also show a highly commendable action on his part in disposing of stocks which he was holding in order to put himself at the disposal of the Government during the War.

"I think that is simply fair on behalf of the committee to Mr. Baruch."

There are two curious points about the comments just quoted from Senator Nye and Senator Clark. One is that Senator Nye completely evaded the issue that Senator Byrnes had made, namely, that there had been an intimation of suspicion about the destruction of some of Baruch's income-tax returns, which had been widely printed and might be calculated to harm Baruch's reputation for integrity and hence his influence on public affairs. Nye was chairman of the committee that sent investigators after Baruch. In view of his previous actions his statement to Senator Byrnes might indicate, to anyone not a mind reader, an eager desire to wipe the slate clean.

The other point is that, according to Senator Clark, it was a committee investigator who was responsible for the unfavorable publicity Baruch had received. This investigator, again according to Senator Clark, apparently had not bothered to ask the Revenue Bureau about the practice in such matters. He had simply picked up a bit of mud and thrown it. Senator Clark, the next day, had investigated and found out that it was common practice, but somehow or other the newspapermen covering the Nye Committee had not learned what Senator Clark had discovered. It was not made public until *after* Senator Byrnes's statement to the committee brought Senator Clark's response.

Washington correspondents and editors generally knew that this lynching by congressional committees was common. What was uncommon was for the person being lynched to win a vindication. It was the proverbial man biting a dog and hence was hot news.

Time magazine in its issue of April 8, 1935, devoted pages to it, mentioning the attacks that Senator Huey Long and Father Coughlin had made on Baruch and pointing out that, as soon as he had disposed of the attacks on his own record, he had steered the committee proceedings back to his idea of taking the profits out of war and keeping the country prepared for eventualities.

Newspapers all over the country devoted editorials as well as news stories to Baruch's defense and the apology of the committee. Down in Baruch's own stamping ground the *Charleston News and Courier* concluded its editorial: "The attacks on Bernard Baruch have been groundless, and even as attacks on public men are considered they have been unusually contemptible."

A short paragraph from an editorial in the *Pittsburgh Post-Gazette:* "It was about time for somebody to call a halt on certain United States Senators who seem to delight in attempts to attack or slur prominent individuals by inference and innuendo. Bernard M. Baruch did it in complete and convincing fashion when the Nye Committee investigating the munitions industry tried to pick on him."

Merryle Stanley Rukeyser, in the *New York American*, said:

"If more men of affairs would show Mr. Baruch's backbone, the people would applaud them.

"Those who had business experience with Mr. Baruch admired his integrity. This remark about him is attributed to the late Thomas Fortune Ryan: 'When I get into a tight spot I can always count on Baruch.' "

"Senator Long and Father Coughlin will have to find a new target," said a Scripps-Howard editorial. "Their charge that Gen. Hugh Johnson is 'Baruch's hired man' doesn't sound like a very harsh indictment in light of Bernard Baruch's performance before the Senate Munitions Investigating Committee."

Actually, this episode was another important milestone in Baruch's life. By it he was definitely graduated into the category of this country's elder statesman. Actually, he had not been attacked directly; he was not to be attacked even indirectly after this.

For all of this he was profoundly grateful to Jimmy Byrnes. It was not the beginning of their friendship. As a young politician in South Carolina, years before, Byrnes had come to know and like Baruch. Some of Byrnes's best personal friends in the Senate were of the Baruch Inner Circle, particularly Pat Harrison, of Mississippi, Joe Robinson, of Arkansas, and Key Pittman, of Nevada.

At the time he went to Baruch's defense Byrnes had become one of the most important figures on Capitol Hill. With the possible exception of Harrison he was the most ingratiating compromiser in Congress. President Roosevelt had discovered his flair for leadership and had begun to make use of it.

So, on top of his gratitude to Byrnes, Baruch discovered in him another avenue of approach to his constant goal, adviser to the White House. From the closing of that hearing there was nothing that Baruch would not gladly do for Byrnes.

When one remembers Baruch's devotion to Woodrow Wilson

and his dream of a League of Nations that would prevent war, there is one little exchange in the Nye Committee hearings that will bear pondering.

"Do you think," asked Senator Bone, of Washington, "that we made the world safe for democracy by going into that war?"

"I will say it could have been made safe for democracy," said Baruch. "If you and I are going to get into that, we will never agree. We can stand up all day and argue. I have changed my views somewhat, because I found that the agreements which have been made are not kept. I was going to say 'scrupulously kept.'"

So far as the Nye Committee was concerned, and for that matter all the other committees before which he appeared in the more than twenty years following 1918, Baruch was a voice crying in the wilderness. People listened, perhaps more politely than the ancient Hebrews did to his ancestors, but nobody *did* anything.

He should be given much of the credit, however, for killing off the plan, so dear to many pacifists, of virtually conscripting all wealth in the event of war—a policy that he pointed out again and again would lead certainly to this country's becoming so defenseless that it would be a constant temptation to any robber nation.

Little was heard of the John T. Flynn plan after that committee hearing. "The Flynn plan," said Baruch in a memorandum submitted to the committee following his personal appearance, "is to limit corporate profit to 3 per cent on declared adjusted capital value. If earnings are 3 per cent or less it takes half of that, or indeed half of any earnings less than 6 per cent and 100 per cent of earnings above 6 per cent. It allows no personal income in excess of $10,000 (this particular phase was to bob up again and again and become the pet of certain labor leaders) and taxes even that $10,000 heavily. It requires these taxes to be paid quarterly in cash.

"This plan has certain characteristics that make it questionable and might defeat every purpose it asserts, and that would probably imperil the defensive power of the United States. . . .

"It is my deliberate and considered judgment that the Flynn plan would insure an exaggerated inflation far greater than if there were no plan at all, paralyze war production and render this nation practically helpless against a major attack by any enemy possessing an economic and industrial system fairly comparable with our own.

"Much as it may be decried, the cold fact remains that ours is an economy activated by profits. A certain return on money is necessary to make our industrial system work. Insofar as a penny of profit derived from war is concerned, I propose to go exactly as far in taking them as we can go without interfering with the free flow of munitions for defense. I am not willing to go one step further than that, any more than I would be willing to impede or hamper or destroy the defensive power of our armies in the field in face of an enemy. One is the same as the other, and, in modern war, I am not sure that industrial effectiveness in war production is not the more important of the two."

Flynn contended that Baruch's general fixing of price ceilings was unnecessary, that the danger of inflation could be taken care of by adequate taxation.

Here are a few of Baruch's sentences in that hearing which caused the Flynn plan to be pigeonholed.

"Higher prices are themselves inflation and not merely the result of it. They are accelerated and not stopped by taxation. Putting on a ceiling is in no sense dependent on cost finding. . . .

"You certainly cannot pay the cost of a war by taking war profits because profit is but a small part of war cost and the whole is greater than any of its parts. [The two-plus-two-equal-four stubbornness again!] . . .

"If there are no profits there will be no tax revenue. If there is no revenue, this plan won't pay as we fight. . . .

"It is clear also that business and industry is in large part activated by the spending and investment of income and that if a war government takes all of income, it will not have to worry about paying for the war. It will not be there to pay for it. Either its conquerors or the Commune will have that problem. . . .

"It isn't high prices that persuade the 'high cost' and 'marginal' producer to make the investment necessary to bring him into production. It is the promise of profit. High prices without profit merely requires more investment to support turnover and inventory. Money will not invest and run the extreme risks of war production for a fraction of 3 per cent."

CHAPTER... TWENTY-EIGHT

NO PROPHET of old ever gave his rulers more accurate warnings, and had less advantage taken of his suggestions as to how to soften the blows he saw coming, than did Baruch in the years from 1934 until Pearl Harbor.

His difficulty through these years was to keep close enough to the throne even to have his advice heard at all, much less heeded. All the left-wingers were constantly shooting at him, needling the President against him, trying to destroy his influence.

It was not too difficult for them. The President had never really warmed to Baruch, always had hated to argue with him, resented his failure to yield to Roosevelt charm on economic questions, still rankled a little over Baruch's failure to help before the 1932 convention, and hence listened grudgingly, though of course with the surface cordiality of which he is such a master.

Every summer until the war broke out Baruch visited Europe. Every autumn he came back more certain that war was coming and that the United States would be involved and full of ideas as to what the government should do to be ready for the storm when it should break. But every time he found the sales resistance at the White House just a little stronger against him. Every time he wormed his way back to the visitor's chair by the President's desk something would happen that would increase the disfavor in which he was held by so many of the President's intimates.

"Stubborn" and "reactionary" were the least things said about him. His two lieutenants, Hugh Johnson and George Peek, lost their inner-circle places when the Supreme Court ruled out the NRA and the AAA in 1935. Johnson at once became embroiled in a palace row over the course the Administration should then pursue, his chief opponent, apparently, being Felix Frankfurter.

Often differing with Frankfurter, Baruch found himself on those occasions the target for the Frankfurter "boys," of which, Tommy Corcoran stated, there were not less than 250 around Washington. Most of them, incidentally, were in "key positions."

But, by dint of always smiling, always coming back, never saying anything harsh that would leave a scar, he managed to stay in the picture. A very proud man—very sure of the soundness of his own judgment on any particular point he undertook to expound—Baruch had frankly no pride when it came to the White House.

"I would crawl on my hands and knees to the White House," he said to a friend who was indignant over what the friend considered was very shabby treatment of the financier by the President, "if I thought it would do my country any good."

Besides this humility, persistence, and charm Baruch had a few other assets that stood him in good stead in this fight to stay near the throne. Those who ignored his advice were generally sorry later, so that the next time a problem arose and Baruch was right on the job with a recommendation, he was apt to get at least a hearing, even if the person advised had no intention of following his advice.

Another considerable element of strength was the known influence he held on Capitol Hill. The young New Dealers ran into it every time they went up to the Senate or House to do a little lobbying for the Administration, not that they found it used against them, but even the most casual conversation over any bit of legislation involving economics was apt to reveal its existence.

Then there was the deplorable human tendency to want something for nothing. Baruch's reputation as a regular wizard of Wall Street clung to him. Even the ardent left-wingers, those who hated Wall Street and all its works, especially those who had tilted their lances at the stock-market windmill without financial success, believed that if Baruch would only tell them what to do, and when to do it, they could make themselves rich. And, much as they might deplore riches in the pockets of the wicked interests, there were quite a sprinkling who were not averse to accumulating some for themselves. This is not to say that very many New Dealers openly asked Baruch for stock-market tips, although *some* did. It was difficult for people to be convinced that Baruch was really out of the market.

For all these reasons, there were a great many who were careful not to go too far in their efforts to bar Baruch from the visitor's chair by the President's desk.

Baruch's own office during pleasant weather in these years was the much-advertised bench in La Fayette Park. There he sat in the sun. There he could be seen by anybody who wanted to talk with him. From there he watched the White House, hoping, paragraphers and cartoonists insisted, that a flag would shortly be displayed that would summon him to lunch.

In June, 1936, Baruch was called in by the President for advice about the acceptance speech F.D.R. was to make at the Philadelphia Convention.

Ray Moley afterward revealed that Baruch had wanted the speech to have as its theme "serenity and service" and that the President had told Moley the suggestion was "splendid." Most of the headline and editorial writers, however, did not seem to get the impression of "serenity and service" from the final text. But that June, at least, Baruch was being asked for advice.

But while he was in Europe, right after that 1936 convention, George Peek, his old lieutenant, took the stump against Roosevelt. After the outlawing of the Triple A, Peek had been appointed by Roosevelt to a post under Secretary of State Hull. He had views about trade agreements and tariffs that clashed sharply with Mr. Hull's ideas. He found out, as Ray Moley had done before him and as Sumner Welles was to do later, that it was not healthy to fight Hull.

Of course when Peek tried to turn the Middle West against F.D.R. and attempted to prove that the President was ruining the farmers, there were some in the White House circle who said Peek was merely reflecting Baruch's private views and that the whole Baruch crowd were a lot of reactionary traitors. This was told the President often enough to produce a bit of coolness toward Baruch.

Then the following spring, just as F.D.R.'s glow over his big victory at the polls was fading, came the Supreme Court "packing" fight. Baruch actually took no part in that, but his friends did. Some of his closest friends in the Senate opposed it, though his best friend there, Joe Robinson, of Arkansas, died as a result of the strain he underwent fighting for the President.

In the summer of 1937 Baruch found Winston Churchill no longer merely "afraid" of war. He was now certain it was coming, and he was bitter about the fumbling of his own government and the lack of preparedness.

"War is coming very soon," said Churchill emphatically. "We will be in it and you [meaning the United States] will be in it. You [meaning Baruch] will be running the show over there, but I will be on the sidelines over here."

Churchill had come to like Baruch very much. He had admired his ability since he watched the operations of the War Industries Board in the First World War. He had visited Baruch in this country and gone crabbing in the little estuaries at

Hobcaw. The two men had come to be close friends and confidants. Baruch admired the Britisher's gift of prophecy as well as his abilities in other lines. Moreover, what Churchill said about the certainty of war checked with everything Baruch had been finding out in his last few trips to Europe.

Shortly after he returned to the United States, Baruch was cornered by Louis Johnson, then Assistant Secretary of War.

"Do you know," said Johnson, "that we have no machinery for the making of smokeless powder?"

"Why don't you buy some?" demanded Baruch.

"We have no appropriation," said Johnson.

"How much would the machinery you need cost?" asked the financier.

"Three million dollars," replied Johnson.

"Go ahead and buy it," said Baruch.

"How in the world can we?" said Johnson with an air of finality.

"My dear fellow," said Baruch, "the country needs that powder-making machinery. Order it at once. Tell the manufacturers that I will pay for it, so they will have no hesitation in accepting the order."

"I think Congress will appropriate the money eventually," said Johnson, "but you never can tell."

"If Congress appropriates the money, well and good," said Baruch. "If Congress does not appropriate the money, that will be all right too. It will just be my contribution to preparedness. But don't hesitate a minute. Order that machinery *now.* Who pays for it is not important."

The machinery was ordered. Congress did appropriate the money, so that the move did not cost Baruch anything. Actually, his risk of his own money resulted not only in providing the United States army with something it vitally needed, and well in advance of shortages and priorities, but it saved the Treasury something. Had the order been withheld until *after* Congress appropriated the money, it would have run into the competition of the belated preparedness purchases that Britain and France began in 1938.

Before Baruch shuttled back to Europe that summer of 1938 he was suspected by the White House of something nearly approaching treason. It was thought that he was aiding, financially, the campaigns of certain Democratic senators the President was trying to defeat. This was the "purge," the attempt to defeat for renomination all Democratic senators who had opposed the President in the court-bill fight.

One of the senators the Administration tried to defeat was Ellison D. Smith, in Baruch's own state of South Carolina. Another was Walter George, in the adjoining state of Georgia. Cotton Ed, as Smith was popularly known, had never been so friendly to Baruch as some other Southern senators. Millard Tydings, of Maryland, another on the purge list, was friendly but not intimate.

Nevertheless, suspicion mounted among the Frankfurter Boys that Baruch was helping the purgees. Maybe they were right; maybe they were mistaken. A man cannot be compelled to testify against himself. There were twigs floating on the water that indicated a strong undercurrent. It could have been popular feeling, of course, and not Baruch influence. The left-wingers convinced the President it was Baruch, plus "other reactionary influences."

This was extremely unfortunate for the country, because it was at this precise moment of his nose dive in popularity in Administration councils that he returned from Europe convinced that stockpiling of strategic materials could not wait.

It will be recalled that Baruch had urged stockpiling of tin and rubber as early as 1934. At that time, however, he thought of its importance in terms of shipping over the long transpacific haul. Also he envisioned it as a happy solution of the war-debt controversy. He thought it would allay some of the bitterness in this country against the very nations, Britain and France, whose Allies we were almost sure to become again in a world war.

But in 1938 he came back from his talks with Churchill and others convinced that the United States was going to become embroiled in a war not only against Germany, but against Japan also. This meant war in the Pacific. Neither he nor Churchill foresaw the extent of the disaster in the Pacific. They did not contemplate the overrunning of all the Dutch East Indies and Malaya, the fall of Singapore, and the crippling of the United States fleet at Pearl Harbor.

But Baruch, on his return from Europe in 1938, told everyone he could get to listen to him that war in the Pacific would mean cutting our shipping lanes in that ocean, and hence it was imperative for this country to lay in stocks of tin, rubber, and other vital materials that we normally get from that quarter of the globe.

Early in his fight for the stockpiling of strategic materials Baruch did succeed in interesting one New Dealer in one phase of the problem. Secretary of Agriculture Henry A. Wallace listened to the warnings about our supplies of rubber being cut off and at once became an enthusiastic advocate of development of new sources of rubber in Latin America.

So from 1934 until 1939 Baruch fought for stockpiles of rubber, while Wallace fought, also in vain, for appropriations that would aid rubber culture in the tropical portions of this hemisphere. By 1939 Baruch, always seeking a hole in whatever wall was blocking him, conceived the idea of swapping cotton for the strategic materials needed. He had been worried about the cotton-surplus problem for years, had tried to do something about it as long before as in the Hoover administration.

Wallace embraced this idea, and, on August 11, 1939, there

was enacted a law as a result of which this country swapped 600,-000 bales of cotton for 90,000 tons of rubber, enough, a witness told the Truman Committee, to make 18,000,000 tires.

Despite his talks with Churchill and others in Europe, Baruch maintained in public statements that it might be possible for the United States to avoid getting into the next world war if proper precautions were taken. These were:

1. To make ourselves so strong that any nation would hesitate to attack us, a policy that would include not only having a strong army, navy, air force, and planned war-industries setup, but also ample stocks of all strategic materials not produced in the United States.

2. To pursue a neutrality policy as near incident-proof as possible.

To this end he appeared before the Senate Foreign Relations Committee in April, 1939, insisting, among other things, that "there ain't no such animal" as international law and that "neutrality" really is just as elusive.

He advocated what has been called the "cash and carry" plan, the chief point of which was that any cargo lost through the destruction of a ship at sea during a war would not bring about any claim for payment to American owners.

But he admitted again and again to the committee that he could not reconcile his heart and his head. His heart inclined him so strongly to avoid war, he said, but his head could not always follow.

Meanwhile the friendship between Baruch and Mrs. Roosevelt had been ripening beautifully. The two had learned that there were several highly controversial subjects on which they agreed heartily. By dint of avoiding economic questions they got along splendidly. Soon Mrs. Roosevelt was interlarding many of her conversations with: "You know, Mr. Baruch says. . . ."

This fitted in perfectly with Baruch's constant attempt to keep in close contact with the White House, but frost again nipped the budding plant. The 1940 campaign brought another of Baruch's "boys" into the firing line against Roosevelt.

Back in 1936 some of the most effective speeches made for Roosevelt were those of Hugh Johnson. But in 1940, Johnson took the stump for Wendell Willkie, and when Johnson talked and when he wrote in his newspaper column, he had none of the suavity and politeness of his beloved chief, Baruch. On the contrary he did what Bob Fitzsimmons had told Baruch to do when boxing, hit with the firm intention of knocking his opponent's block off.

The opponent, in this case, was Franklin D. Roosevelt. Johnson didn't bother much about Willkie's virtues. He concerned himself with Roosevelt's weak spots. Further, Johnson had the gift of phrasing the mildest sort of attack in words that made it hurt a lot worse than a much more serious attack by most other writers and orators. People liked to listen to him on the radio, whether they agreed with him or not. He was definitely good entertainment, no matter what he talked about.

Naturally, Johnson's attacks on the Administration caused resentment in White House circles, and all of it was blamed on Baruch. In fact, Roosevelt and many close to him suspected that Johnson was saying what the suave Baruch would never say, but what he really thought, perhaps even what he was saying, in private, to Johnson.

This again was a very unfortunate combination of circumstances, for the country! It resulted in Baruch's sitting a great many days on that bench in La Fayette Park without the "lunch flag" being raised. It resulted, perhaps unconsciously, in efforts on the part of the President to avoid even the appearance of taking Baruch's advice.

A study of the preparations this country made, as it drifted closer and closer to war from 1938 to December, 1941, reveals a very sharp line of division between what might be called the strictly military classification and the industrial mobilization for which Baruch had been preaching since 1919.

Many critics agree that what was done on the strictly military side was as much as the President could have done, taking into consideration the large pacifist minority and its representation in Congress. It was the ignoring of the lessons Baruch had learned from experience in the First World War that caused Johnson to remark, shortly before he died, that "those kings did not want advice either." Johnson was referring to the ancient Hebrew kings who ignored the advice of Baruch's ancestors.

First there was the Stettinius War Resources Board. It was supposed to lay the groundwork for industrial mobilization. Washington newspapermen understood that this board eventually made a report, but the report was never made public, and key figures in later setups did not seem to know anything about what the Stettinius Board recommended.

Churchill had expected Baruch to be at the head of a new War Industries Board. Plans for such a board, without of course designating any individual members, had been brought up to date by the War Department. With Baruch's advice the War Department had worked out these plans, constantly revising them with changing conditions, through the years since 1919.

Baruch insisted to friends who wanted him to direct the job that he was too old now to take such a responsibility. "But I know who the men are who are capable of doing the various jobs," he would always add, and then, a little impishly, "and they would work for me!"

Baruch's cardinal principle with regard to any such board was that one man should head it and be the boss, responsible only to the President.

In fairness to the President it should be stated that no matter in how high favor Baruch had been at the White House in the period from 1938 to 1941 this particular idea would probably not have been adopted at the outset. In sharp contrast to Woodrow Wilson, who would appoint a man to do a job and then actually protect that man from interference by friends who might be much closer to Wilson, Roosevelt infinitely preferred the plan of getting divergent and sometimes mentally antagonistic groups to work on whatever he was planning. He would then force those in conflict to work out a compromise and thus reach the solution.

This characteristic Roosevelt policy was one reason for the selection of a giant with two heads to run another early substitute for the War Industries Board, now almost forgotten but known at the time as SPAB, directed by William S. Knudsen, former president of General Motors, and Sidney Hillman, labor leader.

It is interesting that every change made in this industrial mobilization setup tended toward the plan that had been waiting, in War Department pigeonholes, since the beginning—the Baruch War Industries Board plan as brought up to date.

It is also interesting, if a little depressing, to note that every step made in the attempts to prevent inflation, by OPA rationing, price fixing, etc., was also back toward the plan that Baruch had preached since 1919. Failure to adopt his general price-ceiling plan, as of some day *before* war pressures began boosting prices and wages, made inevitable the headaches of the Price Administrators, not to mention the War Labor Board's difficulties over the Little Steel formula and other wage controversies.

Baruch's plans for preventing inflation, postwar booms, and the inevitable depressions that followed, had changed very little since 1919, but they were not static. For example, he slowly came to the conclusion that it would be necessary, in fixing price ceilings as of some day prior to the beginning of the emergency, to freeze wages also.

When he opposed Newton D. Baker and others on piecemeal price fixing in the twenties before committees he had not made

Brown Brothers

AT THE PRESIDENT'S BIRTHDAY BALL, 1942

With his daughter Mrs. Samstag (l.) and Mrs. Leonard Plugge of London.

this last point. But on September 19, 1941, before the House Banking and Currency Committee, he said:

"I do not believe in piecemeal price fixing. I think you have first to put a ceiling over the whole price structure, including wages, rents and farm prices, up to the parity level, and no higher, and then to adjust separate price schedules upward separately, if necessary, where justice or governmental policy so require."

The politicians did not like that. Congress passed a bill doing precisely the opposite. Long after Leon Henderson, the first Price Administrator, had run into labor complications he opposed wage fixing, ignoring the simple Baruch two-plus-two-equal-four formula that wages constitute by far the greatest element of cost in everything, and hence must be kept down if prices are to be held down. Henderson was converted—much later.

"They never want to take Baruch's advice until the trouble has become serious," a friend commented. "They wait until it is too late and then do what he advised the year before."

But they kept on asking for it. They remembered that he was right last time, when they had ignored it.

CHAPTER . . . TWENTY-NINE

BARUCH sat on his famous park bench one day in the late spring of 1942 wearing an intent but frustrated expression. Two men were sitting by him, talking earnestly. Baruch was silent. He didn't understand a single idea either of the men was expressing. Every sentence contained some technical term or formula that escaped him. The two men were James B. Conant and Earl T. Compton, who with Baruch constituted the special committee just appointed by the President to work out some solution for the rubber problem.

"When you fellows get through talking Chinese," Baruch finally broke in, "please let me know, as I believe then we can go ahead and declare a dividend."

Baruch had been seeking a solution to this country's rubber problem for nearly forty years. In the hope of a profit he had sent expeditions all over the world and had actually begun profitable production in Mexico, from guayule, though the revolution had put an end to it. Then from 1934 right up to the outbreak of the war he had urged stockpiling of this precious substance but had been only partly successful in bringing about government action.

When, shortly after Pearl Harbor, the Army, Navy, bus and truck operators, and civilians were all frightened to death that there would not be enough tires, he was the logical man to head any group assigned to study the problem.

The committee reported that summer. There is space here for

but a few highlights, but it is interesting to note that there has never been any important criticism of the report from any quarter. The Army, the Navy, the bus operators, the rubber industry —all approved it unqualifiedly.

One item became politically important. This was the recommendation that gasoline rationing should be applied, at once, all over the country instead of merely on the East Coast. The report insisted that the chief reason for limiting gas sales was to save not gas but tires, and hence the restriction should be nationwide. Naturally there was a great outcry against anything of the sort, and as a result there was considerable delay before this recommendation was put into effect. This delay proved very expensive to rubber conservation.

Other recommendations were:

"That no speed above 35 miles an hour be permitted for passenger cars and trucks. (In this way the life of tires will be prolonged by nearly 40 per cent.)

"That the annual average mileage per car now estimated as 6,700 miles be held down to 5,000 miles, a reduction of 25 per cent. (This does not mean that each has a right to 5,000 miles; it applies to necessary driving.)

"That more rubber than is now given to the public be released to fully maintain, by recapping or new tires, necessary civilian driving.

"That a new rationing system of gasoline be devised, based on this 5,000 miles a year to save tires.

"That compulsory periodic tire inspection be instituted.

"That a voluntary tire conservation program be put into effect until gasoline rationing can be established."

Most of these recommendations were carried out by the government.

Another important recommendation that was carried out concerned the administrative setup.

"There have been many adjustments and readjustments—" the report said, "a 'stop and go' policy—in the synthetic rubber program. Some of these were inevitable; some appear to be the result of bad administration."

The committee recommended that a Rubber Administrator be appointed, under the WPB but with a considerable measure of authority. This was done and apparently worked very well.

Why had not this government ascertained from Russia its ten-year-old and successful method of producing synthetic rubber? This question, posed by the committee with considerable emphasis, has never been answered. As a matter of fact it was more than a year after the report was made before satisfactory progress was reported on this.

The report did not name names in its indictment of governmental errors, but it named agencies, and everyone knew who was meant. Thus it stated that the conflict between the Rubber Reserve Company, a subsidiary of the RFC, and the Office of Petroleum Coordinator had "delayed and complicated the bringing in of new facilities for the production of butadiene from oil." It said that it had taken "six weeks of repeated effort for the Rubber Branch of the WPB, desiring to launch a program of education throughout the industry, to get this vital information released by the Rubber Reserve."

Hammering the same line it insisted that "to make certain there are no construction delays because of conflicting authority, the construction of all plants and equipment concerned with the production and purification of butadiene from oil shall be under the direction of the Rubber Administrator."

The Petroleum Coordinator, the report said, could supervise the operation of these plants, after construction, "but he shall not change the presently authorized program (or plans for operation) except as approved by the Rubber Administrator."

"In war," the report stated, "one cannot wait upon perfection.

Any weapon on the battlefield is better than the best weapon on a blueprint. The committee recommends that the present program be pushed forward with the greatest possible speed, without further change, except that if new projects are adopted, they be made *additions* to the present program."

The committee then recommended that there be another increase of 30,000 tons of Buna S, to come from an *additional* plant to be erected in 1943 and be in operation in 1944.

This plant, the committee recommended, should be located in the grain area. Interesting in connection with the later shortage of alcohol for liquor, which promised to cut so seriously into government revenues, was the recommendation also that a plant capable of producing 100,000,000 gallons of alcohol be erected in the grain area accessible to water transportation. The latter was to make it possible, after the war, for molasses to be brought to the plants by barges in the event that manufacture of alcohol from grain should prove uneconomical. Baruch was thinking of reconversion and postwar employment problems.

The report stressed the point that even construction of this plant might not provide enough alcohol-producing capacity. It quoted the Secretary of Agriculture as saying that, after all food requirements that could then be anticipated should be met, there would still be upward of a billion and a quarter bushels of wheat left on this continent. Alcohol plants, it stated, could be produced with little use of scarce materials.

Incidentally, in that report in midsummer of 1942 the need of more fabricating facilities for tires was pointed out. By 1944 WPB discovered this virtually as a new problem!

By this time Baruch had nearly attained the position he craved —Dr. Fixit for his country's problems. His only complaint was that he was usually called in only after a lot of mistakes had been made and precious time, which in war usually means lives, had been wasted.

His next task, the man-power problem occasioned by enormous expansion of shipbuilding, airplane, and other plants on the Pacific Coast, was given him by James F. Byrnes, who had resigned from the Supreme Bench to become Director of the Office of War Mobilization. The report on this was made by Baruch and John M. Hancock, one of the few survivors of the old War Industries Board group, on August 19, 1943.

It was known on Capitol Hill that Baruch and Hancock had made their report, but the legislators and newspapers did not know what was to be done about it, as weeks passed with no public announcement, even of the text. So favorably did congressmen recall the rubber report that they were sure the man-power report would be valuable, and they were afraid it was pigeonholed.

On the floor of the Senate Arthur Vandenberg, of Michigan, a Republican, demanded that the report be made public immediately. Whereupon Director Byrnes wrote the Senator, on September 15, advising him that the Baruch-Hancock report had been translated into action. Mr. Byrnes requested that the text of the report be printed in the Congressional Record, because, he said, though simply an interoffice memorandum, it was "a splendid argument in favor of the action which was taken by the War Mobilization Committee on September 4, which is set forth in the program herewith enclosed."

Baruch and Hancock proposed the application of a simple budget system to the problem—a budget for labor! The WPB should be charged with responsibility, no contracts assigned (as had been done repeatedly) to communities where the supply of labor was already strained, manufacturers limited as to the number of persons they could employ, workers limited in their choice of jobs.

"Without arguing the merits of a National Service Act," the report said, "which is for Congress to decide—it can be said that everything called for in the labor-budget plan would be necessary in the administration of such an act."

Most important, the report insisted that the plan must be enforced by *local* authorities.

"There must be adequate delegation of power from all Washington agencies to their West coast representatives and the communities themselves must get on the team. The job cannot be done from Washington. . . . The time must end when agencies spend their energies battling to build up empires of power. It is time to reassert the fact there is one Federal Government—speaking with one voice—not a 'centimouth.' "

There were gentlemen in high places in Washington who did not like that sort of language and particularly did not like its being published in any document carrying the prestige of Bernard M. Baruch's imprint. It is not surprising, therefore, that Byrnes, eager to carry out Baruch's recommendations, still hesitated to make the document's text available until his hand was forced by Congress.

Cost plus contracts were attacked as being an incentive to the hoarding of labor, and then there was another shrewd businesslike admonition:

"Until now the energies of Government have been directed principally at reducing the five, ten, or fifteen cents of a production dollar that goes into profits. While not relaxing our efforts to prevent profiteering, it is time we turned our attention to reducing the 85, 90, or 95 cents of the production dollar represented by costs."

An amusing illustration of Baruch's stubbornness appeared further along in the text. He knew that Roosevelt's favorite method of attacking any problem, whether it was the writing of one of his speeches or the working out of a new proposal, was to set several different groups to work on it and then reconcile the differences in compromise.

"There are entirely too many agencies," the report said, "studying these problems, arguing abstract issues, and not getting enough done."

He didn't worry about being tactful as to the feelings of congressmen either. One complaint in the report was that too much time of skilled plant managers and workmen was taken up by their being summoned before visiting congressional committees. Some of the West Coast aircraft manufacturers told the committee, and this was duly included in the report, that *one-fourth* of their time was being taken up answering government inquiries and questionnaires and in being interviewed by representatives from different government agencies.

As chairman of the Aircraft Production Board, Charles E. Wilson should take steps to reduce the number of inquiries and interviews to which airplane manufacturers were subjected, the report said.

One paragraph of the report dwelt on the uncertainty of manufacturers about contract termination and urged that the elements of uncertainty on this point be cleared as soon as possible.

Outside of the immediate problem of winning the war, there was concern throughout the country during 1943 over the problems that peace would bring—particularly contract termination, employment in peacetime pursuits of returned soldiers and sailors and ex-warworkers, disposal of government-owned surplus materials at the cessation of hostilities, and disposition of the huge government-owned plants of various types.

Not only in Washington, where many government officials were studying the problem, many with the thought of spreading government ownership, but all through the country this was regarded as the Number One economic, political, and social problem. Many economists were predicting a wild boom right after the armistice, to be followed by a deep depression, with widespread unemployment. An astonishing number added to this the prediction that thereupon we would be forced to abandon the capitalistic system.

Baruch was assigned to study this problem, also, and this time, as in the man-power study, he had John M. Hancock as his coworker.

The resulting report was good news for advocates of individual enterprise.

"It is our conviction," it said, "that we will emerge from the war with the greatest opportunities any people ever had. A post-war depression is not inevitable. One half of the world will need rebuilding. Enormous demands, put aside during the war and added to pre-war demands, await satisfaction. Much depends on the settlement of the peace. If it be one under which men and women can look forward with hope—not fear—there will not be enough hands to do what needs to be done."

Much would depend, the report declared, on the measures approved in planning for peace and, just as important, on the men assigned to carry them out. Mistakes made in mobilization should not be repeated in the demobilization.

Then came a sharp slap for the left-wingers:

"There has been too much loose parroting of the slogan, that if individual enterprise fails to provide jobs for everyone, it must be replaced by some one of the other systems that are around. The war has been a crucible for all of the economic systems of the world, for our own, for Communism, Fascism, Nazism, all the others. And the American system has outproduced the world."

There was a stern warning against special groups and inflation:

"America's productive capacity can perform still another miracle in a fine and lasting peace. It will not do so if pressure groups are permitted to turn that productive capacity into a battleground for their own selfish interests or inflate ourselves out of the world market."

Having watched most of his advice with respect to universal price-ceiling fixing go unheeded, Baruch was more concerned about the dangers of inflation than almost anything else in the economic picture. By the term "inflate ourselves out of the world market," he meant, of course, that if our price structure were permitted to soar, including wages and all other costs of production, we would not be able to sell anything abroad except at a loss.

"Speed in shifting this productive capacity from war to peace," the report declared, "is our most effective attack against the two enemies which threaten in the transition and post-war period—*unemployment and inflation.*"

Baruch and Hancock pulled no punches in attacking Comptroller General Lindsay C. Warren's plan for auditing *before* payment. Warren appeared before congressional committees both before and after the report was made, using spectacular cases of War Department extravagance to justify his position.

The Comptroller's plan, the report said, "would quibble the nation into a panic. . . . It means unemployment by audit. . . .

"If such an audit before payment were decreed, no war contractor would know where he stood, prime contractors would be unable to pay subcontractors, banks would be reluctant to make adequate loans, billions in working capital would be frozen. The delays in settlement could force many concerns into bankruptcy. . . .

"We recommend quick, fair, and final settlement of terminated war contracts through negotiations by the contractors and the procurement agencies. . . . The men who made the contracts or who have administered them are the best persons to unmake them."

Precautions against fraud were recommended, including a requirement that all records should be kept for at least 3 years.

Immediate payment in full for all completed articles was

recommended, as was 100 per cent of the government's estimate of all factual items, where proof ordinarily is simple, such as direct labor or materials, and of other items on which the government is able to satisfy itself, up to 90 per cent of the contractor's estimated costs. Settlements by contractors with subcontractors should be reimbursed in full by the government as soon as approved.

These recommendations for prompt settlements, without waiting for audits by the Comptroller of the Treasury, raised a storm on Capitol Hill. Friends of Comptroller Lindsay Warren rallied to his support. A meeting of the House Military Affairs Committee reported a bill to the House of Representatives providing for audit by the Comptroller's office *before* payments. The report was signed by twelve members of the committee. Within a day or two a "minority" report was filed, signed by the other thirteen members of the committee.

Chairman A. J. May took a lot of kidding about his "majority" report! He was even more annoyed when he learned that the House did not intend to pay any attention to the Military Committee on this legislation, but did intend to follow the Baruch pattern rather closely. Another committee, that on Judiciary, handled the measure.

Baruch and Hancock in their report proposed a system of T (termination) loans to aid manufacturers in converting their plants from war to peacetime production. These were to be made by local banks, and guaranteed by the government, but the government was to make them direct if for any reason bank loans were not forthcoming.

The report also voiced a warning to Congress about the legislation that their termination plan would involve.

"The only purpose of contract settlement," it said, "is to pay what the Government owes. Contract settlement should not be used for punishment or reward, for making better or worse the position of manufacturers, workers, or the public."

Note the significance of those last three words!

"Attempts to turn the settlement legislation into a band wagon for special interests should be fought off. To the extent that the simple purpose of settlement becomes involved with other issues, passage of the legislation will be delayed. The result, should Germany collapse suddenly, might be calamitous."

Government machinery and supplies in private plants must be removed within 60 days after the inventory, in order to clear the plants for peacetime pursuits, the report declared, adding that the contractor should have the right to move and store them sooner at his own risk.

Constant studies should be made by the army, navy, and other agencies to determine what could be sold while the war is still in progress. Everything possible should be sold the moment it becomes certain these particular articles would not be needed for the war.

"Market conditions will never be better," says the report, succinctly. "Effective action now could reduce enormously the likely surpluses that will be left for after the war."

Appointment was recommended of a Surplus Property Administrator, who should be advised, though retaining full and final authority, by a board composed of representatives of all agencies interested. Then, all sales should be made "in a goldfish bowl" as far as publicity is concerned.

Constant study of possible cancellations should be maintained, the report urged, for the same reason that studies of the needs for surplus materials should be continued while the war is still raging, to keep down so far as possible the amount of surplus material peace will find the government holding.

"Where there have been war expansions, far beyond any possible postwar future, it will be better to cancel war contracts earlier, and begin reducing the 'bloat,' than to wait until it has to be done all at once."

Construction of homes, nurseries, and other projects in war communities, it was pointed out, might be avoided by timely information as to cancellations.

"X Day" planning is one of the striking recommendations. The idea is not only to draw up plans including all possible moves, contract cancellations, etc., that will be made on the day Germany stops fighting, but to have the fullest possible publicity for these plans, for the guidance of contractors and communities.

Before selling any war equipment abroad, it is insisted, possible needs for it in this country should be explored. As to plants owned by the government, outright sales were preferred.

"The disposal agencies, though, should exchange properties and lease as well as sell; also sell on credit, not solely for cash. This will assure smaller enterprises opportunities that would otherwise be denied them. . . .

"This red flag of warning is raised. Leasing must not become a hidden device for the Government to compete with private plants; it must not become a hidden device for subsidies—by any name—to anyone. Once plants leave the Government's hands they must stand on their own feet competitively."

Baruch and Hancock hit hard at one large group of economists in this paragraph:

"Let no one feel that precious surpluses will bear down upon us and destroy us; that vast amounts of metals, raw materials, ships and airplanes will smother us and engulf us. These are assets of tremendous value. They will be real forces not alone in making the peace but in opening to the whole world, and therefore to us, vast opportunities. As soon as our Government obtains possession of cotton, or gold, or silver, or ships, or planes, or other evidences of power or wealth, these possessions suddenly seem to become less valuable in the eyes of others. Remember the fox in Aesop's fable, who, when he lost his tail, wanted the other foxes to cut off theirs."

Baruch always mentioned this particular fable, from 1933 on, when anyone asked him about the supposed danger of gold becoming of small value, once this country had bought most of it, with no countries on the gold standard.

"Winston Churchill has said he did not accept his portfolio in order to liquidate His Majesty's empire," Baruch and Hancock said. "No American should accept a portfolio to liquidate American living standards. . . . The living standards of the world must be lifted—and ours go higher—not our standards be dragged down to those of others."

In a speech before the Academy of Political Science in New York on April 12, 1944, Director of War Mobilization James F. Byrnes said: "The constructive report of B. M. Baruch and John Hancock on the problems of postwar readjustments has gone far to dispel the fog of controversy which had hung over the discussions of the termination of war contracts and the disposition of surplus property."

CHAPTER . . . THIRTY

BARUCH'S hold on the imagination of the plain people—the man in the street and the housewife in the home—had become legendary even before he was assigned to the task of working out a postwar economic program. It continued to grow as his recommendations were praised by nearly all commentators, and the Baruch-Hancock report became virtually a blueprint not only for the White House but for Congress.

The left-wingers who did not like it went unheard. To the farmers, little merchants, mechanics, and taxi drivers it *had* to be just what the doctor ordered for the country's good. Hadn't *Baruch* written it? When was Baruch wrong about anything?

There was the butcher in Baltimore, cringing under an attack by some wrought-up housewives who couldn't get what they wanted.

"Listen, ladies," he said, "Barney Baruch just took a job in Washington and soon everything is going to be a lot better."

When told the story Baruch hastened to explain that he was not a miracle man. People must not be led to expect too much. But he could hardly conceal his smile, and his eyes were twinkling. He appreciated that tribute far more than, 50 years earlier, he had valued a huge profit in the stock market. It carried all the savor of a spontaneous burst of applause for an artist's performance.

The financier was similarly pleased with reactions from Capitol Hill. Friends and admirers among the senators and representatives had been numerous for many years, but now he was being recognized as the final arbiter on legislative proposals affecting postwar employment, business, taxes, and economics generally. In fact he was now the Elder Statesman for America.

To make the picture as near perfection as may be, human nature duly considered, he seemed to have won his 12-year campaign to wear Franklin D. Roosevelt down with amiability and good advice. The ups and downs in his relationship with the President, the setbacks and the sniping from the left-wingers, seemed to be over. It appeared that while he had lost a lot of battles he had won the war.

Evidence of this came in April, 1944, while echoes of the chorus of approval of the postwar report were still resounding. The President and Baruch slipped down to Hobcaw for a proposed visit of 2 weeks. Once down there the climate and relaxation proved so beneficial to Mr. Roosevelt's health that the stay was extended to 4 weeks.

Normally it would have been out of season for Hobcaw vacations. There is no hunting in April and May. But the President wanted to fish, to bask in the sun, and rest, and Hobcaw is ideal for such a program in the spring.

After Baruch himself, perhaps the happiest man about this consummation was General E. M. "Pa" Watson, the President's military aide. For years the general had been slowly fitting into the niche made vacant when Admiral Cary T. Grayson died. He had enjoyed many trips down to Hobcaw, loved the hunting, and had become very much attached to Baruch.

While this triangular relationship of Roosevelt, Watson, and Baruch was not precisely similar to that twenty-odd years earlier of Wilson, Grayson, and Baruch, it had many points of similarity. Both Grayson and Watson possessed tremendous personal charm. Both would have denied ever attempting to advise their presi-

Brown Brothers

ELDER STATESMAN

A Recent Portrait.

dents, but both were daily companions and regarded by their chiefs with strong affection.

What the left-wingers in the Administration thought about all this, and particularly what they thought when Mrs. Roosevelt showed strong approval of the President's visiting Baruch's estate for his vacation, may be passed over. Their chief hope, as this is written, is that the summer of 1944 is just another phase—that after the November election things will be different!

This is not feared by those who have known Baruch any length of time.

"Any man who talks to Baruch every day for four weeks," one senator commented after the President's return, "will have an enormous admiration for him the rest of his life. I think this means that Roosevelt has completely forgiven Baruch for not having been in F.D.R.'s corner in his fight for the nomination back in 1932."

At the time of this unexpected vacation at Hobcaw with President Roosevelt, Baruch's physical condition was better than it had been for years. Even his hearing had been aided by a new device. Health and physical fitness had been a fetish with him since his youth. He believed them of the utmost importance even in purely mental contacts.

All through the years he kept up his exercises. Hunting, horseback riding, and walking he loved. Golf he played occasionally, though more frequently for the companionship than because of any devotion to the game. A little shadow boxing and other exercises every morning were routine.

He stopped smoking fairly early in life, for his health's sake. Enjoying food as much as a sixteen-year-old, even in his seventies, he follows a rigorous diet, almost never touching red meat, rich foods, oysters (and he loved to eat the delicious small oysters for which the Hobcaw dinner table is noted), or most desserts. He drinks a brand of bottled water that he believes good for him and eats lots of fruit for the same reason. Actually he loves a drink but he has to have some special excuse to take one, such as sickness in the house!

For years he suffered from "poor man's gout," as Dr. Grayson called it. This was responsible for starting him on the diet he followed, but he practiced self-denial at the table to an extent that aroused admiration from many of his friends, who frankly admitted not having much character in the presence of delectable viands.

While Baruch was in the South, recognition of his services came from another quarter. Dr. Guy Emery Shipler, editor of *The Churchman*, announced, on April 20, that Baruch had been chosen for the 1944 *Churchman* award for "the promotion of good-will and understanding among all peoples." He had been selected, it was announced, "after a nation-wide poll among members of The Churchman Association and leaders of church, industry and the professions." In previous years this award had been bestowed on Mrs. Franklin D. Roosevelt, William Allen White, Wendell L. Willkie, President Roosevelt, and Madame Chiang Kai-shek.

Just before his trip down to Hobcaw with President Roosevelt, Baruch took the first step toward accomplishing another long-cherished ambition, setting up a research foundation that he hoped would be of enormous benefit to mankind in general and returning soldiers in particular.

He provided $1,100,000 for the promotion of "physical medicine," especially for war veterans to whom such treatment might prove beneficial. "If it works out," he said in announcing the gift, "I am prepared to put most of my fortune into it—I believe in it. . . .

"I am convinced that returning men and women now in the armed forces will need the advantages of physical medicine, and

I feel that this program will help restore discharged soldiers to normal physical and mental conditions."

The plan calls for research in massages, water, light, heat, cold, electricity, occupational pursuits, exercises, muscular manipulations, and various mechanical devices in the diagnoses and treatment of diseases.

The money was distributed as follows:

$400,000 to the Columbia University College of Physicians and Surgeons.

$250,000 to New York University College of Medicine.

$250,000 to the Medical College of Virginia, at Richmond.

$100,000 to various other medical schools.

$100,000 to provide fellowships and residencies.

The survey for the program (of course Baruch would get the facts before acting) was made by a committee headed by Dr. Ray Lyman Wilbur, chancellor of Stanford University and an old friend of Baruch. Dr. Frank Krusen, professor of physical medicine at the University of Minnesota, agreed to act as chairman of the committee that will put the program into effect. Dr. Krusen's headquarters, for this assignment, were at the Mayo Clinic, at Rochester, Minnesota.

Baruch announced that the gift was in honor of his father, Dr. Simon Baruch, of whose record and achievements Baruch was enormously proud. It was Dr. Baruch's interest in physical medicine, particularly treatment by water, that resulted in the family's moving to New York from South Carolina. So interested was Dr. Baruch in research that in 1900 Baruch persuaded his father to retire from active practice so as to give all his time to medical research.

Many of the results of his experiments are preserved in the Army Medical Library, in Washington, as is also Dr. Baruch's first effort in print, called "Two Penetrating Bayonet Wounds of the Chest" and published in *The Confederate States Medical and Surgical Journal.*

Fellow Confederate surgeons might well have called Simon Baruch Dr. Facts, as a Virginia-born President later called his son. The doctor insisted on more investigation of the curious differences between the effects of bayonet and gunshot wounds and hence the necessity for entirely dissimilar treatment to get the best results.

In the concluding paragraph of this article Dr. Baruch urged that first-aid instructions be given the soldiers, so that they would not make the mistake of using the same type of treatment for gunshot and for bayonet wounds.

The Army Medical Library also preserves a copy of Dr. Baruch's *Reminiscences of a Confederate Surgeon,* which was published in 1915, and an address by the doctor on January 19, 1918, which was virtually a biography of Robert E. Lee, delivered before the Confederate Veterans Camp of New York at the Hotel Astor.

Baruch's admiration, as well as affection, for his father, was pronounced. The only time he had an important difference of opinion with the doctor he became convinced later that his father was right. Dr. Baruch had insisted that the terms granted Germany at Versailles were too light, that trouble would result. Baruch thought at the time his father wanted to go too far.

CHAPTER . . . THIRTY-ONE

EVEN in his seventies there are indications that Baruch's attraction for women—and theirs for him—is a constant source of worry to his entourage. He never made any bones about liking good-looking women, and, if a touch of glamour were added—for example, if the lady were a grand-opera singer or a famous actress—he would positively purr as he turned on the charm.

He is a fine-looking man, well over 6 feet, straight as the ramrod of his boyhood shotgun, with no trace of a bald spot in his well-kept white hair, not a pound of superfluous fat, and he radiates vigor, so that it is not surprising that his would-be protectors are on the alert.

Baruch not only likes the game that this attempt to protect him provides, but is flattered by it. Nor does he resent intimations that he has cream on his whiskers. It has seemed to some of his friends that he uses this protective ring just as he uses his deafness, as an occasional defense against boredom.

Incidentally, the one enthuiasm of Baruch that is not shared by his children, the love of politics and politicians, is another important bastion against designing females. Many a lady who thought she was making a conquest suddenly found herself almost forgotten when some senator turned Baruch's mind to economics or politics. Romeo would turn Polonius before the lady could mention her telephone number.

When a woman comes along who is not only beautiful and witty, but also important in government, that is a bombshell, or, more accurately, that is Clare Boothe Luce. Mrs. Luce is a Republican, and that is against her from Baruch's standpoint, but then Baruch does not dislike individual Republicans.

It has been said that Baruch is never too busy to chat with a pretty woman and that the girls at the newsstands of hotels where he stays know him and like him. It is also true that Baruch likes to talk with cabdrivers or with any farmer he happens to meet—in fact, with almost anybody.

There are several hundred people in Washington who still tell about the time, in the War Industries Board days, when Baruch picked them up as he drove down to his office and carried them to theirs. The impression on them was tremendous. They always tell you how interested *he* was in what they had to say. Sometimes they remember a sentence or so he said. They have been quoting it ever since. Some few were thus given a ride, in at least two senses of the expression, twice. The second time they were enchanted to find that he remembered them from the first time and remembered something *they* had said.

The man has an amazing memory. In the days when he played bridge he never had to wonder if the ten of diamonds had been played; he knew. This may not seem extraordinary to a good bridge player, but Baruch has that sort of memory about everything in which he is the slightest bit interested and about a great many things in which it would seem unlikely that he could have any concern.

When Baruch would pick up Jim Smith at R and Sixteenth, on his way downtown, he would not only remember that he picked up Jim once before, but that it was at Q Street the former time, and he would ask if the toothache from which Jim was suffering had given him any more trouble. If it was Sally Jones, Baruch would remember the dress or coat she had on last time.

"Certainly I remember you," he said to a man he met casually at a luncheon. "We were both at Union Station trying to get a cab. I was going to the Carleton and you were going to the Statler, so we rode down together. You were worried about axles for busses."

Baruch knows perfectly well the effect of that sort of thing. He knew in the First World War days what Jim Smith and Sally Jones would be saying about him. He knew in the Second World War what the man interested in bus axles would think. He enjoys tremendously the good will of people and constantly works to win it. It is the trait that most good politicians have—the willingness to take a little trouble to produce the good feeling they desire. It seldom happens unless the person exerting the charm *enjoys* the effort as well as the result, which is one answer to why there are so many poor politicians.

In spending all this effort for good will that he has no thought of ever using—in which he differs from the politician, who intends to capitalize it—Baruch does not feel that he is wasting time. He is merely giving the back of his head a chance to function. He is letting his subconscious mind work.

Everyone has had experiences in which his subconscious mind solved a problem he was unable to unravel by conscious cerebration. Whoever first said that he would sleep on it before making a decision may not have been thinking of his subconscious mind, but he knew from experience that he often had the solution in the morning. The reporter who plays poker until the last possible minute before the deadline to write his story often not only writes a better story, but takes an entirely different and more interesting angle than he had planned before being enticed into the card game. The back of his head was working.

Since there has been some public discussion of this, a great many lazy men have used it as an alibi. Baruch is one of the few nonlazy people who actually take a pride in their subconscious mental functioning. In his case he believes it responsible for many of his famous hunches.

Emphatically this does not mean that one should play a hunch without having done any serious thinking, above all not without the necessary gathering of all the facts. It is no question of sticking a pencil in a racing card with one's eyes closed and betting on the horse thus selected.

Once in possession of all the facts obtainable, however, and having given plenty of conscious thought to the problem, one frequently finds that the working of the subconscious mind, Baruch thinks, will suddenly bring the whole picture into focus, and one has the solution.

Be all this as it may, it is very difficult to make a good case against Baruch on it. He has been right too often.

This idea of getting all the impressions, as well as facts, clearly in mind, and then depending on the back of his head for the answer is not a recent development in the Baruch method of operation. In the War Industries Board days, when he had almost the power of life and death over American industry, he early devised the system of refusing to talk with lawyers representing any concern that was trying to present a case. He made it clear to companies that wanted something from the Board that if their presidents or general managers would come to Washington he would be very glad to see them, but if they sent their lawyers he would have to insist on the War Industries Board lawyers seeing them. Many sent their lawyers, feeling safer that way. They discovered, if they had more than one experience with the Board, that they did much better by having their practical men talk with Baruch.

What Baruch wanted, and what he practically forced by this stratagem, was a plain statement of the facts. He would listen to all sides, and suddenly, without a conscious effort to produce it, the answer would pop into his mind. He never had to reduce it to a formula. He didn't have to pile one bit of evidence on another in logical order, as does the supersleuth in the last chapter of a detective story. That is done for him by the back of his head.

The late Clinton W. Gilbert, former assistant editor of the *New York Tribune*, was much impressed by this working of Baruch's mind at the Versailles Peace Conference.

"I would go to Mr. X," he said, naming a very prominent figure, "and pose my problem. Mr. X would at once begin to discuss it, building up one seemingly logical point upon another, until he had erected a structure of such convincing strength that I would be filled with admiration for his logic, and ashamed of myself that I had not been able to reason the thing out so clearly for myself. I would leave him in no doubt whatever as to the answer.

"Then I would go to Baruch. He would listen politely to the question, perhaps ask me a few questions, and then we would get into a conversation which seemed mostly off on tangents from the immediate question. But before I left he would invariably say what he thought the answer was.

"The funny part of this is," Gilbert would conclude in a sort of perplexed way, "was that Mr. X's logical structure was invariably wrong. Baruch's answer, which seemed like a shot in the dark, was invariably right."

In his stock-market days Baruch loved to go to Hobcaw and cut himself off from everything connected with trading. In those days he was not so clear about his subconscious mind. He thought then that it was the rest and freedom from strain, for a few days, that enabled him to come back with renewed vigor and most of the answers to questions that had been bothering him.

Later he realized that the back of his head was working on his problems all the time he was shooting or sitting in the sun gossiping with guides, guests, or retainers or swapping stories before the fire.

It was a matter of great regret to Baruch, when at length President Roosevelt began to pass tough nuts for him to crack, that Hobcaw was not available. His invariable four rides a week between New York and Washington, during the periods when he was working on rubber, man-power, and postwar problems, were fine in their way. He would doze or chat with friends in his drawing room. The longer rides to Hobcaw helped more, and then there were the diversions of the Barony itself at the end of the ride.

But with an acute shortage of tires and gasoline, Hobcaw became practically inaccessible. In the months that followed Pearl Harbor it was believed that rubber would be a problem, but gasoline would not. During that period Baruch tried to solve the transportation situation so far as Hobcaw itself was concerned by buying a launch. That would provide transportation from Georgetown direct to the wharf in front of his house. That had been the method for many years, before the new bridge connecting the peninsula on which the Barony is located from the mainland was built. In early 1942 the launch saved the 6- to 7-mile drive from his house to Georgetown.

It was not possible to go back to the old days. For one thing the Seaboard branch line that ran from Lane, on the Atlantic Coast line, to Georgetown was no longer in operation. This was the route used when Baruch so astounded the House Rules Committee, during the "peace-leak" investigation, as told earlier, by admitting that he had an engine attached to his private car at Georgetown.

Second World War conditions made a trip down to Hobcaw from Washington or New York more trouble than it was worth. It would have needed either special privilege or patronage of the black market, neither of which Baruch would use. He refused to aid his daughter Belle to keep either of her airplanes, being unwilling to say he regarded them as necessary for his travel, even though the Georgetown "airport" is only a short distance from the dock at which his launch could meet him.

This deprivation of his former use of Hobcaw was a real sacrifice to Baruch. He thoroughly enjoyed not only the obvious diversions of the estate, but the role of an old "befo' de wah" Southern planter. The human relationships were positively feudal. Anyone on the place from the overseer, called the "superintendent" as a slight concession to the march of time, could have an audience with "de massa." Only nobody ever called Baruch "Massa," or at least I never heard of it.

There was a sort of Connecticut Yankee at King Arthur's Court twist here, for everybody called him, simply and without affectation, "the Boss."

"What does the Boss say?" or "What does the Boss want?" are constant questions, put scores of times each day. If there is a dispute, and the Boss is in residence, it is brought to him and argued out. It provides all the satisfaction of a lawsuit with a minimum of the trouble a lawsuit would involve and no expense whatever.

The fame of it naturally has spread through the near-by country, and there have been times when troubles originating on neighboring estates were brought to Baruch for settlement.

Baruch was particularly touched by a story he repeated several times in Washington. Two Negro women on his place met, as they walked on one of the dirt roads connecting the three Negro villages in the Barony.

"Say, Mandy," said one, "did you hear about the new job they give the Boss?"

"No," said Mandy. "What they got him doing now?"

"Oh, they got him fixing up everything, the way it's going to be after the war, *everything*."

"My goodness," said Mandy, "they must be going to have to pay him a powerful lot of money for all that."

"No, they ain't going to pay him a cent."

"Not going to pay him nothin'? Whyfor is he doing it then?"

"Oh, just to fix things so poor folk like you and me will be better off."

Mandy paused a moment, then said:

"May Jesus prop him up!"

INDEX

Index

Index

Index